W9-BNF-789

SHOOTING
THE
HIPPO

DEATH BY DEFICIT
AND OTHER CANADIAN MYTHS

VIKING

LINDA McQUAIG

VIKING
Published by the Penguin Group
Penguin Books Canada Ltd, 10 Alcorn Avenue, Toronto, Ontario,
Canada M4V 3B2
Penguin Books Ltd, 27 Wrights Lane, London W8 5TZ, England
Viking Penguin, a division of Penguin Books USA Inc., 375 Hudson
Street, New York, New York 10014, U.S.A.
Penguin Books Australia Ltd, Ringwood, Victoria, Australia
Penguin Books (NZ) Ltd, 182–190 Wairau Road, Auckland 10,
New Zealand

Penguin Books Ltd, Registered Offices: Harmondsworth,
Middlesex, England

First published 1995
1 3 5 7 9 10 8 6 4 2

Printed and bound in Canada on acid free paper ⊜

Canadian Cataloguing in Publication Data

McQuaig, Linda, 1951–
Shooting the hippo: death by deficit and other canadian myths

ISBN 0-670-84767-4

1. Budget deficits - Canada.   2. Government spending
policy - Canada.   I. Title.

HJ8033.C3M37 1995   339.5'23'0971   C95-930627-7

for Amy,
my pride and joy

Acknowledgments

I am greatly indebted to many people who generously contributed their time and knowledge to help me with this book. Although this list is by no means complete, I particularly want to mention Pierre Fortin, Peter Spiro, Ernie Stokes, Michael McCracken, Carl Sonnen, David McQueen, Gideon Rosenbluth and John Smithin. I also want to thank David Slater for his meticulous and extremely useful comments on parts of the manuscript. Andrew Sharpe helped enormously, both in shaping the ideas and making sure that I got the facts right. Of course, any omissions or errors are exclusively my fault.

Jim Laxer was a much appreciated friend and colleague. My thanks, as always, go to my mentor, Neil Brooks, as well as to my lifelong friend and fellow journalist, Tom Walkom.

Thanks also to the excellent Penguin crew, who, after four books, have become my friends: Cynthia Good, Brad Martin, Lori Ledingham, Scott Sellers, Karen Cossar, Martin Gould. Also much appreciated are the efforts of freelance copy editor Jem Bates, my trusted editor, David Kilgour, my dedicated researchers, Linda Manzer and Sarah Ives, and my U.S. adviser, Tim Canova, who provided some key assistance.

I also want to thank my parents, Audrey and Jack McQuaig, for their unfailing support, my extremely thoughtful brother Peter, and my wonderful friends Linda Diebel, Jane Spanton and Ken Finkleman. I should also mention Bhagyavathi Patel, who is perhaps the most generous person I know, and Peter Duffin, who's a close second.

My final thanks go to my daughter Amy. Anyone who thinks a three-year-old doesn't make a good office mate obviously hasn't met Amy. For long periods of time, she would sit quietly and studiously at her little desk in my office, busily drawing or writing long lists, only occasionally raising her head to say: "Mommy, do we need broccoli? What about cauliflower?" and even occasionally: "Mommy, I love you." Amazingly, during the most crucial interview of the book—a surprise return phone call—she saw the look of panic on my face and, without a word, tiptoed quietly out of the room, closing the door gently behind her. Her studiousness, her patience, her companionship were a constant and compelling source of inspiration; it is to her that this book is dedicated.

Linda McQuaig

Contents

CHAPTER ONE

They Shoot Hippos, Don't They?

We never see the shooting of the baby hippo. No hippo blood and guts on national television. Just a quick view of the cuddly newborn pup splashing by her mother in the water. Then the camera cuts to a little school girl assuring us that the baby hippo has indeed been shot.

An animal rights story? A plea for better gun control laws? No. This is a tale about our national deficit.

Eric Malling explains: "What, shoot the baby hippo? That's right. No room at the zoo and they couldn't expand the hippo pen because the government has no money."

Death: the ultimate deficit solution.

Malling, the consummate TV host, makes it all sound necessary, even reasonable. What choice is there but to shoot the baby hippo? The government is in debt. What other possible solution could there be? Isn't this the way humankind has solved its problems from time immemorial? Hippos, line up. Bam, bam, bam.

You can almost feel the confidence of international investors growing with each shot.

The hippo story on CTV's high-profile current affairs program "W5" aired for the first time in February 1993, and had an almost immediate impact on the popular debate in Canada.

Not only did it attract an unusually large audience of 1.7 million, but it quickly became part of the popular mythology of the deficit. Commentators began to refer to what had happened in New Zealand, which figured prominently in the program, as proof of the disasters that lay ahead for debt-ridden Canada. Provincial governments studied the program as they geared up for their own deficit-slashing binges that spring. Ontario premier Bob Rae reportedly watched it numerous times as he put in place the final touches of his "social contract" of pay cuts for the civil service. Nowhere did it have a greater effect than in Alberta, where the Conservative government of Ralph Klein constantly used New Zealand as a model. Vancouver *Sun* columnist Jamie Lamb, commenting on the enormous impact the show had on the 1993 federal election campaign, argued that it had "proven more influential than any political coverage or party advertising in the same medium over the course of the campaign… I can't recall a television documentary or show to match it for effect."

The show is about debt, about what happens when a country hits the "debt wall." Ostensibly, it is a story about New Zealand, but Malling makes clear it is really a story about what lies ahead for Canada.

"It all happened when New Zealand, a country a lot like Canada, suddenly realized it was going broke," says a tanned and relaxed Malling, on location in New Zealand. "It's a little strange to be doing an hour on another country's economy, but have a look and you might see yourself in the mirror."

At the time of the program's first airing, Brian Mulroney had just announced his intention to retire as prime minister. The commentators were busy pondering the Mulroney legacy: unpopular autocrat or visionary who could see where

Canada must go? Whichever, the race was now on to replace the hated despot/visionary. For the foreseeable future, Canadians were to be treated to a steady diet of Conservative politicians trotting out their deficit-reduction strategies to an audience that only a few months later, on election night, would reveal it was never particularly interested in what this Tory gang of deficit-slashers had to say.

In the meantime, TV screens were filled with Conservative politicians talking about the deficit. But Malling knew—as Tory strategists apparently didn't—that men and women in suits talking about the deficit make boring TV. And Malling never bores. He is, above all, a skilled communicator, a popularizer of ideas, a master in the art of persuasion. So while Tory politicians and businessmen droned on about the deficit with charts and graphs and stupefying numbers, Malling presented us with the baby hippo.

He starts by brushing aside all the political yackety-yack of the Tory leadership race and the inevitable election. "Good theatre, I suppose, like a pennant race in baseball," he says, pacing slowly in front of the camera, as if he were pacing thoughtfully around your living room. "But in my opinion none of it really matters."

Now we're ready for Malling to tell us what *does* matter. He looks directly at the camera. He's talking straight to us.

"Economists are predicting that sometime in the next year, maybe two years, the deputy minister of finance is going to walk into cabinet—and it doesn't matter whose cabinet—and announce that Canada's credit has run out. Now *that* matters. Our lives will change dramatically."

Hippos, take cover.

"Can't happen to us? Well, it did happen to a country very much like ours, New Zealand."

For the next hour, Malling gently blends the New Zealand and Canadian situations. The suggestion that we might recognize ourselves in the mirror becomes stronger as the show progresses, and the fate of the two countries becomes virtually identical. "How does a country like New Zealand, like Canada, eventually hit the [debt] wall?" Malling traces the dramatic cuts New Zealand has made in government spending over the last decade, slashing social programs, introducing user fees, removing government regulations and privatizing just about everything the government owned, including the post office and the national airline.

All this has been done, not by choice, but because debt left New Zealanders with no other options, Malling explains. The health minister tells Malling this had to happen because New Zealand was "at the edge of the cliff." Malling quickly tells his audience, "Well now, a lot of Canadians, I think, are getting a view of the cliff too."

The show is a masterpiece of TV journalism. It is Malling at his best, communicating a complex subject in a simple, direct and powerful way, with a touch of scepticism and humour. It is also a fine example of what could perhaps be termed "deficit pornography"—material designed to arouse our fears through the use of provocative imagery. The image of Canada poised precariously at the edge of a cliff, or about to slam into a concrete wall, has the power to stimulate fears about the deficit in a way that all those ponderous politicians and business leaders in suits had failed to. The show was a massive success by any usual measure applied in the media industry—fabulous ratings, a buzz in the corridors of power, a higher profile for Malling, a big effect on public opinion.

Its only shortcoming—which went largely unnoticed— was that it distorted what actually happened in New Zealand. There *is* a fascinating story there, and it is highly relevant to Canada. But it's not the story that Malling told. The real story is about how New Zealand's politicians embarked on a huge experiment in which they transformed their country from an advanced social democracy into a free-market jungle with massive unemployment, growing inequality and a damaged manufacturing base. Have a look and you might see yourself in the mirror.

But, in presenting New Zealand's government-slashing solutions as a desirable model for Canada, Malling used his considerable skills to entice us further down this dangerous path.

—————

This book is about how we are being enticed down this path—and not just by Malling. He is simply one of the most effective salesmen for a pitch that is coming from virtually all established information sources in our lives: from business, government, academia and the media—those who can perhaps be loosely termed "the elite." Dissenting voices are sometimes heard in all these sectors. Nevertheless, a prevailing ideology has taken hold in our culture with a ferocity that has all but eliminated any meaningful debate.

This newly dominant ideology has many threads, but essentially it is about lowering our expectations of what a society can do for its citizens. The experience of the postwar years has left us with a conviction that it is possible to create a society that offers a great deal for all. We have come to believe that we live in a nation in which every citizen has certain rights—to a job, to a certain standard of living, to a high level of health care and education, to fair treatment, to some sort of protection from the ravages of a punishing world. And we have increasingly looked to government to provide and guarantee these rights. For the most part, we like the security of all this so much that we have been reluctant to give it up.

These civic expectations, which have become deeply entrenched in recent decades, are a relatively new development. For much of history, the notion that every member of society had certain intrinsic rights did not exist. There was no sense that *everyone mattered*. The life and death and suffering of large segments of society were not considered to be matters of national concern. Revolutions in the seventeenth and eighteenth centuries established many of the basic political and legal rights in Western countries. But it wasn't until much later—in the twentieth century, and particularly in the last half of the twentieth century—that the idea that everyone also enjoyed certain social rights developed.

It is perhaps worth reminding ourselves how truly significant this development has been. By extending the notion of rights in this way, Western countries have created new possibilities for equality and social inclusiveness. They have created societies in which everyone has a broad set of rights, and those rights are deemed to matter. The idea, for instance, that access to health care and education should be a right enjoyed by every member of society is nothing short of revolutionary. Arguably, these social rights are as far-reaching in their scope and significance in our lives as a long-revered legal concept such as *habeas corpus*, which centuries ago established a safeguard against arbitrary imprisonment. For most people, the prospect of medical care being denied to their dying child—a regular occurrence in past centuries, and still a fact of life in the Third World—is as horrific as the prospect of facing a criminal court without a carefully-spelled-out bill of rights.

This dramatic extension of rights has required a more equal distribution of society's resources than existed, for instance, in feudal times or in the early years of the industrial revolution—or than exists in many Third World countries today. Extensive taxation has been necessary to support these universal public services. Contrary to popular lore, however, this hasn't impoverished us; postwar Western societies, with their broad social welfare systems, are far richer, by any measure, than they were in previous centuries. For most citizens, the price in taxation has been worth paying. But some in the upper income range have begun to feel that they are contributing more than they are receiving in benefits.

In many ways, what the elite wants now is to lower citizens' expectations of what they can count on from society, to roll back the frontiers of government—to return to an earlier focus on enforcing more narrowly defined legal and political rights. It wants to wean us away from the notion of government as provider and equalizer, and re-establish the discipline of the marketplace in meting out these sorts of rewards where they are "earned." Under the harsher discipline of the marketplace, we would have no automatic "rights" or "entitlements;" all we would have is whatever we could get by selling our services to those with the money to pay us.

Presented this way, the new ideology might not sound appealing to most members of society; so it is rarely presented this way. Rather, proponents of rolling back government have focused on finding fault with the system of extended rights that we've come to enjoy, or presenting ordinary citizens as victims of an excessive tax burden apparently caused by government largesse. It has become fashionable to say that all this government assistance has created a dangerous "dependency."

Indeed, the "dependency" argument is particularly compelling; it suggests that by cutting back our social rights, we will transform an allegedly dependent citizenry into a vigorous and self-sufficient one. In fact, the cutbacks are unlikely to affect dependency. Do we somehow imagine that people were never "dependent" in the days before they had social rights? Or that no one is "dependent" today in the Third World? What is likely to change if we cut back social rights is not human behaviour, but the levels of human suffering in our society. We will almost certainly see a return to the greater inequality that prevailed before these social rights were established.

Denunciations of "dependency" are interesting. They imply that people are exclusively self-sufficient creatures, which is only part of the story of human behaviour. They fail to recognize that, in addition to being self-sufficient, we are also social, communal beings who are by nature dependent on each other. Surely any intelligent society would consider the needs of its citizens as dependent and interdependent creatures as well as their talent for self-sufficiency. Rather than downgrading the dependent aspects of human nature, we should perhaps view them as part of the human condition, as a necessary mechanism for survival, even as a source of prosperity. By pooling our resources effectively, we can produce better, more efficient systems that provide for all members of society.

In earlier centuries, for instance, fire protection was often a private business. In some communities in nineteenth-century England and North America, homeowners received a cast-iron plaque when they paid a premium to a private fire insurance company. In the case of a fire, a volunteer fire brigade would come to the rescue. But the volunteers in the brigade would be more likely to stay and actually put out the blaze if they saw the plaque on the house, indicating that the fire insurance company would reimburse them for their trouble. For homeowners who hadn't paid their premiums, the problems were obvious. But the system could pose problems even for those who were fully paid up. If your neighbour's uninsured house was on fire, were you not potentially worse off as well?

Today, of course, our public fire departments are paid for collectively through our taxes. Does this mean we have become hopelessly "dependent" on government, that we should be ashamed of our lack of self-sufficiency? Or does it mean that we have simply recognized a certain degree of positive interdependency in our lives—that when our neighbour's house burns, ours is also put at risk—and opted for a more sensible way of managing our affairs collectively, in the best interests of all? While the urgency of a fire may highlight the point, the principle applies elsewhere too: are we not ultimately worse off as a society if some of us have untreated diseases, are illiterate or otherwise ill-equipped to deal with the world, or grow up in homes wreaked by poverty and violence?

In a column in the *Globe and Mail* in December 1994, Rick Salutin attacked the increasingly prominent notion that government should be restricted to performing only those roles that the private sector can't perform. "Does anyone else feel that society itself is vanishing behind this mindset?" asked Salutin. "We still have the components of society, competing with each other for their own interests. But what of the common interests of us all or, as they said in ancient days, the public interest? Without a vigorous public sector, including government, who looks after that?" That public interest has, in recent decades, come to include the notion that society has a responsibility for all its members, that everyone's well-being matters.

Stripping away our newfound social rights has proved to be a tough sell for those in authority. Spurious arguments about "dependency" have helped weaken the public's support for these rights. The most promising line of attack, however, has proved to be the "debt crisis." Accompanied by vivid and powerful images of dangerous cliffs and concrete walls, the debt argument has enjoyed growing success. The deficit has thus become a key tool for picking away at what many in the elite consider to be our overly generous social welfare system and government policies dedicated to pampering the undeserving, at the expense of the deserving (such as those in the elite). The best evidence of this is how quickly the elite loses its enthusiasm for deficit reduction when the focus shifts from cutting social spending to other approaches to the deficit problem, such as reducing tax breaks, which tend to provide bigger benefits to those on higher incomes. The *Globe and Mail*, the *Financial Post* and the Business Council on National Issues have all condemned suggestions that raising tax revenues could help reduce the deficit. Interestingly, this wasn't the type of deficit reduction that the elite had in mind.

The sense of urgency expressed by many Bay Street analysts over the deficit seems to fluctuate according to the government's willingness to attack social spending, not according to the actual size of the deficit. We heard barely a murmur of protest, for instance, against the former Conservative government's plan to spend a staggering $6 billion on new military helicopters in a deal full of rich payments to private manufacturers, contractors and lobbyists. It was extraordinary that such a major new expenditure should be advanced so calmly in the face of the apparently skyrocketing deficit. (Imagine the reaction if someone had advocated spending $6 billion on, say, setting up a national daycare program; the idea would have been dismissed as ludicrously unrealistic in these days of budget constraint.)

Whatever one may feel about the pros and cons of new military hardware, no one argued the helicopters were essential to the safety of Canada. Rather, supporters of the plan simply insisted that the program was a good investment, because our existing helicopter fleet would otherwise have to be upgraded at a substantially greater cost in the future. Surely this was an argument that could be used to justify upgrading any of our collectively owned facilities, such as our schools, universities, hospitals, museums and public transit systems. And yet these public facilities, which are vital to our way of life, have been allowed to deteriorate in recent years, their funding eroded in the name of deficit reduction and spending restraint.

Despite these anomalies, the anti-deficit campaign has been portrayed as a non-ideological battle against a common foe. We are told, "The debt problem has become so extreme that we have no choice but to cut social spending." This sort of statement is presented as an objective assessment of our situation and often appears in apparently neutral news stories. Now, imagine if a media commentator made the following assertion: "The debt problem has become so extreme that we have no choice but to raise taxes on the rich." Such a statement would clearly, and correctly, be seen as the expression of an opinion, and would not be acceptable in a neutral news story. And yet, both statements express opinions—opinions about how the resources in our society should be divided up. What is remarkable is how, in the first case, the opinion expressed has become so widely endorsed and often repeated that its bias has become all but invisible.

Indeed, rather than being seen as an attempt to turn back the clock to an earlier era of minimal social rights, the anti-deficit campaign is presented as a modern-day morality play, a crusade for the future of the country. Its message is simple but powerful: *We are living beyond our means—and our children will reap the consequences.* Here we are, partying away irresponsibly, running up a credit card bill we can't possibly afford, and our children will be stuck paying for it all. Once again, however, it is hard not to be struck by the selectiveness of the concern for our children's future. Do we seriously believe that leaving our children with a big debt-to-GDP ratio is somehow more serious than, say, leaving them with lakes and rivers full of toxic chemicals, and nuclear wastes that will remain radioactive for thousands of years?

Still, if all this about living beyond our means and hurting our children were true, it would indeed be a damning indictment on our society. But as we shall see in the next chapter, it is—much like the hippo story—a distortion of the real story, a mythologized account designed to persuade us to accept what we don't want.

How is it that this mythologized account has come to dominate the way we look at the deficit? Later in the book we will look at the real story of our debt—where it came from, how serious it is and what can be done about it. But first, it might be useful to look more closely at the distorted story that we're constantly being told. If we have any hope of grasping how we're being led down the wrong road on the debt issue—and on the larger issue of what options lie before us as a nation—we must understand how our view of the issue has been shaped by the elite.

This brings us to the vital role played by the media. To suggest that every word in the media is watched over and controlled by the elite would be naive. The media are made up of tens of thousands of individuals from a variety of backgrounds and outlooks, many of whom view the world very differently than do business leaders and Bay Street brokers, and their views creep into their reports. But to imagine that, because of this, the media constitute an independent marketplace of ideas—where all the salient facts are clearly presented and the best arguments ultimately win—is even more naive. At the most basic level, we must always remember that virtually all media outlets are owned by rich, powerful members of the elite. To assume that this fact has no influence on the ideas they present would be equivalent to assuming that, should the entire media be owned by, say, labour unions, women's groups or social workers, this would have no impact on the editorial content.

It should come as no surprise, then, that the media's position on the deficit has been one that overwhelmingly corresponds with that of the elite. This is not to suggest that dissenting voices are never heard. The media regularly interview social welfare activists who argue against spending cuts, and most newspapers publish "opinion" pieces that present a range of viewpoints, sometimes even contradicting their own editorials. There is a handful of newspaper columnists—notably Thomas Walkom, Frances Russell, Rick Salutin and James Laxer—who frequently pick holes in the prevailing arguments about debt and deficits. Furthermore, struggling little anti-establishment newspapers and magazines are published all across the country. So if this is simple censorship, it's of a slipshod variety.

The point is, however, not that no other viewpoints are heard, but that one viewpoint overwhelmingly dominates. Arrayed against the handful of sceptics mentioned above is an army of commentators, who tirelessly promote the deficit-leaves-us-no-alternative-but-to-cut-social-spending theory and whose views are regularly featured in every major newspaper and magazine, as well as on television and radio news and current affairs programs. This chorus of voices simply overwhelms, not because of the force of their arguments, but through their sheer numbers and the prominence they are given. After a while, their incessant calls for fiscal restraint and spending cuts take on a quality of inevitability. Surely these people, who have presumably been selected as commentators because of their insightful minds, can't all be mischievous or mistaken. To raise a voice in opposition to them—to argue for *more* social programs or *greater* income redistribution—seems naive and unrealistic, almost silly. To argue, for instance, for a national denticare program, in the face of the swelling movement for fiscal restraint, is to put oneself on the outer margins of serious national debate— even though such a program would probably improve our lives and save us all money in the long run.

After a while, the chorus calling for deficit reduction and spending cuts becomes just part of the "clatter in people's heads." This wonderful phrase comes from pollster Donna Dasko, who uses it to describe the way the media bombard us with a message until eventually, through sheer repetition—like the monotonous, incessant banging of plates—it lodges in our heads, becoming a dull background noise, a kind of invisible yet inescapable fact of life. Anything else then comes to sound like a curious, offkey whine. The sound rumbling through our heads tells us: this is just the way things are; there is no alternative.

So before we try to understand the real situation, let's first explore what's behind the clatter.

———

Eric Malling reaches over, plucks a greasy piece of chicken skin off my plate, and eats it.

Drat. I was hoping he wouldn't notice me discreetly slipping the warm, rubbery skin from the chicken breast—an act that has no doubt exposed me to be concerned about health, exactly the kind of stance he loves to mock. Malling has been known to argue that we've been too hard on Chernobyl. "The anti-nukes used it to terrify everyone," he once said in a speech. Clearly someone who takes nuclear meltdown in stride is not going to be overly worried about a little chicken skin.

Malling has even been known to make the case that radiation levels in the Ukraine are no higher than those in high-altitude Denver. (So what if thirty-one people died at Chernobyl? No doubt, there were more people who died that year flossing their teeth.) Other overblown health risks, according to Malling, include pesticides, asbestos and smoking. To Malling, it's all just another "whine of the week."

Sure enough, the sight of me removing the chicken skin is too much for him, and he can't resist challenging me. I mumble something about trying to avoid various diseases that I've heard are linked to eating chicken fat. He scoffs, has another sip of beer and another drag on his cigarette. I realize that I feel embarrassed, caught out doing something so obviously politically correct as trying to be healthy.

Malling, flaunting his political incorrectness, has a large steak and eats the fat on it, too. The grease glistens on his lips, making him look every inch the character I've heard him to be—outdoorsman, ice-fisherman, a rough-hewn Saskatchewan boy who eats red meat and takes no guff. It's an image he cultivates with some success. On camera, of course, he wears suits and doesn't eat steak, but he still manages to come across as an individualist, a sceptic, someone who doesn't buy the party line—a "contrarian," as his executive producer, Peter Rehak, puts it. "He'll take the opposite tack to everybody else on most issues." An anti-pack journalism journalist, a guy who fishes through a hole in the ice while the rest of the mob throngs to the ski hill. His own man.

Malling has indeed cut out some ground of his own, although it's turf that is increasingly crowded these days, with others flocking into the anti–political correctness camp. They're out to take on what they see as the new establishment of "whiners" who have come to dominate the political scene—environmentalists, feminists, poor people, unemployed fishermen, animal rights protestors, anti-smoking activists, people who remove skin from chicken or any other "interest group" with a cause or a grievance. In the view of Malling and others, these traditionally powerless underdogs have somehow taken control.

If you believe that this motley crew is now running the country, then Malling does come across as something of a loner, a brave trooper marching by himself against the well-armed battalions of the new tyranny. And we need him because, as we all know, our institutions—from our local high schools right up to our governments and big corporations, and, of course, our TV stations—are now run by unemployed fishermen, animal rights activists or poor people, etc. And Malling is fearlessly taking them all on, regardless of the consequences.

On the other hand, if you don't believe that the underdog has seized control of the country, then Malling may seem like less of a loner. Because the kinds of policies he actively pushes on "W5"—deficit reduction, social spending cuts, less government—are notions that, to say the least, find favour with many of those who actually *do* run governments, corporations and, no doubt, even TV stations.

Malling's active promotion of these sorts of ideas has

given a fresh and effective voice to familiar causes long espoused by business. Indeed, Malling has done a lot to diminish what little voice was given to the underdog and replace it once again with the loud and confident voice of the establishment. As a host on CBC TV's "The Fifth Estate" before he moved to CTV, Malling used to rail to his colleagues against "victim" journalism, by which he meant the kind of journalism that focuses on the grievances and suffering of the powerless. With his rapier wit, he would mock and criticize those proposing "victim" story ideas at "The Fifth Estate." "After a while, we became like a unit of victims," commented one who clashed with him there.

When he was lured to "W5," Malling was given more leeway to put his stamp on the show, which he did in short order. For years, "W5" had focused on issues that could be broadly termed "social"—stories about abortion, AIDS, sexual harassment, pensions or the handicapped. Victims abounded. People cried on TV. There was a strong sense of outrage over injustice, often from the viewpoint of the "little guy." Ideas for the stories were often drawn from letters from viewers, who had their own tales of injustice. According to one former employee, "W5" had become "a voice for people who didn't have a voice."

TV lends itself to this, partly because victims are human and their real emotions are more interesting to watch than, say, footage of a grain elevator or a deficit chart. Malling, who understands TV well, complains about how these victims are able to win so much television time. And in a sense, he's right; real people with real feelings do have a leg-up over men in suits talking about the deficit. The media, and particularly television, have put the spotlight on the powerless and their grievances in a way that has never happened before.

But it would be wrong to confuse air time with real power. Just because poor people or unemployed fishermen or day care advocates are sometimes seen on TV doesn't mean these people exercise real power, even the power to improve their own situations. Apart from the rare heart-wrenching personal story that captures public sympathy and pushes government to act in some limited way, these people simply return to their powerless, impoverished lives the minute the camera stops rolling. Malling's gripe against them seems to have less to do with any real power they wield than with the presumptuous nature of their demands.

At the root of their whining is a belief that they have a *right* to something they're not getting, and that government should step in and make sure that they *do* get it, in the interests of fairness and equality. For Malling and other comfortably ensconced members of the elite—Malling, at the top of his profession, draws a six-figure income—these demands for greater equality from less talented and less deserving people are irritating and vexatious. All these people demanding more means a bigger tax bite out of that six-figure income. Why can't they be content with their traditional lot as beggars?

It's almost as if democracy has gotten out of control; the people are getting too uppity. Where does it all stop? Once the egalitarian impulses of the public have been stimulated, can they be controlled? It's not surprising that this has created a backlash among members of the elite, whose power base could be disturbed by the new challenge from below. It is perhaps unrealistic to expect people to give up—or even share—power, position and status without some resistance.

If "W5" once focused on the powerless, Malling has turned it into a showcase for the issues that concern the truly powerful. If it was once a voice for the voiceless, it could now perhaps be called a voice for the C.D. Howe Institute, the prominent Toronto think tank funded by Bay Street. With his considerable skills as a popularizer, Malling is able to take up Bay Street's political objectives—deficit reduction, a reduced role for government, more power to the private sector—and present them in a way that is convincing, accessible and even entertaining to a mass audience.

Together, Malling and the C.D. Howe Institute provide a kind of one-two punch, each playing an important yet different role in creating the "clatter" that ends up in people's heads. Malling transforms the message into a saleable package; the institute provides the technical arguments and data to back up the case and give it credibility.

The C.D. Howe Institute, known in financial circles as simply "the Howe," is particularly effective in this back-up role because it has the air of an academic body. Its role as an "institute" suggests a kind of value-free, scientific approach that the Business Council on National Issues, for instance, lacks. Whereas statements from the BCNI are readily identifiable as the self-serving voice of business, the Howe is able to present itself as neutral and public-spirited—even though it, too, represents big financial and business interests. In fact, the Howe is funded entirely by its members, which include the country's five big banks, major corporations, investment houses, life insurance and trust companies, as well as law and accounting firms.

Howe commentators are identified with the institute, but the institute is not identified as a lobby group for business or financial interests. This omission is very helpful to the Howe—and ultimately to its sponsors—because it gives its message more credibility. It's like a form of idea-laundering: by transferring the message into the mouth of someone not apparently on the payroll of Bay Street, the fact that the message has been funded by Bay Street is effectively obscured.

The credibility enjoyed by the Howe perhaps explains why the media have given such prominence to its "reports" and statements in recent years. The media have come to treat Howe publications with a seriousness that is quite striking, and that often leaves the public with the impression that Howe statements are objectively authoritative, rather than simply representing a very conservative business viewpoint.

In January 1993, for instance, the Howe called together a band of conservative Bay Street economists for an informal discussion on Canada's debt situation. The economists, mostly from banks and brokerage houses, repeated many of the concerns that they regularly express on the subject. The institute taped the session and then released a transcript to the media. The *Globe and Mail*, always eager to highlight a story about the dangers of the deficit, ran a major article about the meeting as the paper's banner front-page story, under the headline "Debt crisis looms, study warns: Experts worry government bonds could lose appeal to foreign investors." The article left the impression that the country was facing a sudden crisis, which had prompted this important meeting. No hint was given of the Howe's long-standing bias in favour of slashing government spending to reduce the deficit—the solution advocated by most of the assembled economists. The Howe was identified only as a "private Toronto-based research organization."

The sense of urgency communicated by the article was odd, considering that the points made by the economists were not new and had already been covered extensively in the media (including, of course, in countless columns and editorials in the *Globe and Mail*). Furthermore, the transcript of the meeting showed that, while they all agreed that the debt situation was serious, even some of these carefully hand-picked economists were reluctant to say that the situation was actually a crisis. "I would counsel against overuse of the word 'crisis,'" cautioned Ted Carmichael, a deficit hawk at Burns Fry Ltd. "It's best to avoid being a Cassandra— enough to say that we're into territory where a crisis is a higher probability than it was two or three years ago." As for the contention that foreign investors might lose interest in government bonds, Warren Jestin, senior economist at the Bank of Nova Scotia, noted that there actually hadn't been any signs of this so far, and that Ontario's recently issued bonds had sold like hotcakes: "It is true that international markets have been receptive to Canadian issues... Ontario's recent $3 billion global offering was a barn burner. But this shouldn't give us a false sense of security."

The Howe meeting had managed to generate a sense of crisis despite its unremarkable conclusions. It was followed later in the month by the airing of Malling's odyssey to New Zealand, encouraging a building sense of crisis. Interestingly, the Howe proved to be the source of one of the key images in Malling's documentary, as we shall see. The point of all this is not to suggest that the Howe and the media are involved in a conspiracy, but rather to show how news is generated, and what an influential role a partisan organization like the Howe can play in convincing Canadians that the country is about to hit the "debt wall."

"Hitting the wall" is an image that crops up in much of Malling's work as well as in the literature put out by the Howe. It's a vivid way of describing what happens when your debt has become so big that your creditors won't lend you any more. The end of the road, with nothing but a wall in front of you. But while it's a great image, it proved difficult to find an authentic example in the real world.

Of course, there were Third World countries that could be said to have "hit the wall," that are no longer able to borrow money on foreign markets. But nobody would take them as offering serious precedents for Canada. What was needed was a real industrialized, Canadian-type country in crisis. Unfortunately, none existed.

Enter New Zealand, a tiny country of 3 million people, so far away, so little known in Canada. New Zealand hadn't hit the wall either, but a short-term crisis back in 1984 could pass for a hit. Malling was off to New Zealand in hot pursuit of a nine-year-old example of his elusive objective.

Over in New Zealand, Malling apparently found what he

was looking for. As he told his audience: "New Zealand had been topping up with borrowed money, and its credit finally ran out. That sounds like Latin America or Africa. But how does a country like New Zealand, like Canada, eventually hit the wall?"

At last! There it was: a real example of the debt wall!

To illustrate the concept of the debt wall in Canadian terms, Malling presents us with an image of Canada's deputy finance minister walking into a cabinet meeting and declaring that Canada's credit has run out. Malling only tells us that this is what "economists are predicting." Over lunch, however, Malling volunteers that the image in fact came from Howe president Tom Kierans, who is actually a former investment banker and bond dealer.

Nevertheless, the image was a powerful one. And Malling skilfully tied it in with the New Zealand story, with references to how New Zealand's government had suddenly found itself confronted with similar credit problems. Malling left the clear impression that New Zealand had gone broke and was no longer able to borrow on international markets. But the real situation was quite different. What Malling was referring to was not the bankruptcy of the country, which never happened, but a very short-term currency crisis. "It is simply not true that New Zealand has ever gone broke. And it is not true that we reached the limits of our borrowing capacity," said Jonathan Boston, associate professor of public policy at Victoria University in Wellington, New Zealand, after reading the transcript of Malling's New Zealand program.

Boston explained that, prior to the 1984 election, New Zealand's currency was overvalued, but the government was reluctant to devalue it in the middle of an election campaign, since this might signal a lack of confidence in its own economic policies. Still, international markets anticipated a post-election devaluation—particularly after a prominent member of the leading opposition party suggested publicly that his party would consider a devaluation.

As a result, there was a run on the New Zealand dollar as currency traders sought to cash in on the devaluation, until eventually the country's foreign reserves were exhausted. Days after the election, the new government devalued the currency by 20 per cent. "The crisis was over within a few minutes of the devaluation," Boston explained. "It was essentially a currency crisis, compounded by an election. Indeed, it would not have happened except for the election ... this is light years away from countries like Somalia and Bangladesh. There's no comparison." A recent study of New Zealand's debt by the New Zealand Institute of Economic Research confirms this. The study, prepared by two economists, one of whom works for New Zealand's central bank, notes, "At no stage has New Zealand defaulted, or threatened to default, on its debt obligations." Its international credit rating by Moody's, one of the big New York credit rating agencies, never dropped below Aa3—the rough equivalent of an A minus—making it one of only twenty-four countries in the world to receive a ranking in the "low-risk" range. So much for the debt wall.

Of course Malling wanted to make the case that debt-ridden New Zealand had its credit cut off, forcing it to cut government spending dramatically, just as would happen to debt-ridden Canada when its time came. What was needed, therefore, was a full-fledged debt crisis leading to the end of credit—the elusive debt wall!—not some boring run on the currency that was over within minutes of a devaluation. Some crisis! That would create no terror in Canada, would do nothing to convince Canadians to accept user fees and pension cuts. Indeed, the New Zealand example would be largely irrelevant to Canada. The show would be hardly worth doing.

When asked over lunch about his contention that New Zealand had had its credit cut off, Malling simply shrugs. "They had a currency crisis," he says, revealing that he is aware of the distinction. Then, as if to head off any further probing along these lines, he quickly adds: "You can really split hairs over this. I'm not an economist."

Perhaps. But the difference between a currency crisis and hitting the debt wall is significant. And, as we've seen, the premise of the show was that New Zealand and Canada faced similar problems because of their dangerously high debt levels. It was about the dangers of over-indebtedness, not the dangers of an overvalued currency—a theme not even mentioned in the program. By failing to accurately present the nature of the New Zealand crisis of 1984, Malling's program drove home to Canadians the same tired old message: we must cut our government spending.

All this is not to suggest that what happened in New Zealand a decade ago has no relevance to Canada. It does, although it is not the message that Malling presents us with. Rather, New Zealand is of interest because it embarked on a dramatic program of changes similar to reforms introduced in recent years in Canada: free trade, deregulation, government downsizing, inflation control, even the imposition of a goods and services tax.

New Zealand in recent years has been like a laboratory experiment in new right economics. For most of the twentieth century, New Zealand had one of the world's most advanced social welfare systems (considerably more generous than Canada's) and an unusually strong government commitment to equality and full employment. Interestingly, it consistently had some of the lowest unemployment rates in the world; legend has it that at one point there were only two unemployed workers in the country, and the minister of internal affairs knew them both by name!

By the early eighties, New Zealand was facing an economic crunch; it had lost a key export market when Britain joined the European Community in 1973, and it had invested large sums in what turned out to be unproductive energy megaprojects. When the Labour Party came to power in 1984, it began implementing many of the new right solutions that were becoming popular fare in other English-speaking countries, including Britain, the United States and Canada. Over the following decade, Labour and later the more conservative National Party put in place an extreme version of this new right agenda.

The results of the New Zealand economic experiment are therefore of considerable interest to Canadians. But surprisingly, Malling doesn't tell us much about them. The little he does tell us is rather discouraging: "So, for all it's been through, New Zealand is still ailing. That's the trouble with strong medicine. Even when you're forced to take it, you don't get better right away."

Once again, Malling has turned the focus back to how New Zealand was "forced"—presumably by the cut-off of international credit—to take its medicine, passing quickly over the fact that, nine years after the experiment began, the country was still ailing. Just how badly was New Zealand ailing? And was the country worse or better off after a decade of new right solutions?

These presumably would be crucial questions for a Canadian audience, but they're never posed by Malling, perhaps because the results of the experiment have so far been mostly negative and might destroy the notion that New Zealand should be used as a model for Canada. Bill Southworth, a New Zealand TV producer who was hired by "W5" to produce the New Zealand show, recalls that Malling seemed somewhat disappointed when he arrived in New Zealand and learned about the bleak results. "His initial outlook was that there were great changes taking place here which were philosophically in tune with his own ideas," said Southworth in a telephone interview from New Zealand. "What he hadn't realized was that the outcomes were not quite as bright and shining as the theory said."

Indeed, the results have been disappointing. Growth rates have recently started to pick up, but this follows almost a decade of stagnation. A study by two economists at the Paris-based Organization for Economic Co-operation and Development (OECD) found that the economic reforms contributed to the decline in New Zealand's manufacturing exports and the rise in unemployment. "New Zealand's economic reform programme has added to the unavoidable stabilisation costs in terms of lost output and employment. As the overshooting unwinds, it leaves the country with a persistent loss in manufactured exports and hence a less diversified export base."

A 1993 report by the United Nations Children's Fund was even more critical, describing New Zealand's experiment as a "cautionary tale." "Long regarded as one of the world's most enlightened social democracies, New Zealand has, since 1984, demolished a cradle-to-grave social welfare system in the name of economic efficiency. Nevertheless, untrammelled markets have not produced vigorous growth. On the contrary, eight years of stringent monetarist policies have produced massive unemployment, rising crime rates, a widening gap between rich and poor and a declining GDP. Between 1985 and 1990, New Zealand's GNP fell by 0.7 per cent, the worst record of any industrialized country, while unemployment more than doubled."

But Malling apparently didn't feel that unemployment or a declining GDP fit with a story about the debt wall. So he confined the interviews in the program to those who were generally enthusiastic about the new experiment—mostly politicians who had had a hand in bringing it about and who, not surprisingly, found merit in what they'd done. According to Jonathan Boston, those interviewed on the program were by no means representative of the broad sweep of opinion in New Zealand. Even Rehak, Malling's executive producer, acknowledged that: "I gather not everybody in

New Zealand is as enthusiastic about what's happened as some of us over here are."

Southworth was disappointed that the "W5" program didn't show the downside of the New Zealand experiment. "I wanted more about the effects on unemployment and social disruption. But [Malling] would make the point constantly that it's the 'process' not the 'pain' we're interested in." This fits, of course, with Malling's distaste for showing victims and pain. But does it fit with what a Canadian audience might want to know? Surely, the extent to which the economic experiment has produced victims would be of considerable interest to Canadians, many of whom already feel like victims themselves. By omitting the New Zealand victims, the program left the mistaken impression that things were working out fine. In doing so, he left out a key part of the story—perhaps *the* key part of the story.

Even more bizarre, however, is the failure of the show to look at the results even in the one area that it focuses on: debt. We're told that New Zealand was driven to make radical cuts because its debt became so big that its international credit ran out. It would therefore seem to be of more than passing interest to discover what had happened to this monstrous debt a decade later. Did a heavy dose of new right medicine cause it to shrink? Malling never tells us.

If he had, he would have had a hard time making the case that Canada should follow in New Zealand's tracks. After almost a decade of drastic cuts and the sale of more than $8 billion worth of Crown assets, New Zealand has finally started producing budget surpluses. But its overall debt situation has actually deteriorated since the reforms began. A 1993 study by the New Zealand Institute of Economic Research examined New Zealand's debt in comparison with the debts of six other countries of similar size and situation. The study concluded: "Most of the statistical ratios used to measure a country's ability to pay indicate that

New Zealand has a heavy overseas debt burden. Debt to GDP is the highest of the countries we looked at... when New Zealand is compared to similar economies, according to most indicators both its relative and absolute position have deteriorated since 1985."

Despite all this, Malling's show seems to have been enormously successful in selling the deficit-cutting message. Certainly, the show was a godsend to those in the business and financial world who had been trying in their own dull way to get the message across to the Canadian public. In Edmonton, car dealer Ken Haywood could barely control his enthusiasm. Haywood contacted Rehak to urge a rerun. He explained that he sat on the boards of the Edmonton Chamber of Commerce and the Alberta Taxpayers Association—organizations that had been actively pushing for government spending cuts—and he pledged that both groups would help publicize the rerun. Haywood himself sent out 670 faxes urging people to watch the show and advertised it on the large billboard at his car dealership. He also sent fifty copies of the show to influential Albertans.

Back at the Howe, Kierans was so impressed by the New Zealand show that he took the unusual step of sending a video of it to all Howe members. Included was a personal endorsement from Kierans. At the Howe's request, Rehak had provided a CTV cameraman to record Kierans presenting an introduction and conclusion to the video version sent to Howe members. In a sense, things had come full circle. Kierans had provided the key image for the show, which Malling had turned into a popular TV program, which Kierans, in turn, had endorsed. It looked as if the issue was building, but it was really just circling around the loop, apparently picking up momentum as it went.

By the summer of '93, with an election in the air, "W5" came up with a new spin on the deficit story: how about handing the debt crisis over to a group of representative

Canadians to see what they would do about it? The concept had worked well on another occasion, when "W5," teaming up with *Maclean's* magazine, brought together twelve Canadians in a weekend session to hammer out a solution to the country's constitutional crisis.

With the deficit show likely to air—and appear as a *Maclean's* cover story—during the election campaign, it promised to have a significant impact. Here was the flagship news program of a national TV network teaming up with the national newsmagazine for a huge feature on how ordinary Canadians would tackle the deficit problem. Hundreds of thousands—perhaps millions—of Canadians would see the show or read the magazine article, or both, just when they were trying to make up their minds about how to vote in an election campaign that was heavily focused on the dangers of the debt problem.

The group assembled was a careful cross-section; it looked like something out of a handbook for political correctness. It was gender-balanced, regionally balanced, age balanced (from twenty-six to seventy-six), ethnically balanced (white, black, Oriental, native); there was a farmer, a nurse, a union leader, a small businessman, a computer specialist, a lawyer, a shopkeeper, even an unemployed woman. And after an intense weekend, this diverse group ended up unanimously recommending deep cuts that were not far from what was being advocated by the Reform Party.

For Donna Dasko, the results were surprising. For more than a decade, Dasko, vice-president of Environics, a national polling company, had been tracking Canadians' attitudes on political issues, including the deficit. Her research showed that the deficit, while attracting more attention in recent years, was not the number one issue for Canadians. Rather, unemployment consistently and dramatically dwarfed deficit reduction as the most important issue. The apparent willingness of the "W5"–*Maclean's* panel to slash government programs—including health care spending—by about 30 per cent also didn't jibe with the opinion samplings Dasko had seen over the years.

"It seemed much more extreme than I would have thought," said Dasko. Was it just that this group had taken the time to sort through the facts, and had reached conclusions that all Canadians would come to, given the same time to study the numbers?

Dasko would have been less surprised by the results had she known that the apparently typical Canadians on the panel weren't as typical as they appeared.

It would be hard for anyone to watch the CTV deficit show without being somewhat surprised. Although the panel includes a one-time labour organizer, an unemployed person, a nurse and two senior citizens, it advocates taking an axe to much of our social welfare system. Barely has the panel settled in for its weekend retreat at a picturesque resort north of Toronto than bizarre things start happening: the unemployed woman urges the dismantling of the unemployment insurance system, even though she herself is collecting UI benefits. The nurse urges dramatic cuts in health care spending, and a Philippine immigrant calls for user fees and large cuts in our social welfare system.

Who are these people? Have we slipped into a meeting of the Chamber of Commerce by mistake? Malling assures us that this is a representative group. "Only a few of those twelve people were selected because they believed in less government or even that the deficit was the main issue in the country. Rather, most of them came to that conclusion after looking at the numbers."

What Malling doesn't tell his audience is that at least half of the people were in fact selected because they had contacted "W5" to express their enthusiasm about his New Zealand debt program. Among the twelve panelists, looking every bit like a randomly selected small businessman, is Ken Haywood, the Edmonton car dealer who had contacted CTV with his enthusiastic plans for publicizing the New Zealand show. "I'd spread the gospel so well on New Zealand; that's how I got selected," Haywood told me in an interview. He was a dominant force throughout the weekend retreat, providing literature about the deficit to other panelists and acting as a catalyst for deeper cuts.

Indeed, much of what appears puzzling about the show becomes less so when we know how these people were selected. Chantal Biron, the unemployed woman who advocates abolishing UI, may not seem typical of the 1.6 million unemployed workers in Canada. That's because she probably isn't. A graduate of a university commerce course, Biron was deeply moved when she saw Malling's show on New Zealand with its government-slashing message. "My first reaction was that I wanted to leave the country," she told me. She wrote to "W5" to voice her approval and soon afterwards was asked if she would like to sit on the "W5"–*Maclean's* deficit panel.

Kit Krasemann, a communications specialist from Dartmouth, N.S., had also watched the New Zealand show, which he considered "first rate." Soon after he wrote to "W5" to express his approval, he was contacted about joining the deficit panel. Others on the panel who had also written to CTV to praise the New Zealand show included Ed Lim, the Philippine immigrant, Bill Barker, the farmer (who liked the show's warnings about the deficit but thought it was too hard on New Zealand farmers), and Carol Meredith, a computer consultant from Quebec.

Not all of the panelists had been selected from the CTV mailbag. Margaret Black, a nursing professor at a Toronto community college, was found by the polling firm Decima Research, which had been retained by CTV and *Maclean's* to help come up with prospective panelists. As a nurse, Black comes across as surprisingly willing to chop health care spending. But then Black, who had past ties with the Conservative party, may not be representative of Canadian nurses. By what criteria was she selected? She recalls being asked by the Decima interviewer what the most important problem facing Canadians was. "I answered: the deficit," she explained. That put her clearly in the small camp of Canadians—less than 20 per cent—who have reached the same conclusion. Clearly, however, she was going to feel right at home with the other panelists.

Rehak insists that the group was fairly diverse and that there was no intent to stack the deck. If anything, he says, he was disappointed that there wasn't more of a clash on the show, which would have made for better theatre. He regrets, for instance, that the unemployed woman didn't defend UI, and the nurse didn't defend health care spending. "They all turned out to be fairly hawkish, although not by design." But Rehak must have realized that he risked getting an unemployed person with a fairly hawkish viewpoint when he chose someone who had written praising Eric Malling's hawkish New Zealand show. There were many other unemployed individuals in the country who might have defended Canada's unemployment insurance system, which most unemployed people rely on for feeding themselves and their families.

Yet even if we assume that the panelists came to the weekend with relatively open minds, they were fed a carefully controlled diet of information that would lead them to believe that Canada's debt situation was acute and that the only solution lay in drastic cuts in government spending. As preparation for the weekend, each panelist was provided with videos of Malling's New Zealand show (in case they'd forgotten the details), Malling's shows on the Saskatchewan debt, and an article about the debt situation written by freelance writer Mary Janigan. While Janigan is an experienced and capable journalist, choosing her to write a "debt handbook" was perhaps a bit odd: she is married to Tom Kierans, the Howe president, who for years has been telling Canadians that we must make significant cuts in government spending in order to reduce the debt. Janigan's article makes the same point.

There seems to have been little attempt to provide another point of view. This was something that worried Ben Hoffman, an Ottawa-based negotiator who was hired by CTV and *Maclean's* to act as mediator for the event. Hoffman says that one of his big concerns when mediating an event is that participants have enough information to understand the issue they are trying to resolve.

So, while he was preparing for the weekend, Hoffman dug up material that might offer the panelists a different perspective on the issue. He got a copy of a short handbook on the deficit put out by the Canadian Centre for Policy Alternatives, an Ottawa think tank that receives some of its funding from labour unions. The handbook, called *The Deficit Made Me Do It*, is an easy-to-read critique of the deficit issue, written by three economists, that attempts to refute many of the arguments put out by conservative organizations like the C.D. Howe Institute. Hoffman said that he sent copies of *The Deficit Made Me Do It* to "W5" and *Maclean's*, but that it was not included in the package of material sent to panelists.

Rehak insists that, in an attempt to provide balance, four experts were on hand at the weekend retreat to answer questions from the panelists, and two of these experts took a moderate line on the deficit. Hoffman agrees that there was no attempt to cook the results. Perhaps it was simply more convenient to turn to the CTV mailbag to select panelists. Still, it is hard to imagine CTV and *Maclean's* turning to, say, the Canadian Centre for Policy Alternatives to suggest possible panelists. There would surely have been fears that candidates recommended by the centre might have a bias on the issue. Why were there no fears that selecting names from

Eric Malling's fan mail might result in a different sort of bias?

Sheila Simpson—one of the few panelists who apparently was not chosen on the basis of her strong views on the deficit—said she felt "manipulated" by the events. "It was as if they had a pre-set story line and we had to adhere to it. It wasn't like an exploratory thing." Simpson said that it became clear to her what the agenda was when she first received the package of background material. "When I finally watched the New Zealand thing: aha, the penny dropped."

Whatever the intent of the show's creators, the effect was to distort reality on a crucial political issue. The show left the audience with the clear but erroneous impression that a consensus exists among Canadians for massive spending cuts. Indeed, we are left with the impression that these cuts are simply tough medicine that all reasonable people would agree must be taken, no matter how unpleasant. A jury of our peers—people just like us—has weighed the evidence and come to a clear finding: the deficit must go!

It was enough to convince even those who might have been sceptical about the dire warnings coming from pin-striped deficit crusaders. In a sense, it was the ultimate distortion. Not only had these powerful media outlets failed to present any sense of the alternatives available, but they had also airbrushed away the fact that many Canadians support such alternatives. Anyone looking for hope of an alternative was presented with nothing but an army of blank faces marching in lock-step to the same deficit-reduction tune. It's all over! Resist no longer! Everyone from Bob Rae to the unemployed now agrees: *there is no alternative*.

In fact, the notion that a consensus existed on cutting social spending was misleading. If anything, a consensus appeared to exist *not* to cut social spending. An Angus Reid poll, taken in late April 1993—only a few months before the

CTV-*Maclean's* panel held its deliberations—found that almost 80 per cent of Canadians opposed any funding cuts to medicare, and almost 90 per cent opposed any funding cuts to education.

This fits with the results of polls done by Environics. Dasko said that support for social programs remains strong. She said that polling done by Environics in October '94 indicated that the public supported the idea of reforming—rather than cutting—social programs. "People think there are inefficiencies and abuses in social programs and strongly feel that those should be ferreted out," said Dasko. "But when we ask about cutting levels of benefits, there is a lot of resistance." She says that this is even true with controversial programs like unemployment insurance.

Dasko also notes that while the public supports the idea of reforming programs, it is not primarily motivated by a desire to save money. When Environics asked people what they felt should be the priorities in the Liberal government's social policy reform, the goal of ending inefficiencies ranked above the goal of saving money. "People seem to be primarily motivated by making the programs work better," says Dasko. Interestingly, however, the polling showed that people suspect that the *government's* main motivation in overhauling the programs is to save money.

The Environics results also reveal that, while Canadians feel the deficit is important, it does not rank at the top of their concerns about the country. Rather, most Canadians seem to be more concerned about unemployment and problems in the economy in general. Dasko says that Environics conducts a regular poll in which it asks Canadians what they consider to be the most important issue facing the nation. Throughout most of the '80s, the deficit barely even registered on this poll, despite the fact that the Conservative government began focusing heavily on the issue as soon as it took office in September 1984. Dasko said that no more than 1 to 2 per cent of Canadians considered the deficit the most important issue before 1988. Even after the anti-deficit campaign gained ground in business, government and the media over the following four years, still only 3 to 5 per cent of Canadians ranked it as the country's top problem.

By the spring of 1993, the deficit issue was soaring to new prominence in the rhetoric of the establishment, partly due to the incredibly high profile the issue received during the televised Conservative leadership debates that spring. Dasko says that by June 1993, when the Tory leadership race wound up with its big convention, selecting Kim Campbell, the deficit issue had picked up momentum, with 9 to 10 per cent of Canadians ranking it as the country's most serious problem—which still, however, amounts to only one in ten. During the election campaign, with almost obsessive focus on the deficit from both the Conservatives and the Reform party, it was considered most important by 14 per cent and, in late campaign, 20 per cent of Canadians. Two months later, however, it had dropped back to being the top issue for just 12 per cent of Canadians.

Dasko notes that concerns about the deficit, even at their election high point, have consistently taken a backseat to concerns about unemployment and the economy. Unemployment was ranked as the top issue by 36 per cent of Canadians during the early part of the election and, in late campaign, by 41 per cent. A year later, unemployment continued to rank well ahead of the deficit. By October 1994, as the Liberal government pledged its soul to the anti-deficit crusade with ever more feverish rhetoric, a mere 10 per cent of Canadians said the deficit was the most important issue facing the country, while 38 per cent ranked unemployment first, followed by 15 per cent who considered the economy most important.

What these polls appear to indicate, among other things, is that there is a considerable gap between the attitudes of

Canadians in general and those in the elite. While the polls consistently indicate that most Canadians consider unemployment the number one problem facing the country, the views of the elite, as reflected in the concerns expressed by the BCNI and the C.D. Howe Institute, for instance, place much greater emphasis on reducing the deficit. This gap can also be seen in Environics' poll results showing that, for Canadians with incomes below $15,000, unemployment was ranked the top issue by 40 per cent, compared to only 5 per cent concerned primarily about the deficit. For Canadians with incomes above $50,000, however, the deficit was chosen by 13 per cent, and unemployment by 34 per cent.

The deep concern over unemployment felt by ordinary Canadians was certainly visible in the dramatic line-up of an estimated 25,000 people in Pickering, just outside Toronto, when General Motors announced it would accept job applications in January 1995. There were actually no openings at the plant, and the company would only say that it anticipated hiring about 700 people over the next year for $22-an-hour assembly line jobs. Yet people, bundled in blankets and snow suits, camped out overnight in sub-zero weather, starting Friday, to be in line when the doors opened Monday morning. Indeed, the spectacle, captured in an enormous aerial photograph reproduced on the front page of *The Toronto Star*, may have come as a surprise to many members of the elite who appear to believe that the unemployed choose not to work. As a report in the *Star* vividly described:

> By Monday, the centre looked like a suburban version of Lourdes, ringed by thousands hoping to have their faith redeemed by the modern miracle of a permanent job... the crowd had assumed mythic proportions, winding for more than a kilometre around the building and through the parking lots, inching forward hour after endless hour in the steely cold...

Nobody laughed when 24-year-old Luciano Pichea described his feelings, as he finally approached the door where he would fill out an application after 12 hours of waiting. "This is a moment in history."

The different priorities of so-called ordinary people and the elite raise some interesting questions about democracy. The people seem to want jobs, and seem to be less enthusiastic about deficit reduction. The elite, on the other hand, seems to be primarily concerned about deficit reduction. If the democratic will of the people were the key factor, then presumably the government would focus its energy on jobs. It would re-examine all its policies and approaches as part of an all-out effort to figure out how to create jobs, how to come as close as we can to the goal of full employment.

To this end, for instance, it would re-examine policies like deregulation and free trade and tax policy in light of their impact on jobs. It would ask whether our obsession with inflation control was killing jobs, and whether we could increase employment through an industrial policy aimed at developing certain industries.

But rather than go through this sort of exercise in order to deliver what people evidently want, the government seems intent instead on trying to *alter* what people want. In a revealing comment shortly after the October 1993 election, a Chrétien adviser explained some of the strategic difficulties the new prime minister faced on the deficit reduction issue: "You have to remember that we weren't elected on the deficit in any way, shape or form," the adviser told *Globe and Mail* reporter Edward Greenspon. "So he has to bring everyone on side—caucus, cabinet, everyone."

This is a fascinating statement. Here we have a Chrétien adviser acknowledging that deficit reduction wasn't what Canadians voted for in the election that gave the Liberals a massive majority. Yet it never seems to occur to the adviser that the government should try to deliver what—in every way, shape and form—the people voted for. Rather, without any apparent embarrassment, the adviser goes on to define the prime minister's task as "to bring everyone on side." In other words, forget what Canadians voted for and trusted the new government to deliver (jobs), and concentrate on cajoling them into accepting what the elite wants (deficit reduction).

Some might justify this approach by arguing that the government and the experts know what is best for "ordinary people." But there is another way of looking at the situation. Perhaps ordinary people want the government to focus on jobs while the elite wants it to focus on deficit reduction, because the two groups have somewhat different interests. Jobs are the highest priority of ordinary people, who rely on a buoyant labour market to give them greater job security and prevent downward pressure on their wages. Thus, a vast army of unemployed workers is a scary sight; the spectacle of 25,000 people lined up to fill out job applications leaves even the employed feeling insecure. The deficit, on the other hand, seems like a more remote problem. Their lack of enthusiasm over the issue also has something to do with the fact that the solutions proposed always involve removing public services that they rely on.

Members of the elite, however, generally have jobs or ample means of support, and a vast army of unemployed workers means lower wages for those they employ. The deficit, on the other hand, represents a potential for higher taxes, which scares the elite, partly because there is always the danger that the public will demand that the tax system be made more progressive. Furthermore, the solutions proposed for deficit reduction—cutting back government spending—are exactly what the elite wants anyway. It is quite willing to pay for its own services privately—from private medical insurance to private schools—if it can be spared having to contribute to the cost of providing these services for everyone else.

Perhaps, then, the public's support for jobs over deficit reduction isn't just the product of ignorance or short-sightedness. Perhaps it reflects the ability of ordinary people to see through the deficit rhetoric, and appreciate that their interests may be different from those who are so keenly proposing deficit reduction. Dalton Camp, a former top-level Conservative adviser who appears to have become cynical of elites since leaving politics, put it this way: "There is a growing suspicion in the land—among common folk—that much of this public keening about how much 'they' owe, and the clever inflation thereof, is meant to soften public opinion in advance of the assault being prepared against Canadian social policy."

In other words, the public may be growing suspicious that the real goal of the deficit slashers is cutting back the size and scope of government and particularly its social welfare system. Although mainstream commentators tend to focus on the horrors of indebtedness, occasionally they reveal this deeper goal. *Globe and Mail* business columnist Peter Cook, for instance, suggested in a column that the recent rise in interest rates wasn't necessarily the bad development that everyone seemed to believe. Cook's reasoning was revealing. First, he noted, high interest rates benefit those with financial assets (generally the well-to-do, who are likely well represented among Cook's readers). Second, he argued, high interest rates greatly increase the deficit, and therefore would bring more pressure on Ottawa to start cutting spending. "Rising rates make it less easy to postpone the inevitable," wrote Cook. "The level of government in Canada is simply too large for the private sector to support and must be cut back to what is affordable. And the sooner the better.

"Is it in the national interest that Paul Martin be forced to come to terms with rising debt earlier and cut more drastically?" Cook continued. "Could this come about because rising interest rates wreck his inadequate deficit reduction plans? The answer to both is yes. Which is…two reasons to rejoice."

So increasing the deficit—normally considered an almost treasonable act by commentators like Cook—is apparently all right when the benefits go to the rich and the result is greater pressure for social cuts. Indeed, Cook's enthusiasm for higher interest rates is striking in the midst of an apparently wrenching national debate on how to bring down the deficit. Higher interest rates add billions of dollars to the deficit, making deeper spending cuts more likely and resulting in more pain for millions of Canadians. Cook's almost gleeful approach—let's tighten the deficit screws until the victim breaks under pressure!—suggests not only an indifference to the deficit, but also a more dangerous sort of indifference.

This sort of commentary, indicating a degree of nonchalance about the size of the deficit, is of course rare. Generally, commentators stick to the script that the deficit will crush us if we don't eliminate it immediately.

Certainly, the occasional attempt by labour leaders or social welfare activists to launch an attack against the heavily fortified positions of the deficit-reduction camp produces petulance among Bay Street types. And that petulance turns to anger when the attack is made by one of their own—in one case, as we shall see, by a man who, from the elegance of his Wall Street office, exercises amazing power over who will end up facing the dreaded debt wall.

CHAPTER TWO
Scissorhands Meets the Deficit Slayer

Vincent Truglia is not a man to mess with. According to Bay Street lore, at least, he is someone all Canadians should fear. From his Manhattan office, Truglia is assumed to wield more power over our collective fate than does, say, our elected prime minister. Unlike the prime minister, who ultimately must answer to the Canadian public, Truglia answers to the people who apparently make the real decisions about Canada—the international investment community. As senior analyst specializing in Canada for Moody's Investors Services, one of the two biggest debt rating agencies in the world, Truglia has a big influence on whether or not investors around the world are willing to buy Canadian government bonds. If he gives Canada the thumbs down, the country might well expect to see the debt wall coming into view.

Bay Street commentators rarely miss an opportunity to remind us how powerless we are, how real power lies in the hands of these international investors. As Tom Kierans puts it, "We're losing our sovereignty. We are living on the edge...[we are] prisoners to the international financial markets." In this "prison world" in which we live, Truglia holds the key.

So it is with considerable misgivings that a Canadian

enters the impressive Wall Street building that houses
Moody's, in search of the fearsome Mr. Truglia. The air outside on this blistering hot July day spreads over New York
like heavy steam, closing in with an almost suffocating
thickness. But inside Moody's, there is an instant feeling of
spacious coolness, of cold, gleaming marble everywhere. The
coolness tingles the skin; one could almost wear a scarf and
gloves in here. The reception area on the main floor is full of
dark panelling and plush carpeting, and has the feel of a discreet European bank.

On the elevator up to Truglia's office, I brace myself for a
lecture on the dangers of piling up mountains of debt. Surely
the very sight of a Canadian will provoke him into a tirade
against those who are unwilling to live within their means. I
feel certain that a conversation about the "debt wall" is
imminent.

But Truglia will have none of it. Animated and articu-
late, he launches almost immediately into a modest little
tirade, and yet, to my surprise, it is not against the Canadian
debt, but rather against members of the Canadian investment community for overblowing Canada's debt problems.
Can this be real? Is this actually Wall Street? Have I wan-
dered into the wrong place?

"In Canada, the tone of the debate—I handle a lot of
countries—sometimes borders on the extreme," he says.
"The vocabulary used to describe problems, from a foreign
observer's point of view, is unusual."

Truglia points out that Moody's assigns Canada a triple A
(Aaa) credit rating—its top rating. "The risk of a default on
a Triple A is something under three-tenths of one per cent
over ten years," he says, suggesting that the debt wall may be
more remote than Eric Malling would have us believe.

Even if Canada's debt were downgraded a notch to Aa1,
this would only raise the probability of a default very slightly
to five-tenths of one per cent over ten years. Truglia notes

that Aa1 is still an "extremely high rating," and is far from the debt wall. (By comparison, Truglia points out, Mexico's debt is many notches below at Baa3.) Similarly, a downgrade on the small portion of Canadian debt that is denominated in foreign currency would still leave Canada among the top 24 nations whose foreign currency debt is considered "low-risk" by Moody's. Below this group, another nine countries are considered "medium-risk." Below this is the "high-risk" category, with eleven nations, such as Brazil, India, Uruguay, and the Philippines,. Below *these*, we find dozens more—the desperately poor nations in Africa and the Middle East—that don't even get a ranking from Moody's. So uncreditworthy are they considered that international financial markets cut them off years ago. Now, *that's* the debt wall.

On the corporate side, the picture is much the same: only a small group of companies qualify for a Triple A credit rating for their corporate bonds, and the number has been declining. Back in 1926, fifty-nine industrial companies enjoyed a Triple A rating. By 1989, the number had fallen to fifteen, and included such giants as Exxon, General Electric, IBM and Kellogg. Today, in the aftermath of the corporate debt binges of the eighties, the number has fallen to six.

So for investors scouring the global horizon in search of a reliable place to invest their money, Canadian government bonds are about as safe as anything the world has to offer.

But Truglia says this message seems to irk the Canadian financial community, which is anxious to portray Canada's debt situation as far more precarious than it is. Indeed, he notes that the Canadian financial community is always hounding him to *downgrade* Canada's credit rating. "It's the only country that I handle where, usually, nationals from that country want the country downgraded even more—on a regular basis. They think it's rated too highly."

In his seventeen years as an analyst, Truglia has dealt with a wide array of countries, but he has found this attitude unique to the investment community in Canada. "If I'm giving a speech in Australia, New Zealand, Italy or Singapore, you're not going to get people arguing that you should be downgrading the country more; it just isn't done. In Canada, that's the norm. It's constant…all the time."

All the rhetoric about the Canadian debt in recent years has led to a great deal of confusion, Truglia says, and he is constantly questioned about just how serious the Canadian situation is. In an attempt to clarify some of the misunderstanding, he issued a Moody's "special commentary" in June 1993—right in the midst of a particularly strong bout of deficit hysteria in Canada. The commentary described Canada's debt as "grossly exaggerated" and pointed out that Ottawa's fiscal position was "not out of control." This was not at all what the Canadian investment community wanted to hear. It was almost like waving a red flag in front of an angry bull.

"I remember when we put out [the special commentary], one Canadian…from a very large financial institution in Canada called me up on the telephone screaming at me, literally screaming at me. That was unique. Not that people don't scream at us. They scream at us all the time. But it's usually because they're complaining that we have downgraded something and that we're not taking into account the underlying strength of the country. But Canadians usually, if anything, disparage their country far more than foreigners do."

Even if the investment community didn't like what Moody's had to say, it seemed odd that it didn't pay more attention. After all, it was Bay Street that constantly hyped the importance of international financial markets and how much control these faraway investors wielded over our economy. The slightest hint that a bond rating agency might consider downgrading Canada's credit rating usually provoked dire warnings from investors about the serious consequences for Canada. Yet here was Moody's issuing a "special commentary" on the subject of Canada's creditworthiness. Surely Truglia's words would echo through financial markets around the world, determining all sorts of things about Canada's future. If Moody's, one of the key arbiters of Canada's credit rating, was as powerful as Bay Street legend had it, then clearly Truglia's special commentary was the secular equivalent of an edict from the Pope.

Oddly, despite this mythical power, Truglia's message had almost no impact. The business press reported it briefly and largely without comment. Bay Street seemed indifferent to what most Canadians would have considered very good news. It wasn't that there were other distractions on the political horizon. The deficit was virtually the only distraction in town. June 1993 saw the culmination of the long Conservative leadership-deficit fest that selected Kim Campbell over the other equally deficit-obsessed candidates. The deficit was the subject of the day, the toast of Bay Street. And yet here were words on the deficit from an international authority, the warden of our "prison," and nobody seemed interested.

The reason for Bay Street's indifference clearly lay in the irritating content of Truglia's message. Rather than reinforcing the deficit hysteria that Bay Street had carefully been drumming up over the preceding months and years, Truglia was essentially pricking holes in this hot-air balloon. "Moody's sees no significantly negative trends in the Federal or public-sector debt outlooks which would justify changing the Aaa ratings on C$ debt of the Government of Canada." That kind of talk, if it spread, could make it a lot harder to whip up deficit mania in the future.

Truglia noted that some commentators had claimed that Canada's public-sector debt was equal to 98.1 per cent of our gross domestic product in 1992. He dismissed this number, describing it as "incredible but meaningless." One of the reasons that the number was meaningless, he explained, was that the public-sector debt package included debt run up to finance costly hydro-electric projects on behalf of provincially owned utilities. In the United States, most hydro utilities are privately owned, while in Canada they are owned by provincial governments, so the debt remains private in the U.S., while public in Canada. But Truglia pointed out that this does not represent a greater burden for Canadian taxpayers. On the contrary, he noted, "The hydros are profitable entities which can service their debt from their own generation of revenue... These companies are not a drain on provincial budgets." Indeed, they have been a boon to Canadians, generating cheap electricity for both businesses and consumers here. Truglia noted that it was a "serious flaw in the analysis" to simply add the Canadian hydro debt— worth $84.9 billion—to the country's overall debt without taking into consideration the enormous revenue the utilities generate for the Canadian provinces.

But Truglia went further, provocatively suggesting that the sense of crisis over the Canadian debt had been deliberately orchestrated through the use of invalid numbers and comparisons. Although he diplomatically mentioned no names, Truglia minced no words about the extent and nature of the deception. "Several recently published reports have grossly exaggerated Canada's fiscal debt position. Some of them have double counted numbers, while others have made inappropriate international comparisons, e.g. comparing Canadian gross debt to other countries' net debt. These inaccurate measurements may have played a role in exaggerated evaluations of the severity of Canada's debt problems."

A curious calm prevailed on Bay Street. It was the day after the new Liberal government's first budget in the winter of 1994, and in many ways, this should have been a good day for hysteria—something the gloomy bunch on Bay Street was more than capable of stirring up, particularly when the subject was the deficit. The budget confirmed the bleak news that Paul Martin had been warning us about since taking over as finance minister several months earlier—the deficit had swelled to a huge $45 billion. Such a gigantic number! More than enough to cover the salaries of a whole league of professional baseball players for decades to come.

For the brokers, currency traders, analysts and other assorted types who make up the financial markets of Toronto's Bay Street, this should have been a glum day indeed. The deficit was their obsession; the slightest change in its size or shape could cause a big change in their collective mood, a major alteration in their outlook about the country's fate. They constantly reminded us that if the deficit got too big, investors would no longer think Canada was a safe place to put their money, and they'd cut off our credit. Only a few months earlier, the deficit was said to be $30 billion, and the market types were warning that the end was approaching. How much longer would long-suffering foreign investors continue to put up with our disgraceful national profligacy?

Now, suddenly, it seemed that things had taken a dramatic turn for the worse! The deficit had gone haywire, shooting up to an incomprehensible $45 billion virtually overnight. Not a sight for the faint of heart. Truly this must be the end. All those who had sinned, all those who had benefited from government largesse, all those who had failed to pay homage to the god of a balanced budget, were surely about to pay the price. Off in the distance somewhere, officials of the International Monetary Fund (IMF) were no doubt putting on their snowsuits for the flight to Ottawa in order to take control of the nation's finances, just as they did when Third World countries went bankrupt.

Yet somehow, it didn't happen. The day after budget day, everything more or less continued as before. The IMF officials never showed up. Perhaps they were too busy in

Burundi. And, strangely, the New York-based bond rating agencies didn't even downgrade the rating on Canadian government bonds, which continued to enjoy the prestigious Triple A rating, sending a clear message to investors that Canada was still a safe place to invest money.

What's more, there was even an undercurrent of optimism in the air. "No revolution but first shot at deficit" screamed a headline on the front of a special pull-out section on the budget in the *Financial Post*. Inside, an upbeat column by Lisa Grogan-Green, the bond market reporter, was headlined: "Optimism about budget attack on deficit feeds rally." What was going on here? Hadn't the deficit just shot up almost overnight from $30 billion to $45 billion? Why wasn't everyone on Bay Street jumping off the CN Tower? Instead, they were now apparently pleased to hear that next year the deficit would "drop" to $39 billion.

If it all sounded a little suspicious, that's because it all *was* a little suspicious. The Bay Street types weren't panicking because, among other things, they understood that the deficit numbers were highly suspect. The numbers could be manipulated, almost like Play-Doh, into whatever shape government and Bay Street desired.

It was all understood to be a game, and the players were all supposed to know the rules. When Tory finance minister Don Mazankowski, in his final budget in the spring of 1993, offered up some big deficit numbers, he never expected that anyone who mattered would take him seriously. So he was outraged when the small, Montreal-based Canadian Bond Rating Service decided to downgrade its rating of Canada's bonds the day after the budget. Mazankowski harangued the little Canadian agency for its irresponsible behaviour, noting that the big New York agencies—the ones that really mattered—hadn't touched Canada's Triple A rating. What was this silly upstart Canadian agency trying to prove? Didn't it know how the game worked? Didn't it realize that those big deficit numbers were only there to scare the public?

This is not difficult to do, since the deficit is essentially a measurement, and its size can change according to what is included in the measurement. The Canadian government uses two different methods and comes up with two different-sized deficits, explains Stewart Wells, assistant chief statistician at Statistics Canada.

The first method, which is most publicized by the government, is known as the "Public Accounts." One of the features of the Public Accounts method, explains Wells, is that it makes no distinction between government spending on its operating costs, such as salaries or pension cheques, and government spending on projects that add to the country's overall physical infrastructure and provide an ongoing benefit over time, such as building a bridge or creating a harbour. In the corporate world, this distinction between "operating" and "capital" expenses is always made. Salaries and other operating expenses are accounted for separately and paid for out of current income. If the company generates more income than these operating costs over the year, it shows a profit that year.

But, even if it shows a profit, the corporation may still be deeply in debt because it has borrowed money to finance investments in new capital projects, which it expects will lead to future growth. These investments are treated differently in the company's books from current operating expenses. Since they are considered to provide an ongoing benefit over time, their costs are spread out over a number of years. If corporations simply lumped these expenditures together, as our government does, companies would almost never show a profit, since any successful corporation is almost continually going into debt to finance new capital projects.

The Public Accounts method of accounting makes the deficit look much bigger, since it lumps together all government expenditures, making it much more difficult for us to come up with the revenue to pay for it all each year. One consequence of this is that we have dramatically cut back the amount we spend on these capital investments, which will almost certainly undermine our ability to increase our productivity in the future.

The other accounting method, used by most countries around the world, is called the "National Accounts," and gives us a leaner deficit. We can see how much leaner this version looks, since Statistics Canada conveniently publishes annual figures for both the Public Accounts and the National Accounts. If we take the years from 1983 to 1992, for instance, we find that the deficit according to the Public Accounts is significantly bigger than the deficit according to the more widely used measure of the National Accounts. In 1985, it is bigger by $4 billion; in 1989, it is bigger by $9 billion. Over the ten-year period, the Public Accounts deficit is larger than the National Accounts deficit by a combined total of $59 billion.

But apparently it still wasn't big enough for the new government. So the Liberals, who had spent years in opposition pooh-poohing the Conservatives' deficit obsession, themselves made some quick adjustments in the way the Public Accounts were calculated and came up with a more satisfactory result—a simply gigantic deficit! Interestingly, the National Accounts deficit stayed about the same, hovering just below $30 billion from 1992 to 1994. But the Public Accounts deficit, which the government uses to flog its case for cutbacks, skyrocketed suddenly in 1994 to a mouthwatering $45 billion. Now that's a deficit!

Something is odd here. If our indebtedness was really growing, why was it only growing in the Public Accounts? The government was expecting us to believe that the gap between the two deficits, which had averaged $5.9 billion a year over the last decade, suddenly ballooned in 1994 to an astonishing $15 billion—all due to accounting differences!

Does this mean that if we switched over to the National Accounts method, we could afford to set up national daycare and denticare programs, feed and house all the homeless and still have money left over for pensions for senators?

Perhaps this explains why no one on Bay Street was jumping off the CN Tower the day after the budget. Nobody took the alleged $45 billion for anything other than what it was—a clever new ploy in the game. The new number was really a coded message, a sign of good faith on the part of the Liberals. It gave a signal to the financial community that the Liberals were prepared to be just as hysterical about the deficit as the Conservatives had been.

None of this is meant to suggest that Canada does not have a deficit problem. It does. Our deficit—and our debt, which is the accumulation of our deficits—are certainly among the most important economic problems we face. But, as Truglia's comments reveal and as the discrepancy between the government's two sets of accounts suggest, the numbers have been manipulated and exaggerated, leaving us with the false notion that we are staring at a "debt wall," which we are not.

The distortion has been not just about the magnitude of the problem, but also about its nature. There *is* a factor that is driving our deficit, but this factor—which we will turn to in the next chapter—has been virtually left out of the deficit debate. Instead, our focus has been restricted to the role of government spending in driving up the deficit, and the proposed solutions have focused almost exclusively on the need for spending cuts.

This view was adopted by the Liberals almost as soon as they took office, despite the fact that they had never signalled an intention to cut social spending during their highly successful election campaign in the fall of 1993. The "red book" outlining the Liberal platform never mentioned a major review of social programs. Yet one of the first big initiatives of the new government was its announcement that it intended to begin immediately conducting such a review. This was a significant turnaround. The Liberals had been in power when most of Canada's major social programs were established, and from the opposition benches they had defended these programs staunchly for years as the Conservatives implemented major cutbacks.

But, as Paul Martin made clear in his first budget in February 1994, deficit reduction was to become the new government's top priority, and it would involve a two-year package, with the big reductions coming in the form of social spending cuts in the next budget. As the *Financial Post* noted on its front page, "Rather than a deficit knock-out, [Martin] delivered what he said will be a two-pronged attack—with real change coming in the next budget, when social programs will be better defined."

Bay Street understood that "better defined" meant "reduced." As the *Post* said in a prominent analysis piece, "If there is any cause for optimism from the first budget of the new Liberal government it is from the tough defence policy and the stand on social spending." The Liberals were dangling the prospect of major social spending cuts and Bay Street was waiting to see if they would deliver results.

After running a campaign focused almost exclusively on job creation, the Liberals had made a smooth transition to deficit mania. There was to be no overhaul of government employment strategies, no cross-country consultation on how to tackle joblessness, no national soul-searching about how to put the country back to work. Social programs alone were on the table, and it looked very much like a cutting table. The Liberals had come to regard social programs as being responsible for the deficit.

It was a view they shared with many in the elite. The only problem was that it was wrong.

The ugly modern building in the heart of bureaucratic Ottawa was perhaps the last place one would expect to find controversy. Far from the bluster of the House of Commons and the push-and-shove of the media pack on Parliament Hill, this grey complex was the centre for the collection and processing of perhaps the dullest of human inventions: the statistic. And if ever a quiet, studious and humble individual suited the painstaking, detailed work of the statistician, it was Hideo Mimoto. A career civil servant in his early sixties, Mimoto had long been involved in preparing endless reams of statistics on social security—statistics that, needless to say, few Canadians ever looked at or cared about.

But Mimoto cared deeply. During the eighties, he had become increasingly concerned and perplexed. Like everyone else, he kept hearing business, government and media commentators call for social spending restraint in order to reduce the deficit. People seemed to feel that social spending was out of control and had to be cut back. But, as chief of the small social security section at Statistics Canada, Mimoto couldn't help but notice that all the talk about runaway social spending didn't seem to match the numbers. He decided to look deeper.

No one was better equipped to tackle this kind of investigation than Mimoto. From his quiet corner inside Statistics Canada, he had been something of a pioneer in expanding the department's data base on social spending, and also in making it accessible to the public. When he first joined the department in 1964, Statistics Canada made little attempt to communicate with the public, or even to provide information that ordinary people could understand. It produced mounds of data—on countless obscure subjects involving trade, production and the economy—with little or no analysis to give the data meaning. And in the vast field of social welfare, the department collected surprisingly little information.

From his early days at Statistics Canada, Mimoto showed

an interest in gathering more information on social programs, and making it publicly accessible. In this, he was influenced by Miles Wisenthal, a director general in the department with a strong commitment to public access. An educational psychologist by training, rather than a statistician, Wisenthal felt that Statistics Canada shouldn't simply be a "figure factory," churning out data that had little meaning for the non-specialist. Rather, he saw the department as playing a key educational role, helping Canadians understand their society by providing them with data and research material that was "issue-oriented." Only through knowledge and understanding could the citizenry be well informed enough to make proper democratic choices.

Mimoto was inspired by Wisenthal's commitment to public education. The work of a statistician seemed more interesting—even exciting—when linked with socially significant ideals like public education and democracy. All this appealed to Mimoto, who, despite a background that was traditional and conservative, had a strong bent for democracy and social justice. He had grown up in a Japanese-Canadian family in British Columbia, where his father ran a contracting business and held views not unlike those espoused today by the Reform Party. Mimoto Senior had resisted signing up for his Old Age Security pension on the grounds that such government handouts smacked of socialism.

Unlike his father, Mimoto had been impressed by the growth of Canada's social programs in the postwar period. And under the influence of Wisenthal, he took an interest in expanding the department's social spending statistics. Using data often collected from other federal departments, Mimoto turned out a massive 600-page report on Canadian social security programs in the late seventies. Further encouraged by Wisenthal, Mimoto went on to produce a series of reports on specific programs like unemployment insurance, public pensions and family benefits. Using simple, coloured charts, the reports made details of these little-known areas of public spending comprehensible to interested members of the public, notably teachers and students. The 300-page report on unemployment insurance, for instance, contained charts and diagrams that graphically illustrated, among other things, the sources of revenue for the unemployment insurance fund, the changing benefit and contribution levels over time, the average weekly benefit for each region and how it compared to the average weekly wage in that region.

By the mid-eighties, when the deficit debate was heating up and increasingly focused on cutting social spending, Mimoto was probably the most knowledgeable person in the country on the subject of government spending on social programs. But he hardly recognized some of the claims made in the debate, which seemed to take it for granted that social spending was growing at explosive rates. He decided to put together another report to set the record straight.

This time, however, he was wading into potentially dangerous political waters. His earlier reports on social programs had been non-contentious descriptions of programs and their costs, and had largely ended up in libraries or as reference material for university courses. Now he was tackling a much more volatile subject—whether or not social programs could be blamed for the deficit. It was a subject that had come to obsess influential segments of the business community, not to mention members of the government, Mimoto's employer.

Mimoto was also without his mentor, who had retired from Statistics Canada. But before leaving, Wisenthal had put him into a new job working on health statistics, where he was mostly left on his own. Mimoto used that freedom to assign himself the somewhat daunting task of determining the truth about what had caused the deficit. For more than a year, Mimoto quietly beavered away at his self-appointed task. By the late spring of 1991, he had pulled together an impressive array of statistics that, in essence, contradicted popular perceptions of the deficit. Indeed, Mimoto's study had the potential to turn the deficit debate on its head.

What it showed was that government spending was not really the root cause of our debt problems. Contrary to the popular image of government spending careening wildly out of control, the study showed that our spending had been quite restrained since the onset of deficit problems in the mid-seventies. And this was particularly true in the area that had been taking the most heat politically—social spending.

Mimoto had come up with an interesting way to demonstrate this. He singled out a number of social programs—including unemployment insurance, old age pensions, family benefits, and welfare—and examined how much spending had increased in each one of these programs. He then calculated how much the increased spending in each program had contributed to the growth of the federal debt.

What he found was surprising. Consider the case of unemployment insurance. If there was a popular bad boy on the social program scene, it was unemployment insurance, which was routinely attacked for encouraging idleness, dependency and outright fraud. Not surprisingly, the program had been a favourite target for cuts by the deficit slashers in the Mulroney government—a pattern that was quickly emulated by the Liberals in their first budget. Given the degree of hostility directed at unemployment insurance over the last decade, we might expect to find that the program had been a major contributor to the growth of the federal debt. So how much of the debt growth could be blamed on unemployment insurance? Perhaps 10 per cent? Or 20 per cent?

Mimoto dug into the numbers and found a very different answer: only *1 per cent* of the debt growth was due to unemployment insurance costs! Whatever mud one wanted to sling at all those idle workers, it wasn't fair to blame them for the deficit.

Mimoto made the same calculations for welfare programs across the country, and found that only 4.5 per cent of the growth of the federal debt could be attributed to them. The old age pension accounted for 6 per cent, and housing programs for 3.4 per cent.

Interestingly, the bigger spending increases were in areas that had not been the focus of public attacks or even public discussion. For instance, about 8 per cent of the debt growth, he found, could be attributed to increased spending on "protection of persons and property," a category that included the military, the police and the prison system. This raised the curious possibility that we were following the uninspiring example of the United States. After deep social spending cuts, the biggest item on many U.S. state budgets was now the cost of imprisoning people. (Of course, this begs the question of whether there is a connection between the two. If we spend less on social programs, do we encourage the kind of social breakdown that leads to higher spending on police and prisons? We may be not only undermining the social order with these spending cuts, but also engaging in an ultimately fruitless attempt at deficit control.)

The story becomes more interesting still when we look at the case of family benefits—that is, payments Ottawa made to families with children, including family allowance cheques and tax credits. During the eighties, the Mulroney government carried out a series of revisions in the family benefits area, always insisting that it was redesigning the system to provide better protection for children. We might, therefore, expect to find that benefits were increased and that the whole area of family benefits contributed significantly to the growth of the debt. But Mimoto found just the opposite: family benefits were not a major contributor to debt growth. In fact, they didn't contribute to it at all. Rather, family benefits were cut back so severely after 1975 that the cuts actually helped *reduce* the debt growth by 11 per cent!

Mimoto found other areas where we "saved" money. For instance, our cuts in spending on public transit and communications systems, including VIA Rail and postal services, helped reduce the deficit by 8.2 per cent. We also "saved" money by cutting back on spending in resource conservation, the environment, industrial development and regional planning and development—areas that by almost any standard would be regarded as important. Indeed, just about every area that would potentially contribute to the growth and development of the country seems to have been singled out by the government as a prime target for deficit reduction.

Let's look closer, for instance, at the environment. As public concern and understanding of the scope of environmental problems grew in the late sixties and early seventies, Ottawa responded with dramatic increases in spending in areas such as pollution control, water purification, sewage treatment and waste disposal. After the mid-seventies, however, with deficits growing, Ottawa's enthusiasm for environmental issues waned and spending declined, even though the scope of our environmental problems had clearly not diminished. Spending on the environment became yet another casualty of the deficit squeeze—without any real public debate about the long-term implications for the country.

Mimoto's tracking of the increases and decreases in various government programs led him to some startling conclusions. As he noted, the amount we spent on social programs had not been growing any faster than the growth in the overall economy. In other words, we were spending roughly the same proportion of our Gross Domestic Product on social programs as we had in the mid-seventies, when our deficits were very small. In some crucial areas, like child benefits, we were spending a smaller proportion than before. As Mimoto bluntly concluded, "it was not explosive growth in social spending that caused the increase in deficits." (We will return later to what Mimoto concluded did cause the deficit.)

Mimoto's findings had the potential to alter the debate in a crucial way. If social programs were not really the cause of the deficit, was slashing them the solution? Or had we gone off on a tangent that was unlikely to solve our deficit problems but that threatened to disturb the social fabric of the country in the process? Mimoto decided to try to get his data out to the public in the only way he knew—by publishing them in Statistics Canada's quasi-academic journal, the *Canadian Economic Observer*. It wouldn't be as effective as a cover story in *Maclean's* or a special on "W5," but at least the information might find its way into the work of academics or others who could eventually draw it to public attention.

So, in typically scholarly fashion, Mimoto sent a draft of his report to a number of experts for review and comment. Among those receiving it were David Perry, senior researcher for the Canadian Tax Foundation, and Eden Cloutier, an economist with the Economic Council of Canada. Some of the experts sent back suggestions, but none had any fundamental problems. Indeed, they were generally encouraging. In a letter, David Perry called it "a useful and well-done study that identified clearly the factors contributing to the current fiscal position of the federal government." Cloutier, at the Economic Council, said that he read the study three or four times and found no problems with it. "To me, it was very straightforward," he recalls. He wrote back an encouraging note to Mimoto: "The paper provides a very useful perspective on the recent growth in federal revenues and expenditures. *The study makes a contribution to current discussions on the deficit...and should be made widely available*" [italics added].

After months in the bureaucratic hopper of Statistics Canada, the study was reworked and rewritten and eventually appeared, in a modified and toned-down version, in the *Canadian Economic Observer* in June 1991. Much of the most interesting material—showing how much various programs had contributed or not contributed to the deficit—was gone from the final version. Still, it made the basic point that social spending had not been the cause of the explosive debt growth in recent years.

The publication of the Mimoto study caused barely a ripple. Academics who read the journal already knew the gist of the story, and the public, who didn't, didn't read statistical journals. But if Mimoto's efforts seemed to have little effect, there was at least one place in the country where they were noted. Across town, in the department of Finance, the report had touched a nerve. It had been the department's role to sell the government's message about the need for spending cuts. And it had been difficult enough to sell that message to an unreceptive public without some upstart statistician in the government's own bureaucracy trying to undermine the case.

The Finance department swung into action. Kevin Lynch, a powerful assistant deputy minister there, wrote a scathing letter to Statistics Canada head Ivan Fellegi outlining the department's objections to the study. Essentially, the department insisted that the study was badly flawed, even though a number of economists, including one in the Finance department itself, had read it and found no fault. Indeed, the research department of the Bank of Canada had done a study in the early eighties that had used a similar methodology and come to similar conclusions. But that was before the topic had become so sensitive. Lynch wanted to make sure the study was effectively removed from public debate.

Fellegi was also a powerful mandarin in the Ottawa bureaucracy, with an international reputation. He had worked his way up through the ranks, and served on the prestigious commission appointed by President Jimmy Carter to reorganize the U.S. statistics system in the late seventies. Since 1985, Fellegi had held the job of chief statistician within Statistics Canada. If it came to a showdown between Fellegi and Lynch, however, Fellegi was unlikely to win.

Within the Ottawa pecking order, Finance was the most powerful department, and deficit management was its bailiwick, as well as being perhaps the highest priority of the government in power. Besides, Lynch was clearly speaking with the authority of those at the very top of Finance. Sometimes referred to behind his back as "Kevin Scissorhands," Lynch had a reputation for being the hatchet man within Finance. He was also known to be close to the department's extremely powerful minister, Michael Wilson, the man most responsible for shaping the government's crusade against the deficit. Fellegi, who understood the nuances of the Ottawa scene, realized that he was not in a promising situation. One of his statisticians had just tweaked the nose of Ottawa's powerful deficit establishment.

Retreat seemed like the best option. And it could be done without much loss of face since this wasn't Fellegi's area of expertise. He was a survey statistician. No doubt he would have gone to bat over a matter of principle involving the proper handling of statistical surveys. But calculations about the deficit and what did and didn't contribute to it were not within his area of interest. He was content to leave the field to Finance. Besides, political survival in the Ottawa jungle demanded nothing less.

Fellegi resolved to beat a quick retreat and take the unusual step of disassociating his department from one of its own studies. He called assistant chief statistician Stewart Wells back from holidays in the middle of July and told him to write a retraction. Wells, who was in charge of Mimoto's section, had seen earlier drafts of the study and had been involved in getting it published. Like Mimoto, he believed that the study contained important information that was being overlooked in the deficit debate. Wells shared Mimoto's frustration over the public's misunderstanding of the deficit issue, and the popular belief that social programs were to blame. Finance's objections seemed frivolous and politically motivated.

But Wells could see that it was a lost cause, with Finance and his own department head lined up against him. After a few heated verbal battles with Fellegi, he complied. The August 1991 edition of the *Canadian Economic Observer* contained an odd disclaimer that expressed regret that the Mimoto article appeared to have "added to controversy rather than reduced it." It then raised a number of obscure objections, none of which contradicted the basic finding of Mimoto's study. The disclaimer concluded by saying "Statistics Canada regrets any inconvenience that may have been caused by these aspects of the article." The deficit establishment had succeeded in squelching Mimoto's bold attempt to bring a little light into the dark reaches of the deficit debate.

Perhaps this is simply the way things are always done in government, or in any bureaucracy. But it is worth considering whether things couldn't have been done differently. The government might have used Mimoto's study as an opportunity to educate the public about an important matter of public concern. This, of course, was the approach that would have been advocated by Miles Wisenthal, who had always argued that government information should be allowed to enrich public debate, and thereby empower the citizenry to make informed choices. In this case, government information, painstakingly assembled at public expense, was disclaimed in order to prevent the public from seeing potential weaknesses in the government's deficit argument.

The experts who were consulted on the report felt that it should have received wider attention. David Perry, from the tax foundation, said that it was "a shame that it got buried." Certainly, from the public's point of view, it would have been healthy to "add to the controversy" about the deficit, rather than have us all simply accept the version of reality offered up by the Finance department or the C.D. Howe Institute or the *Globe and Mail* editorial page. But that would be risky. If Canadians learned that social spending wasn't really the deficit culprit, they might be less willing to accept the drastic social spending cuts that the government had in mind. And they might also start asking the question that, above all, the government did not want to answer—*what then, for God's sake, was the culprit?*

To continue our quest, let's return to the Moody's special commentary on Canada. Its most telling point was simple and basic, yet almost always ignored by deficit commentators: that the Canadian deficit was largely a product of the recession. Truglia noted, for instance, that Canada's debt was essentially manageable in the late eighties, and was not much bigger proportionately than the U.S. debt. But our debt spurted up suddenly in the early nineties. He explains that this was "mainly because of the economic downturn. Such a development is normal during a recession."

Such a development is normal during a recession.

This calm assessment of the situation is so simple that it almost passes by without notice. At first, it just sounds as if Truglia's saying recessions are bad. In fact, he's saying much more than that. What he's saying amounts to a fundamentally different perspective on the deficit. Rather than its being the product of overspending, overindulgence, gorging on rich food, all the images captured by the familiar phrase "living beyond our means," the deficit is actually caused by the fact that we have been—and in many ways continue to be—mired in a recession. With so many Canadians unemployed and underemployed, we are just not generating the kind of economic activity we need for a healthy economy. And that is producing a number of serious consequences, including driving up our deficit and debt.

In our obsessive focus on the costs of maintaining our social programs, we overlook the enormous costs of maintaining such a high rate of unemployment. The simple truth is that having large numbers of people idle is very expensive for us. To begin with, if people are not working, they are paying a great deal less income tax and a great deal less sales tax into the federal treasury. Also, since they have less money to spend on all the goods and services that other Canadians produce, these other Canadians also end up with less income, and therefore pay less in the way of income and sales taxes. And since the unemployed now have no income from jobs, we have to pay out money to care for many of their needs—through unemployment insurance, welfare or myriad programs that provide special supplements for low-income people to cover the costs of the GST, dental bills, housing, drug plans, day care and so on. Instead of being contributors to our economy, they become a drain on the economy.

The costs of all this are staggering. A study by two Quebec economists, Diane Bellemare and Lise Poulin-Simon, estimated that unemployment cost the total Canadian economy $109 billion in the fiscal year 1992–93. The cost to federal and provincial treasuries in lost tax revenue alone amounted to $39 billion, they found. In addition, unemployment obliged us to spend an additional $10 billion in unemployment insurance and social assistance costs. Unemployment costs us all money, and offers nothing in the way of extra goods and services that would improve our lives. It has become nothing but a deadweight on our shoulders.

This is very demoralizing to those who have had to live with the stigma of being a deadweight on society—a message constantly driven home by those who pontificate about the alleged overgenerosity in our unemployment insurance system. But the point here is that this deadweight is costly for the rest of society, too. Indeed, as Truglia points out, it is the main reason for our deficit problems. Significant numbers of people who used to contribute to our economy and our national treasury are no longer contributing their share (and their diminished incomes have also reduced the incomes of others who relied on selling to them). Those without work are draining our collective resources. The result has been a sudden surge in our deficit, as the costs of financing our debt have outstripped the growth of our economy, like a bushfire consuming a dry forest.

In some ways, we have compounded the problem with our obsessive quest to cut government spending. We have reduced government spending substantially in the last decade, cutting back in almost every area, and this has given us the illusion that we are saving more than we really are. We think that if the government sheds thousands of employees, this will reduce our costs and therefore our deficit. But it is not that simple. It might be, if all the government employees who lost their jobs could find work elsewhere. But the private sector, too, has been shedding its own workers in a drive to downsize and restructure its operations. So, with nowhere to go, these casualties of government restraint have simply swollen the ranks of the unemployed, and thereby exacerbated the deficit problem. The result is that, despite massive government spending cuts over the past decade, the deficit stubbornly refuses to subside—because unemployment has failed to subside.

Even the widely trumpeted "recovery" of '93 and '94 has been little help in bringing down the deficit, because, unlike past recoveries, it has been largely a "jobless recovery." Truglia argues that with both the private and public sectors "shedding workers," there just hasn't been the overall rise in incomes that would normally accompany a recovery. "If you don't get sharp improvements in income, you don't get improvement in government tax receipts which governments normally count on to improve their fiscal positions," says Truglia. This also suggests that, as long as we have high unemployment and underemployment in Canada, we will continue to suffer deficit problems.

The Canadian public seems to have instinctively figured this out, which is apparently why it voted massively in the 1993 federal election for the party that promised to focus, above all, on creating jobs, and to reject the governing party, which had focused, almost exclusively, on the goal of cutting government spending. But, as we've seen, the Liberals, once in power, changed their focus. And certainly, influential segments of the business and financial community have kept their gaze fixed resolutely on spending cuts.

The focus on spending cuts is apparently rooted in the assumption that our national finances are fundamentally unsound, and that our financial house must be put back in order. And yet, it is important to assess in what way our financial house is in disorder. We should remember that our social spending is not out of line with that of other industrial nations; in fact, it is lower than the social spending in the advanced nations of western Europe. We raise more than enough money through our tax system to pay for all our government spending programs—*when enough people are working*. In other words, without the massive unemployment that has plagued us in recent years, we have been "living within our means."

We can see this most clearly if we compare ourselves to some other countries that are not "living within their means." The Paris-based Organization of Economic Co-operation and Development (OECD), which measures all aspects of the economies of the advanced industrial nations, produces an interesting set of calculations to determine the *nature* of each country's deficit. The calculation shows the extent to which each country is "living within its means"— that is, the extent to which its revenues are sufficient to cover its spending, as long as sufficient numbers of people are working.

To obtain an accurate measure of this, the OECD considers it necessary to identify how much of a country's deficit is caused by recession, since recessions, as we've just seen, cause deficits to balloon. This allows the OECD to measure what it calls the "structural" deficit—the gap between the revenue a government collects and the amount it spends when the economy is operating properly, free of recession. A large structural deficit indicates something is truly wrong with the nation's finances, like the foundations of a house not being strong enough to hold it up. To see how solid a country's foundations are, the OECD separates out the part of the deficit caused by the recession. "Strip out that [recession] portion and the true financial health of governments is easier to measure," as the *Economist* explains it.

Interestingly, when the OECD applies this approach to Canada's economy, our national finances take on a very different look. Yes, Canada's *overall* deficit is relatively large, compared to those of the other top industrial nations. In 1993, our deficit (as a percentage of our GDP) was the third largest among the top seven nations, after Italy and Britain. Not impressive.

When, however, we strip out the portion of the deficit due to the recession, the picture changes: Canada's finances start to look much healthier. For instance, the OECD shows that our overall deficit was 5.8 per cent of our GDP, while the United States had a deficit that year of only 3.8 per cent of its GDP. But when the OECD stripped out the recession component, the U.S. deficit shrank by only 0.8 per cent, leaving it with a "structural" deficit of 3 per cent. When the recession component was stripped out of Canada's deficit, however, our deficit shrank by a significant 3.7 percentage points, leaving us with a "structural" deficit of only 2.1 per cent. In other words, when "true financial health" is measured, Canada does better than the U.S. Indeed, according to the OECD's calculations, Canada ranks second only to

Japan in "true financial health"!

Furthermore, Canada's "true" deficit of 2.1 per cent is not only small by international comparisons, it is, in a sense, dangerously small. Its smallness reflects the fact that the federal government in recent years has been investing too little in our public infrastructure. From the mid-fifties to the mid-seventies, Canada was investing almost 4 per cent of the nation's GDP each year in public infrastructure, which includes everything from highways, airports, bridges, canals, public transit systems, power plants and sewage systems to all our public buildings for schools, universities, libraries and hospitals. But that investment began to decline and, by 1990, was less than 2.5 per cent of GDP. Pierre Fortin, an economist at the Université du Québec à Montréal, notes that this lower spending in recent years is due to our failure to keep updating and improving our infrastructure.

Incidentally, this decline is cause for concern because investments in public infrastructure are the means by which a society prepares itself for the future. Just like a business that fails to invest adequately in its future, a government that fails to make the necessary public investments can end up stunting the country's growth potential, not to mention diminishing the quality of life of Canadians. In an era of apparently fierce global competition, the development and maintenance of a good public infrastructure is crucial to remaining competitive with other nations. An excellent transportation system, for instance, is an essential tool for an advanced industrial economy to function effectively; inadequate, poorly maintained road systems result in traffic jams and flat tires, and this drives up the costs of doing business.

It is also interesting to note that the "recession component" measured by the OECD was larger in the Canadian deficit than in the deficits of any of the other top seven nations. There is a very simple but little-known reason for this: the recession and unemployment have been more severe in Canada than in any of the G7 nations. We can see this clearly if we look at another OECD measurement—something called the "output gap," which is the difference between what an economy actually produces and what it is capable of producing with full employment. A big output gap indicates that a country is failing badly to live up to its full-employment potential. And of the seven top industrial nations, Canada has had the biggest output gap of all!

In 1992, for instance, the output gap of the United States was a mere 1.98 per cent, meaning that the United States was operating at almost its full employment potential. (Japan's output gap was even smaller, at 1.41 per cent, while Germany's was 0.54 per cent and France's was 2.43.) Meanwhile, Canada's was a whopping 10.32 per cent—more than five times larger than that of the U.S. This was also the largest output gap Canada had experienced in the postwar period, and the largest any OECD country had experienced in thirty years. What this indicated was that Canada's severe unemployment crisis had left it operating far below its potential. And this was exactly why our overall deficit was so large. In other words, just as Truglia indicated in the Moody's special commentary, it was unemployment and the recession, not social spending, that were the real cause of our deficit woes.

But what was the cause of the recession? Why, among the seven most advanced nations, has Canada had the most severe recession, with the highest unemployment rate and, as a result, one of the biggest overall deficits? To understand the real story behind the deficit we must figure out what has been creating our unemployment problem. Our search for the real deficit culprit continues.

Globalization, one might assume, would be a likely candidate. The vague term summed up all that seemed to threaten Canadian jobs: the internationalization of markets, the flight of capital to the Third World, the intense competitiveness of the global marketplace. This certainly sounded like the root cause of Canada's unemployment problems. As we were constantly reminded, high-wage Canada was having trouble competing in a low-wage world in an age of disappearing national boundaries and tariff walls. It seemed clear that we Canadians were victims of the sweeping powers of globalization, and our only choice was to get our wages down low enough to compete with the hungry tigers of the Far East.

This was the conventional wisdom, and it was more or less what a team of academic economists at the University of Toronto's Institute for Policy Analysis expected to find when they applied their computer model to the question of what had created Canada's recession. What they discovered surprised them. Rather than Canada being driven into recession by the globalization juggernaut, the U of T team came up with strong evidence to show that the Canadian recession had in fact been caused by something much closer to home, something right here within our borders. We'll return to this subject.

As we continue our search, it is important to remember that, as recently as the late eighties, the deficit situation looked very different. As the economy experienced a mini-boom, the deficit was actually falling—from 8.7 per cent of GDP in 1984–85 down to 4.5 per cent in 1989–90. In early 1991, George Vasic, a Bay Street financial analyst, noted in a column in *Canadian Business* that Ottawa had cut government spending considerably and, he suggested, the deficit was now on its way to oblivion. Vasic predicted that by the mid-nineties, we would have turned the corner and, after that, the debt load would be much more manageable: "It will be all downhill." Vasic went on to suggest, somewhat whimsically, that Finance Minister Michael Wilson would probably not be around to get the credit he so richly deserved, as his clever strategy of spending cuts paid off with a rapidly disappearing deficit by the end of the decade.

In retrospect, Vasic's analysis sounds like naive wishful thinking, but in fact, its assumptions were sound, given the situation at the time. The deficit *was* falling in the late eighties, and if things had simply stayed on track, the deficit would have become less and less of a problem over time. "We were almost there," says Pierre Fortin. "But the recession blew us out of the water."

Indeed, out of the water we went. The recession derailed everything: hundreds of thousands of jobs disappeared, forcing desperate families onto social assistance, and much of the rest of the workforce, fearful for their jobs, cut back their consumption. House buyers who had bought in the frenzied market of the late eighties found themselves owning properties that suddenly lost as much as one-third of their value. And, as a result of all this contraction, the deficit took a beating too. Rather than melting away in the warm afternoon sun, the deficit iceberg began to grow again in the wake of the recession, reaching dramatic proportions once again by 1993, when the Conservative government was inconveniently obliged to call an election.

In a sense, Wilson and the entire Mulroney cabinet had been blindsided, caught off guard by a surging recession that ultimately brought down their government with an unrelenting vengeance. It was a recession the Conservatives had not anticipated, a recession they had allowed someone else to create.

CHAPTER THREE
John Crow and the
Politics of Obsession

Sitting in the audience along with local Halifax digni-
taries in June 1987, Stanley Hartt heard words that set his
political antennae throbbing.

Hartt, the federal deputy minister of finance who later
served as chief of staff to the prime minister, was a political
animal. A former labour lawyer and Montreal crony of Brian
Mulroney, Hartt had been selected by Mulroney to fill the
crucial job of running the Finance department not because
of his grasp of economics; his expertise lay elsewhere. A
sophisticated operator, with a track record for solving hostile
labour disputes, he had a knack for feeling his way deftly
through difficult situations. His task as deputy minister was
clear: to sell his old friend's ambitious economic agenda to a
sceptical public. What he heard at the Halifax dinner that
warm June day made him realize his job was about to get a
lot tougher.

"We cannot afford to give up the hard-won ground we
have gained against inflation," said John Crow, who, months
earlier, had been appointed by the Mulroney government to
head the Bank of Canada. "Further gains in restoring price
stability are essential if we are to make the progress we all
want to see on other economic fronts."

The Halifax gathering was a largely ceremonial affair attended by several hundred people. The Bank's board of directors traditionally held one meeting a year outside Ottawa, and that year it was in Halifax. All the major figures of Nova Scotia business and politics were there. Hartt was flanked on one side by Premier John Buchanan and on the other by NDP leader Alexa McDonagh.

Crow had apparently chosen the sedate Halifax setting to announce a significant policy change. Although his language was somewhat oblique, the new governor was signalling that Canada's central bank was about to get a great deal tougher on inflation. Hartt was no economist, but he was familiar enough with the subject to know that this meant higher interest rates and, inevitably, tougher economic times. It also spelled serious trouble for the two key economic policies that the Mulroney government was most intent on implementing: free trade and the GST.

But what was truly amazing about the whole situation was that Hartt, who was charged with overseeing the country's economic policies, was hearing about this highly significant development—which would affect every area of the economy—for the first time while sitting in the audience at a public event. This wasn't the normal way that government business was conducted.

Back in Ottawa, Hartt reported the highlights of the speech to his boss, Finance Minister Michael Wilson. Wilson was not surprised. He knew of Crow's intentions because he and Crow had held private discussions prior to the Halifax speech and had broadly agreed. "It was pretty consistent with what we had been talking about in our meetings," Wilson recalled in a recent interview. Like Crow, Wilson had a staunch, almost obsessive commitment to fighting inflation, and the two men had agreed in the spring of 1987 that the battle should be stepped up. Still, Wilson was also interested in Hartt's strong instinctive reaction about the political dangers of launching such a battle—something he apparently hadn't sensed himself. Wilson decided that officials in the Finance department should investigate the matter independently, partly to determine how great the danger of inflation really was, and partly to keep an eye on Crow—and to let him know they were doing so.

It was almost like dealing with a foreign government.

Six months later, Crow was more explicit about his intentions. It was a Monday in the dead cold of Edmonton in January 1988, when he spoke to a largely student audience at the University of Alberta. It is probably safe to say that most of the students would rather have been at the campus pub; fighting off boredom promised to be the major challenge of the event. No one in the audience seemed to be aware of the momentous nature of what they were about to hear.

Many of the students had come because they were specializing in economics, and assumed that some of the material might be on an exam. The more serious among them realized that, if they were genuinely interested in economics, they shouldn't pass up an opportunity to hear a speech by the governor of the Bank of Canada, no matter how tedious it promised to be. After only a few minutes, it seemed that their worst fears were about to be realized.

"I realize that parts of what I have to say might seem somewhat technical to some of you," said the governor. Hardly a great way to warm up an audience, but then Crow, a tall, imposing character in a dark, conservative suit, was no stand-up comic. Still, this was shaping up to be even duller than expected. The speech droned on. A beer would sure taste good right now.

"What pace of monetary expansion is most helpful to the development of the Canadian economy?" asked Crow rhetorically, as the students, serious and dilettantes both, shifted in their seats and struggled to focus their attention. An important question, no doubt. But the lure of the pub seemed increasingly irresistible. Could this really be on the exam?

"Monetary policy should be conducted so as to achieve a pace of monetary expansion that promotes price stability in the value of money," Crow said. "This means pursuing a policy aimed at achieving and maintaining stable prices."

His words were greeted with little more than a stifled yawn or two. There were certainly no gasps. No one in the room even seemed aware that this man—whose command over the economy was enormous—had just revealed in those brief sentences his intention to overturn decades of Canadian policy and take the country on an odyssey into uncharted waters. In essence, he had just announced that Canada's economy was to become a laboratory for an experiment never before conducted in any major country in the world.

If the students missed the significance of Crow's words that night, it would have been unfair to punish them on the exam. In the months and years to come, Crow's statements in that speech, the Eric J. Hanson Memorial Lecture, came to be seen as marking the beginning of his bold policy shift. But nobody seemed to notice it at the time. The media paid little attention. The *Globe* ran a story about the speech the next day at the bottom of page 7 of its business section, beneath an article about a regulatory board ruling affecting natural gas prices for hospitals and school boards. There was no mention in the *Globe* story about Crow's crucial policy shift.

Even back in the Finance department, there was still little understanding of where Crow was headed. This was odd, since the department kept close tabs on everything that was going on in the government. Because it was considered the most powerful and important department in the Ottawa hierarchy, other parts of the government generally sought Finance's approval before doing much of anything that would affect the economy. Here was a policy, if ever there was one, that promised to have a lasting, far-reaching impact on the Canadian economy and on the lives of all Canadians. And yet Finance officials had surprisingly little information about what the Bank was doing.

The Bank of Canada was a curious institution, which performed a vital, if little-known function in the Canadian economy. It was the nation's central bank, owned by the federal government and ultimately accountable to the federal government, and it presided over the nation's money, or its monetary policy. It was responsible for protecting the value of the national currency abroad, and for regulating the amount of money in circulation at home. These were crucial functions. Far more than most Canadians realized, the Bank played a vital role in determining the health of the Canadian economy and in mediating between the competing interests of different segments of Canadian society. Yet, despite its awesome powers, it operated as a semi-autonomous institution in virtual obscurity, only remotely controlled by the elected government and poorly understood by the Canadian public.

And Crow's bold policy shift was anything but benign. The goal of achieving "stable prices" may not have sounded earth-shattering. Indeed, it would have sounded more shocking had Crow announced an intention to pursue *unstable* prices. Price stability meant an absence of inflation: a dollar would hold the same value in the future that it held today. That certainly sounded like a reasonable goal. The only problem was, how was it to be achieved? The apparently innocuous concept of price stability rested on a minefield.

In fact, there were a number of ways that rising prices could be curbed. But perhaps the most potent method—a method which, if applied with sufficient force, could stop inflation dead in its tracks—was to raise interest rates. When John Crow spoke of pursuing a policy aimed at price stability, what he meant was that the Bank of Canada would take measures that would have the effect of raising interest rates enough to eliminate inflation.

Before we go any further, we should clarify that the Bank does not have full control over interest rates, but it does however control levers that strongly influence them. Essentially, the interest rate was the cost attached to borrowing money, and it was therefore determined heavily by the desires of those with money to lend. If these lenders felt their loans weren't safe—that the borrower might fail to repay them, for instance—they would demand a higher premium on their money. Political uncertainties—fears about the separation of Quebec or the financial solvency of the government or events abroad—could drive up interest rates. The other key factor in determining interest rates was the amount of money in circulation in the economy. If there was a shortage of funds available to be loaned, and many people wanting to borrow these limited funds, the price of borrowing rose—that is, the interest rate rose.

It was in the second crucial way that the Bank of Canada strongly influenced interest rates. One of the functions that the Bank performed was to lend money to the commercial banks and other financial institutions, which then loaned these funds to members of the public. So by increasing or decreasing the amount of money it lent to financial institutions, the central bank was able to control the amount of money in circulation, which had an enormous impact on interest rates in the country. This gave the bank an almost direct control over short-term interest rates, and an indirect but still potent influence on interest rates on long-term investments of all sorts—an influence even the Bank acknowledged. As Crow himself put it in the Hanson lecture, "The Bank of Canada, by increasing or decreasing the supply of settlement balances to financial institutions, directly influences the very shortest-term interest rates in the Canadian money market. Movements in these rates in turn influence the whole spectrum of market and administered interest rates and rates of return on a wide variety of assets and liabilities."

Exerting such a strong influence over interest rates was like exercising a life-and-death power over the economy. In a sense, controlling interest rates was like controlling the country's supply of air. Money was the economy's oxygen; it allowed the system to function, to breathe. If oxygen became scarce, the economy would start gasping for air. This is exactly what higher interest rates did; by driving up the cost of borrowing money, higher interest rates made it harder for people to get access to money. Thus, businesses couldn't expand their operations and perhaps couldn't even pay their employees, consumers couldn't buy houses and cars and large appliances, and perhaps could no longer afford even little expenses like having their clothes dry-cleaned or their hair cut. If the interest rate lever was cranked up high enough and oxygen became sufficiently scarce, the economy would start choking and reeling in a desperate struggle to breathe.

For most people, the significant result of all this was a recession. Unemployment rose, wages fell, economic prospects seemed grim. But what interested the Bank of Canada most was another result: inflation fell. Indeed, this was true. As the economy writhed in a slow dance of death, rising prices were stopped in their tracks. This happened because the weakened economy and high unemployment eventually convinced frightened workers to moderate their wage demands. Similarly, merchants who wanted to stay in business had no choice but to drop their prices in order to make a sale. Eventually, all wages and prices were pulled down. Along with every other moving thing out there in the economy, inflation fell victim to the tightened levers on the oxygen pump.

For many, this posed an obvious question: Was the whole effort worthwhile? Was it worth wiping out inflation, if we had to lay waste the economy in the process? We will return later to this central question, but for now it is enough to say that this is not a question that generally preoccupied those at the Bank of Canada. Rather, their focus remained rigidly fixed on one goal: controlling inflation. In the Hanson lecture, John Crow signalled that this focus was to become even more rigidly fixed, even though the goal was more remote and difficult to attain. Controlling inflation was no longer enough. Now the target was *eliminating* inflation. In Crow's war on inflation, there would be no prisoners.

In many ways, this represented a crucial turning point, a final abandonment of any notion that the Bank had a responsibility to balance the interests of all members of society. There was a perennial clash between the interests of those primarily concerned with fighting inflation and those primarily concerned with keeping the economy buoyant and growing. This is a simplified characterization; the country didn't divide neatly into these two factions. Most people wanted both low inflation *and* a growing economy. But, more than was generally appreciated, these goals were often in conflict.

Anti-inflation proponents insisted that the goals were not in conflict, that, *in the long term*, low inflation would usher in an era of greater growth. It was one of those theories that could never really be proven right or wrong. What was not disputed, however, was that, *in the short term*, there was a trade-off between controlling inflation and encouraging growth and employment. A major assault on inflation could bring the economy sputtering to a halt, just as a highly revved-up economy could set off a round of inflation. And since most people tended to focus on the state of their lives in the short term—that is, right now and in the immediate future, not at some distant, unspecified time over the horizon—the potential for conflict was significant.

Everyone, of course, would be united in opposition to very high levels of inflation; the experiences of Latin

America, pre-war Germany or, more recently, the former Soviet republics are ample testimony to the destabilizing effects of raging, out-of-control inflation. But it is fair to say that, when it came to moderate or low levels of inflation, there were two opposing factions on the inflation issue. And, while there was some overlap between the two, they broke down roughly as follows: those with financial assets had a strong and well-founded desire to prevent inflation from eroding the value of their assets. Those without financial assets were far more likely to be concerned that the economy keep growing, so that they could get a share of the action. Although this second group generally didn't like inflation either, they considered it the lesser of two evils— less serious than unemployment.

In the ongoing battle, central banks played a key role because they effectively controlled the crucial variable: the interest rate, or the cost of access to money. The Bank of Canada was, in a sense, the referee, the supposedly neutral, superior force with ultimate power over just how much oxygen would be allowed into the economy. By tilting towards a tight-money policy with high interest rates, the Bank would be coming down on the side of those with financial assets. By loosening up the flow of money with lower interest rates, the Bank would be favouring those—generally the less affluent members of society—who stood to benefit from an expanding economy with more jobs.

It was these poorer members of society who had pushed hard in the early part of the century for the establishment of a publicly owned central bank in Canada, in the hope that it would tilt the balance more in their favour, and less in the favour of the extremely powerful financial elite. We will return to this history later, but for now it is important to note that the Ottawa mandarins who designed the Bank of Canada in the thirties were conscious of the diverging interests of different segments of society and were careful to set a mandate for the Bank that would allow it to strike a balance between these conflicting goals and concerns. In the preamble of the Bank of Canada bill, the Bank's architects called for it to "mitigate by its influence fluctuations in the general level of production, trade, *prices and employment*" [italics added].

John Crow's decision to pursue the goal of eliminating inflation was a repudiation of this broad set of goals in the Bank's original mandate. It was a dramatic declaration that the Bank was about to formally abandon an even-handed approach striking a balance between controlling inflation and encouraging economic growth. From now on, Crow was announcing, the Bank would tilt in only one direction. This single-minded focus on stopping inflation was sure to have staggering consequences on economic growth and employment, and on all those Canadians who relied on a buoyant economy for their livelihood.

Crow's decision to actively pursue the goal of price stability meant that, in practical terms, the Bank was serving the interests of the financial elite. Inflation was the nemesis of those with money, since it undermined the value of their savings over time. A $1 bill had no intrinsic value; it was all a question of what it would buy. The erosion of the value of money of course affected everyone who had any money. A dollar in the wallet of a bank teller lost its value as quickly as a dollar in the wallet of a bank president. This simple fact often led people to conclude, incorrectly, that inflation took its toll equally on all.

A key factor often overlooked was that, in reality, dollar bills didn't just sit forever in wallets, or under mattresses, until they eventually lost their value. They were either spent or put somewhere to earn interest. The rate of interest was generally set high enough to compensate moneyholders for the loss of the value of their money due to inflation. It was often set high enough to more than compensate moneyholders for their inflationary losses.

The interest rate became the key variable in the question of who won and who lost from inflation. Although the rate was the same for everyone, there was a great difference between how it affected each individual, depending on whether the individual was primarily a creditor or a debtor. Creditors benefited from high interest rates because they got a bigger return on their money. Debtors were hurt by them because they had to pay higher borrowing costs. In a war on inflation, with inevitably higher interest rates, creditors stood to gain, while debtors were likely to become cannon fodder.

But who were the creditors? Clearly, they included wealthy individuals who owned large financial assets. Yet advocates of price stability or zero inflation, as it is sometimes called, often confused the issue by keeping the focus almost exclusively trained on another group of creditors— senior citizens who had accumulated savings over their life-time. Seniors were the baby seals of the inflation debate. Just as the thought of seal pups being clubbed to death rallied support against the Newfoundland seal hunt, the thought of pensioners being robbed of their life savings through inflation rallied support for the anti-inflation crusade.

Sometimes single mothers were also included in the list of inflation's victims, on the grounds that their support payments were often not fully indexed to inflation. (While this was true, single mothers were generally more adversely affected by anti-inflation policies that drove up interest rates and, consequently, eliminated jobs.) But if pensioners and single mothers stirred sympathetic emotions in the public akin to suffering baby seals, the wealthy aroused about as much public sympathy as the baby seal clubbers. If the public suspected that the anti-inflation war had the effect of further enriching the rich, there would be even less support for it; indeed, there would likely be a backlash against it.

So arguments about the benefits of controlling inflation usually omitted any mention of the wealthy. In outlining the evils of inflation, for instance, *The Great Canadian Disinflation*, one of the key anti-inflation tracts published by the C.D. Howe Institute, lists as the number one evil the way inflation redistributes resources among different members of society. But authors David Laidler and William Robson leave the impression that the main effect of this redistribution is to harm pensioners and single parents: "Thus, even apparently moderate inflation severely erodes the real incomes of old people, of many single-parent households, and of others who depend on fixed nominal payments for a large proportion of their incomes—many of whom live in or close to poverty." (The authors fail to mention that Ottawa's main pension programs—the Old Age Security and the Guaranteed Income Supplement—are fully indexed to inflation.) Instead, Laidler and Robson skilfully touch buzzwords that evoke sympathy—old people, single parents, poverty. Just like seal pups, bleeding, helpless. Strangely absent is any hint of investors, rich people, seal clubbers.

The tract leaves the impression that the only people worried about inflation are old people and single mothers. Are we then to conclude that the C.D. Howe Institute, which is funded by large corporations, banks, investment dealers, life insurance companies, brokerage houses and wealthy individuals, has carried out its lengthy campaign against inflation primarily because it is concerned about the plight of pensioners and single mothers?

Although this has helped confuse ordinary citizens about inflation, the financial community seems to be less confused about the issue. *Business Week* was blunt in describing the situation to its business audience: "When the Federal Reserve Board officials meet on Nov. 15 to consider yet another interest-rate hike, they will carefully weigh the benefits of damping inflation vs. the costs from slowing growth. They probably won't give more than a fleeting thought to how higher interest rates affect families in different income brackets and actually change the distribution of income in the economy. But they should. The evidence is overwhelming that higher interest rates hurt the middle class a lot more, because it shells out a greater portion of its income in interest payments than do the affluent."

Business Week is really just stating the obvious, although it is a point often left out of the debate in Canada—that high interest rates are kind to creditors and harsh on debtors, and that the affluent tend to be creditors and the less affluent tend to be debtors. Thus, the high interest rates in Canada have given a disproportionate benefit to the rich. In 1991, Canadians with incomes between $15,000 and $20,000 received interest income averaging $1,500 per person—an amount that largely reflected the interest collected by seniors in this low-income group. But rich Canadians, with incomes over $250,000, enjoyed interest income that year averaging $51,000 per person. The benefit enjoyed by this upper income group was thus thirty-four times the size of that received by the lower income group.

So if high interest rates were a boon to the affluent, a war on inflation was wonderful news for them. This might seem contradictory at first. Wouldn't lower inflation bring lower interest rates, and wouldn't that hurt the affluent? Not exactly. It was true that lower inflation would bring interest rates down, but ironically, this didn't hurt the affluent, owing to an important factor that we haven't yet discussed. What really mattered was not the interest rate, but the *real* interest rate—that is, the interest rate minus the inflation rate. If the interest rate was 10 per cent, and the inflation rate was 6 per cent, the real interest rate was the difference—4 per cent. This represented the real return on money. A high real interest rate was a bonanza for those with financial assets, because it meant that they were receiving a high return—over and above the rate of inflation.

It was high real interest rates, above all, that interested

the financial community. And low inflation was the key to achieving high real interest rates. Peter Spiro, a former Wood Gundy economist who now heads the macroeconomic policy section of the Ontario Ministry of Finance, explains that low inflation is invariably accompanied by high real interest rates. "Worldwide, lower inflation is always associated with higher real interest rates," said Spiro, who has written extensively on real interest rates and investment patterns in international markets.

Bay Street's enthusiasm for the Bank of Canada's war on inflation is thus closely linked to its impact on real interest rates. Since Crow began tightening monetary policy in earnest, real interest rates in Canada have gone up to historic levels. In the 1960s, for instance, the real interest rate averaged 3.2 per cent, Statistics Canada data show. In the seventies, when inflation was much higher, it fell to 1.2 per cent. Then in the eighties, as the Bank of Canada tightened its monetary policy in response to inflation, the real interest rate shot up to an average of 6.6 per cent. But under Crow's extreme tightening during the 1990–92 period, the real interest rate went all the way up to 8 per cent. Although this pattern is found in other advanced countries as well, it has been most pronounced in Canada. The Canadian real interest rate was above 6 per cent, for instance, in July 1994. In comparison, France had a real interest rate of 4 per cent, while the U.S. real rate was under 3 per cent and Japan's was under 2 per cent.

It should be noted that the interests of the business community and the financial community are not always the same when it comes to inflation. While both like the stability of low inflation, the measures that are taken to reduce inflation affect the two communities differently. For the financial community, the war against inflation means high real interest rates, which are very desirable, as we've seen. For business, however, high interest rates pose problems:

they lead to sluggish growth and reduced consumer spending, thereby reducing the market for the products business wants to sell. Furthermore, corporations rely on borrowing to expand their operations, and high interest rates contribute enormously to their borrowing costs.

On the other hand, business generally likes the way strong anti-inflation measures drive down workers' wages. Furthermore, business owners also often have large financial investments themselves and therefore benefit from a low inflation environment. For business, then, inflation and the measures taken to control it are a mixed bag, and indeed some industries, such as the pulp and paper sector, opposed Crow's strong anti-inflation measures. It was really in the financial community that Crow's tight-money policies won unqualified support.

While Crow's war on inflation has been a boon to creditors, but it has been a disaster for debtors. As real interest rates rise, the real cost of debt rises, because inflation is no longer whittling away the value of the debt load. It is sometimes argued that high real interest rates indirectly benefit all members of society by increasing the savings rate, and thereby encouraging investment in the economy. Spiro says that there is no evidence to support this contention. He argues that high real interest rates have "relatively little effect on the savings rate." But, he says, they do have a significant effect "on the way the national income is shared among different income classes."

A strong distaste for inflation thus pervaded the financial community, but nowhere was it more pronounced than among bondholders. Bondholders were generally major financial players—wealthy individuals or pension funds—who loaned their money for long time periods, anywhere from two to thirty years. And this made them highly vulnerable to inflation. Their bonds had fixed interest rates; if inflation rose, they could end up with their money locked in at a painfully low rate of interest. There was always the option of selling the bond, but if inflation had driven up interest rates, a bond with a lower interest rate would be less valuable and would have to be sold at a loss.

On the other hand, if inflation fell, bondholders could end up collecting extraordinarily high rates of interest on their bonds, long after interest rates on everything else had dropped. In 1981, when Ontario Hydro issued a thirty-year bond with an interest rate of 17.5 per cent, there was no way of knowing what a valuable bond this would turn out to be. At that point, inflation was running at 12.5 per cent and many believed it would keep rising, making the future real rate of return on the bond uncertain. In fact, 1981 was the high point of inflation; a sharp tightening by the central bank brought inflation and interest rates tumbling dramatically, making those thirty-year Hydro bonds seem like gold. Today, more than a decade later, the bonds are still paying out interest rates of 17.5 percent—almost ten percentage points above the going rate.

For bondholders, then, inflation was everything. So it was little wonder that they were constantly scanning the horizon for the slightest hint that it was about to raise its head. Even changes of a fraction of a percentage point made a big difference in the financial planning of those with large bond portfolios. And pension fund managers who were off slightly in their calculations and failed to deliver the expected rates of return, quickly found themselves dumped.

From a bondholder's perspective, one worrisome sign was a rapidly growing economy, with a high rate of employment. While investors weren't exactly against growth, they were deeply frightened by the prospect that growth would lead to inflation, that with most people working, wages and prices would start rising again.

This gave bondholders a somewhat bizarre worldview. They often prospered when the rest of the economy was in recession. Similarly, a buoyant, growing economy that cheered most of the population often turned bondholders sour, since they feared that the onset of inflation would erode the value of their bonds. In the spring of 1994, for instance, the U.S. Commerce Department issued some long-awaited good news for Americans: the economy was growing faster than anyone had predicted. As the *Wall Street Journal* noted, "Consumers were buying more, corporations investing more and factories exporting more than anyone had initially believed." But while this was good news for millions of Americans, it was not at all what bondholders wanted to hear. Indeed, the news sent bond markets reeling. "In reaction, bondholders took a shellacking," continued the *Journal*.

On another occasion *Business Week* was even blunter, pointing out that an upbeat report from the U.S. Commerce Department put an end to what had been a very strong bond market. "Terrified as it is of a strong economy, the bond market has taken a look at some of the snappy data in recent weeks and decided to tone down its euphoria." Conversely, when growth expectations started to look bleaker in July '94, the bond market revived. As the *Financial Post* headline put it, "Investors take heart in U.S. slowdown." The *Post* article reported "soaring bond prices Friday after a report of weaker-than-expected U.S. economic growth." The *Post*'s bond market reporter, Lisa Grogan-Green, continued on the same upbeat theme about the lower growth expectations in an article headlined "Finally something to cheer."

These articles captured the ironic fact that when the economy gets stronger, bondholders often lose money. None of the articles went on to draw an important inference from this: bondholders apparently have different interests from those of ordinary citizens. What's good for ordinary citizens isn't necessarily good for bondholders. Michael McCracken, president of Informetrica, an Ottawa-based economic forecasting firm, underlines this point by noting that there may have been some truth in the old saying "What's good for General Motors is good for the country." But, McCracken insists, "You could never say: 'what's good for bondholders is good for the country.' Bondholders thrive on bad news. No group in the world loves misery more than bondholders."

Of course, outside the bond markets, the world looked like a very different place. What mattered for most people wasn't preserving the value of their past accumulations of wealth—which most people didn't have anyway—but ensuring an ongoing source of income. What mattered to them was growth and prosperity and a job with a wage high enough to support a family. But, to some extent, this meant gaining access to the wealth accumulated in the hands of those grumpy, sour bondholders who revelled in the misery of others. They were the ones with the capital that the rest of the population needed to grow and prosper. Their capital represented the accumulations of past growth and prosperity. But these accumulations also held the key to future growth. It was only by tapping into these vast sources of funds—which were concentrated in the hands of relatively few—that the rest of the population could finance the future growth it so needed.

But at what price would the closely held accumulations of the past be made widely available for the future? What would be the real cost of gaining access to that money? In many ways, this price represented a broad social contract—between creditors and debtors, between the haves and have-nots of society, between finance capital and would-be entrepreneurs. If the price were too low, those with capital would find the value of their accumulated wealth whittled away over time—a situation that they would obviously fiercely resist. But if the price were too high, the masses would never have a shot at prosperity, they would never get a chance to join in the party. In many ways, this was the central question of how society's resources would be divided.

And who would decide the terms of this broad social

contract, who would assume this almost god-like power over society? How could anyone be sufficiently even-handed to preside over such a sweeping contract, which would touch the lives of everyone in the country at the most basic level?

To a large extent, that role belonged to the governor of the Bank of Canada. Certainly, the financial elite looked to the central bank as their protector against the ravages of inflation. Elected governments were not considered trustworthy on the inflation front. They were thought to be too likely to bend to the prevailing winds and give the public what it wanted—more growth, good times, a bigger party for all. Only the central banker, with his distance from the public and independence from electoral fortune, could be trusted to hold the line, to be the party killer who, according to banking legend, removed the punch bowl just when the party was getting going. As Paul Volcker, former chairman of the Federal Reserve Board, the U.S. central bank, once quipped about central bankers, "We have a haunting fear that someone, someplace may be happy."

As John Crow set about presiding over the social contract in Canada, the Canadian party was about to get a lot smaller, and people in many parts of the country were about to be a lot less happy.

Few events were more dreaded by Latin American finance ministers than the annual visit from a delegation of the International Monetary Fund (IMF). And few members of those IMF delegations were more dreaded than John Crow.

Latin American countries had good reason to fear these visits. Among all the international agencies that kept tabs on national economies around the world, the Washington-based IMF was the heavyweight. Its assessment of a country's economic situation had wide-ranging implications. A poor assessment from the IMF, for instance, could affect a country's credit rating as well as its ability to attract foreigners to invest in its economy. And the IMF was the lender of last resort, making loans to countries unable to raise funds on their own. But when the IMF made loans, it extracted punishing conditions. Borrowing countries were required to reorganize their economies to suit foreign investors. One of the things that foreign investors most disliked was a high inflation rate.

Since the IMF wielded such power, countries were inclined to co-operate when it came calling. Visiting delegations were generally given full access to the country's officials, including a private meeting with the minister of finance, without even his officials being present. It was at these meetings that John Crow was particularly effective.

Throughout the 1960s, Crow worked as an IMF economist, specializing in Latin America. Though he had arrived at the IMF straight out of university, Crow rose quickly through the ranks to become, in 1967, assistant chief of the Grancolombian Division, which oversaw Colombia, Venezuela, Ecuador and Panama. Crow had a gift for languages and was fluent in Spanish—a facility that made him unusually effective in dealings in Latin American countries. With his strong grasp of technical monetary issues, Crow could probe deeply into complex areas at meetings with Latin American finance ministers, while other IMF officials usually had to grope about somewhat clumsily in these technical areas through interpreters. He became one of the most highly regarded—and intimidating—members of the IMF's Latin American team.

Thus, Crow learned the ropes of monetary policy on the disciplinary side, as a member of a heavyweight, no-nonsense team that laid down the law to wayward countries. Some Latin American countries, such as Brazil, experienced inflation of 100 per cent a year in the sixties. Inflation rates of 20 to 30 per cent a year were not unusual. At times, it almost seemed that these countries were living laboratories on how much could go wrong with a country when inflation got out of control.

Later, Crow was promoted to chief of the IMF's North American division, which oversaw Canada, the United States and Mexico. Crow's obsession with inflation, acquired in those IMF years before he joined the Bank of Canada in 1973, remained with him after he became the Bank's governor in 1987. Michael Wilson acknowledged that intense vigilance on the inflation front was a factor in the Mulroney government's decision to select him for the job of overseeing Canada's money. Wilson shared this obsession, in part because of his own background as a bond dealer on Bay Street, where he had absorbed the virulent anti-inflation sentiments of the financial markets. He had served as executive vice-president of Dominion Securities through most of the seventies, when inflation was wreaking havoc in the bond market, and he still carried with him the intense anti-inflation sentiments of the bond market after a decade in politics.

Wilson's obsession about inflation had even deeper roots. He recalls that it began in his childhood, when he often heard tales from his father of the German hyperinflation in the 1920s. His father, Harry Wilson, had worked at National Trust and "saw the impact of inflation on people's money during that period." When Michael Wilson became finance minister in 1984, his father gave him a souvenir of the German hyperinflation—a five-mark note from the twenties on which the "5" had been overprinted with "2,000,000."

"One thing he said to me was, 'Okay, you're finance minister. Don't ever forget about the difficulties, the disruption and the unfairness that inflation can bring to an economy,'" recalled Wilson. "And we were seeing that in a number of South American economies, where they were going through the same experience. And I was determined that that wasn't going to happen to me on my watch. Fortunately, I had a governor of the Bank of Canada who felt the same way."

Certainly, Wilson and Crow, both steeped in the lessons of foreign hyperinflations, were of one mind when it came to the need for vigilance over inflation. And, although disagreements later developed between them over the speed of inflation reduction, their views were fundamentally in accord. In their private weekly meetings—usually with no other officials present—they shared a sense of purpose and determination about stamping out the scourge of inflation.

So Crow was confident of Wilson's support in January 1988 as he prepared, on the eve of the Hanson lecture, to launch a strike against the relatively buoyant Canadian economy. In a sense, he was following in the steps of his predecessor, former Bank of Canada governor Gerald Bouey, who had carried out a brutal war against inflation—with devastating consequences for the economy—in the early eighties. But Crow's war would be different.

Bouey's war was conducted in response to a significant inflationary momentum that had developed in the seventies and early eighties. As inflation kept rising through the 1970s, particularly after the oil price shocks of 1973, the bond market in particular took a beating. Throughout the decade, the interest on bonds kept rising, but not fast enough to keep ahead of inflation. Bondholders, who had been accustomed to relatively reliable returns, found themselves holding bonds purchased in the sixties at rates of interest that, a decade later, seemed absurdly low. Buying bonds, which had traditionally been regarded as a conservative form of investment with a guaranteed fixed rate of return, suddenly seemed about as safe and reliable as playing blackjack with a cardshark. By the late seventies, it was getting more and more difficult to entice investors to play the game.

The response of central banks became fierce in the early eighties. Led by the U.S. Federal Reserve Board, central banks throughout the Western world launched major assaults on inflation, tightening the spigots on the oxygen supply and throwing their gasping economies into recession. We'll return later to these important developments and how they changed the world economy. The important point here is that the situation in 1981 was very different from that in 1987, when Crow prepared to launch his war on inflation. Whereas Bouey had faced a real inflation problem, with inflation rising to 12.5 per cent in 1981, Crow faced a relatively benign, low-gear inflation.

Since 1983, inflation had averaged about 4 per cent a year—less than one-third of what it had been. Some economists and investors still considered 4 per cent too high, but for most people inflation was no longer a matter of pressing national urgency. For most developed countries, average inflation rates had ranged between 4 and 11 per cent since the sixties, so 4 per cent was certainly not out of line. Even the inflation-obsessed investment community was relatively calm about the issue. The improvement over the seventies and the newfound stability of the eighties were both a welcome relief. A relatively stable 4 per cent inflation rate wasn't perfect, but it was generally acceptable.

That wasn't the view, however, of the two men who ultimately controlled the nation's oxygen supply. "Four per cent on an ongoing basis wasn't good enough," recalls Michael Wilson. "Credit growth was too fast and was inconsistent with the need for controlling inflation."

Crow certainly agreed, as did his top officials. The seventies had had a traumatic effect on the Bank, as well as on the bond market. Bank analysts looked back on the seventies as a time when the Bank had failed to take sufficient action—action that might have headed off the severity of the eventual response. Crow was part of the Bank's establishment. He had been in its senior ranks since 1979, when he was appointed adviser to the governor, and he had been a deputy governor when the Bank had relentlessly jacked up interest rates and helped bring on the 1981–82 recession. Those tough actions, in Crow's mind, had helped stave off Latin American–style inflation.

Of course, Latin American–style inflation had little relevance to Canada, where inflation was effectively under control and was apparently doing little harm to the economy. "The issue in Canada [was] not the evils of 400 per cent inflation, or 40 per cent inflation or 10 per cent inflation," says economist Lars Osberg of Dalhousie University in Halifax. "The issue in Canada [was] the benefits and costs of the Bank of Canada's decision in 1988 to try to go from 4 per cent to 0 per cent inflation."

In early 1988, the inflation rate in Canada was still declining, bottoming out at 3.8 per cent in July 1988. With the national unemployment rate at about 8 per cent, there was still some slack in the economy, and little prospect for a big inflationary surge. As Peter Spiro notes, "There can be no denying that high inflation is an economic evil which is harmful to virtually everyone in the country. However, at the time that the Bank of Canada's price stability program was launched, the Canadian economy was not suffering by most standards from an inflation problem." So, while Bouey had taken a sledgehammer to the economy when inflation was at least a real menace, Crow resolved to do so when there was no dangerous inflation in sight. The new governor was prepared to make a massive pre-emptive strike against an enemy that hadn't even shown signs of raising its head.

Indeed, Crow himself acknowledged that it was not clear that inflation was really gaining steam. "By some measures the rate of inflation has risen slightly over the past year," he told his Halifax audience in June 1987. "One can indeed argue that this has been more the product of transient factors than of any persistent or self-sustaining cause... It may be that inflation will be drawn back to a declining trend... There is some basis for such a view. Figures for the country as a whole indicate that increases in wage costs to date have stayed quite moderate." But what became clear, both in Halifax and later in his Hanson lecture in Edmonton, was that Crow's aim wasn't merely to head off an inflationary surge, but to achieve a purer, loftier goal—"price stability." As he quickly took control of the Bank, this revolutionary target became the focus.

It was not going to be easy. Although Crow had a solid grasp of the intricacies of monetary policy, the path he was setting out on was uncharted, and the merits of his ultimate goal of price stability were far from clear. The Bank of Canada's own research indicated that no country had achieved an inflation rate close to zero over an extended period of time. Of 62 countries surveyed between 1960 and 1985, the lowest average inflation rate over the period had been 3.6 per cent a year, in Malaysia. Even Germany and Switzerland, known for their tight-money policies, had slightly higher average inflation rates throughout the period; Japan's average rate stood at 6.2 per cent.

Crow liked to present his notion of price stability as simply a continuation of a policy initiated by his predecessor, Gerald Bouey. In his 1983 annual report, Bouey had asserted that "the proper goal of monetary policy is monetary stability." But while Bouey may have initiated talk of price stability in Canada, in practice, he was content to leave inflation in the 4 per cent range. Crow, on the other hand, was determined to push inflation well below 4 per cent. And he was prepared to push up interest rates high enough to achieve his goal. In fact, he pushed Canadian interest rates well above any in the G7 countries. By 1990, real interest rates in Canada were 7.6 per cent, compared to 5.6 per cent in Germany, 4.5 per cent in Japan and only 2.5 per cent in the U.S.

Crow's initiative thus involved a great leap of faith and enormous confidence in his own ability to understand and steer the economy. But Crow had that kind of inner confidence. Although he was shy in some social situations, that shyness masked a confidence in himself and his abilities—a confidence that, to many, came across as arrogance. He had always trusted his own intelligence and his own instincts and, thus far in his life, they had performed brilliantly for him.

It had been solely his brains and instincts that had delivered him to the prestigious post at the top of the Bank of Canada from the humblest of origins on the other side of the Atlantic. Crow had started life as the son of a janitor in Bethnal Green, the grotty east London borough where, a century earlier, the wretched workhouses for orphans had inspired Charles Dickens's depiction of Victorian bleakness and cruelty in *Oliver Twist*. The horrors of Bethnal Green had also partly prompted the establishment in 1869 of the charity Action for Children, with Queen Victoria as patron. In the 1930s and '40s, when Crow was growing up there, it was still one of the grimmest and toughest neighbourhoods in that severely class-divided city.

Crow seemed destined to follow in the footsteps of his working-class parents until, at the age of eleven, he scored well enough on an entrance exam to get accepted into Parmiter's, a local private school for East End boys. Parmiter's was a lifeline out of the neighbourhood. Established two centuries earlier by a wealthy merchant, it provided gifted local boys with not only superb academic training but all the trappings of a real upper-class education: teachers in black robes, sports fraternities and Shakespeare productions. Crow thrived at Parmiter's, proving himself disciplined and hardworking, eventually winning the school's top academic honours, as well as excelling at cricket and football.

Still, after his impressive record at Parmiter's, it was by no means clear where Crow would end up. He received training that could have led to his becoming a British spy in Russia. Upon graduation from Parmiter's he did two years of military service in the British air force. Partly because of his natural talent for languages, he applied for and was accepted into a language program run by the military's intelligence arm, where he was given intensive training in Russian—both ordinary and military. At the end of his two years, Crow was fluent in Russian.

But, upon completing his service, Crow headed instead for Oxford University's exclusive Balliol College where he studied philosophy, politics and economics. If Parmiter's had had all the trappings of upper-class life, Balliol was the real thing, with people very different from anyone he had encountered at Parmiter's. Crow soon discovered that merely excelling at things often wasn't enough to gain acceptance in these sorts of circles. His sports skills were sufficient to win him a coveted position on the Balliol football team, and he even became team captain. But getting into the twenty-four-member sports fraternity, known as the Gordouli Boat Club, was something that required more than athletic prowess.

After all, Crow still had vestiges of his East End accent and demeanour, which prevented him from blending easily with the high-brow Balliol crowd. Some fraternity members were not keen on having Crow in their exclusive club. In the end, he only gained admittance because most fraternity members felt it would be unseemly not to include someone who held the prestigious post of captain of the football team. Despite their evident reticence, Crow readily accepted their invitation.

The social hurdles to gaining acceptance at Balliol were in some ways more daunting than the mental and physical hurdles that Crow had encountered in his days at Parmiter's. For all his talents at intellectual and sports activities, Crow lacked the easy old-boys' manner that was so much a part of moving in elite circles. It was partly his humble origins and partly his nature as a loner. He was clearly much more comfortable when he could retreat into a world where his abilities carried the day—vigorously arguing a point in a tutorial or moving the ball expertly around a soccer field. He was less at ease when it came to hobnobbing with the socially over-advantaged crowd at Balliol, which was known for having produced a number of British prime ministers and senior cabinet ministers.

The job of running a central bank was in many ways ideal for Crow. And the central bank in Canada—where the circumstances of one's birth were more easily forgotten—couldn't have been better. The task was an enormous intellectual challenge, something Crow thrived on. It would take diligence, discipline and hard work, all qualities that Crow had in abundance. It required a willingness to remain apart, even aloof, from the rest of society, something that fitted Crow perfectly. And, in an odd sort of way, Crow was even prepared, from his days at Balliol, for the elite sort of world that central banking represented.

With its role as protector of the nation's money, a central bank always took on a conservative character. The world of central banking was a world in itself, a throwback to earlier, more refined and less hurried times. One former Bank of Canada staffer recalled experiencing that otherworldliness of central banking when he was part of a small Canadian delegation visiting the senior deputy governor of the Bank of France less than a decade ago. The delegation was greeted at the senior deputy governor's office by two men dressed in tails, and ushered into a magnificent room decorated with lavish furnishings from a bygone era and a huge antique clock. "There wasn't a phone in his office. We met with him for over an hour. There were no disturbances, no one knocking on the door. All you could hear was the ticking of the clock."

This refinement and detachment from the hustle and bustle of daily life were part of the tradition of the Bank of Canada. The Bank is still very much a separate world, with its own dining room, and an elegance and peacefulness that set it apart from the other Ottawa corridors of power. In keeping with this refinement, the men's washrooms at the

Bank contain no urinals, only full cubicles, apparently to provide greater comfort and privacy. And, in one legendary story recounted by a former Bank of Canada governor, a private banker from Montreal was paying an official visit in the 1930s to Graham Towers, the Bank of Canada's first governor. When the man got off the elevator at the executive office floor, he was greeted by a distinguished-looking butler dressed in tails. The Montreal banker warmly shook the man's hand, and said, "Mr. Towers, I would recognize you anywhere."

Into this world of elegance and old world charm, John Crow, the janitor's son, entered with surprising grace. Certainly, after Balliol, nothing was too elitist for Crow to handle. The job brought him into formal contact with the Canadian financial elite who regularly advanced their concerns about preserving the value of money. Crow responded with his Balliol manners and sophistication, but also with some reserve. He was never a hobnobber or a chummy old boy who relied on connections—either at Oxford or in Ottawa.

Just as Crow had been accepted into the Gordouli Boat Club strictly on the basis of the skill that made him captain of the football team, so had he landed his job in Ottawa. He had been brought to the Bank from the IMF in Washington strictly on merit. He owed no favours anywhere on Bay Street. He had developed his obsession with inflation honestly, in his dealings with Latin American countries, not at the behest of the Canadian financial elite. If his obsession meshed neatly with that of members of the elite, it wasn't because of his willingness to do their bidding. He was his own man—self-reliant, aloof, arrogant, stubborn, intellectually rigorous and independent.

As the Bank prepared itself for a new assault on inflation—any inflation—there was considerable debate about how to bring the country on side. Some in the Bank argued that it was only necessary to show that inflation offered no benefits. Others felt that this was a rather weak case on which to hang a policy as ambitious as eliminating inflation. There was going to be considerable pain involved, they argued, so there had to be a real carrot to dangle in front of people's eyes, something to make all that suffering seem worthwhile. Merely arguing that inflation was essentially neutral—that it wasn't particularly good or particularly bad—would hardly make a zero inflation policy seem like a reasonable trade-off to people faced with losing their jobs.

In fairness, even those at the Bank didn't fully anticipate the recession they were about to induce. There was optimism within the Bank that the Canadian public had learned its lesson back in 1981, that it had seen how tough the Bank was prepared to get to bring inflation under control. Now that this lesson had been learned, it wouldn't have to be relearned so painfully the second time. This time, when the Bank showed its resolve, people would quickly knuckle under; labour would reduce its wage demands and business would avoid raising prices. The Bank would be able to slay the inflation monster simply by showing its teeth.

Inside the Finance department, there were greater doubts. Two opposing factions had emerged. The first centred around Associate Deputy Minister Michel Caron, a former deputy finance minister in the Quebec government. Caron took the view that parts of the country—including, notably, Quebec—had still not recovered fully from the effects of the 1981–82 recession and that this was not the time for more harsh medicine. The other faction was led by another associate deputy minister, Wendy Dobson, a former president of the C.D. Howe Institute, who strongly supported Crow.

But despite the reservations expressed by Caron and others within Finance, Michael Wilson was unwilling to do anything to stop Crow's anti-inflation crusade. Wilson was not indifferent to the political consequences, but he was convinced that a failure to fight inflation now would mean a bigger fight later.

So, without Wilson restraining him, Crow charged ahead. After an initial round of interest rate hikes in 1988, the Bank found itself paradoxically facing a slightly higher inflation rate in the spring of 1989. But this wasn't the classic kind of inflation, produced by an over-revved economy operating at close to full capacity. That sort of inflation usually prompted central banks to intervene with higher interest rates, in the hope of dampening the inflationary psychology by convincing the public to moderate its wage and price demands.

This time, Canadians couldn't be accused of developing an inflationary psychology. In fact, this round of inflation clearly wasn't their fault. Spiro notes that on this occasion inflation was up because the Bank's higher interest rates had driven up mortgage rates, which are a significant element in the inflation rate. Tax increases had also helped push up inflation, which was now at 5 per cent. Spiro explains that if we factor out the higher mortgage rates and higher taxes, the inflation rate in 1989 would actually have been only 3.9 per cent.

In other words, there was no evidence of an inflationary momentum that might have required a tightening of credit. All that was happening was that the Bank's tightening and the government's tax increases were driving up the cost of living. It hardly seemed appropriate, under the circumstances, to begin a brutal assault on the economy in the name of disciplining Canadians out of an inflationary cycle that they were not even responsible for creating.

Crow's decision to launch the war in earnest at this point was even more bizarre when developments in the United States are taken into consideration. While the Bank of Canada was raising interest rates, the Federal Reserve was doing the opposite, lowering its rates. The result was a sudden, huge gap between interest rates in Canada and the United States. Traditionally, interest rates in Canada have been closely in line with those in the U.S., generally just slightly above U.S. rates. But in 1990, as Crow pushed up the Canadian rate, the difference between interest rates on Canadian and U.S. short-term treasury bills rose to an aston-ishing five percentage points.

This discrepancy had enormous implications for Canada. The higher Canadian interest rates attracted foreign money into Canada, and the sudden flood of foreign money drove up the value of our dollar. The process then began to feed on itself, as yet more foreign money flowed in, attracted by the high interest rates and also now by the opportunity to specu-late on the rising Canadian dollar—an incredibly lucrative proposition.

Indeed, this was where the real money was made. High interest rates were great, but the really spectacular gains were made in currency speculation. When foreign investors cashed in their bonds, they were repaid the principal and interest in Canadian dollars, which had become more valu-able. When they converted these more valuable Canadian dollars back into their own currencies, they realized a healthy profit on the exchange. And this profit was particu-larly significant because it applied to the entire invest-ment—the bond plus interest, not just the interest portion.

In fact, our bonds became almost irresistible to foreigners. The combination of high interest rates and profits on the exchange rate produced returns for U.S. investors, for instance, that were often as high as 35 per cent, says Ernie Stokes, managing director of WEFA Canada, the Canadian subsidiary of an international economic forecasting firm. Stokes says that if those same investors had put their money into U.S. bonds they would have earned about 8 per cent— less than one-quarter of what they could earn on Canadian bonds.

There was one more way that investing in our bonds paid off. As Crow's war on inflation brought inflation down, Canadian interest rates would eventually fall, too. This meant that future bonds would pay a lower rate of interest. Therefore the earlier bonds, with their higher interest rates, would be more valuable and could be sold at a profit, or capital gain.

So Crow's war on inflation produced healthy returns for investors in three different ways: an unusually high interest rate, an exchange rate bonanza and a capital gain to boot! Canadian investors could take advantage of the first and last of these benefits, but the exchange rate boondoggle mostly benefited foreigners. The particularly lucrative returns to foreigners helps explain why a rising proportion of our debt came to be held by foreigners—a phenomenon that has caused much concern in Canada.

Crow's inflation battle was clearly delightful, then, to foreign investors and their Bay Street brokers, who staunchly defended the wisdom of the policy. But while foreign investors rushed to collect the vats of money that we seemed determined to hand over to them, the policy was a disaster for the Canadian economy. As more and more foreign money was sucked into the country in what amounted to a giant currency speculation—with a sure winner—the Canadian dollar soared. From below 75 cents (U.S.) in the mid-eighties, it climbed to 89 cents (U.S.) in the fall of 1991—a rise of about 20 per cent. This meant that Canadian goods being sold to U.S. customers effectively went up in price by about 20 per cent. It would be hard to imagine a more damaging scenario for Canadian producers trying to compete in U.S. markets.

To appreciate the foolhardiness of the policy, it must be remembered that this was all happening right after the intro-duction of the free trade agreement between Canada and the United States. Suddenly, Canadian manufacturers were in a more competitive trading environment than they'd ever

been with the U.S., and at the same time, they were confronted with what amounted to a crippling price increase on
all their products. Oddly, Canada had insisted on a ten-year
period to phase out its tariffs as part of the free trade deal, so
that Canadian industry wouldn't be too suddenly exposed to
the full onslaught of competition with U.S. companies. But
the sudden appreciation of the Canadian dollar made that
slow phaseout of tariffs irrelevant. Even with tariffs, Canada
was hopelessly uncompetitive now that its goods were so
overpriced.

The overvalued dollar—the direct result of Crow's war
on inflation—made it virtually impossible for Canada to
make an effective adjustment to the more competitive era
that was being ushered in. Government and business leaders
were busy urging Canadians to be more competitive, to
become ever leaner and meaner. Yet any competitive gains
that resulted from downsizing and restructuring were more
than wiped out by the overvalued dollar. John Crow's inflation war was shooting the country in the foot.

Wilson acknowledges that the high Canadian dollar
made it harder for Canada to compete, but he insists that
there was a hidden benefit to this. "It forced decisions to be
taken that maybe companies, if the dollar had been low,
would have put off making." In other words, the handicap of
the high dollar forced companies to become more efficient
sooner to overcome the incredible disadvantage they were
operating under. But this seems like an odd argument from a
former minister of a government that had turned the quest
for competitiveness into a fetish. Was the strategy, then, to
deliberately create handicaps for our companies in the hope
of driving them to a point of desperation so that they would
take dramatic action in order to survive?

Despite Wilson's apparent satisfaction with Crow's policies, it seemed almost as if the Bank and the government
were operating at cross-purposes much of the time. This was

certainly the case with free trade, as we've just seen, but it was also the case with the Goods and Services Tax. The GST threatened to set off a spiral of rising prices just as the Bank was setting out to kill inflation permanently. The two policies were headed for a collision. Fears that the GST would generate inflation meant that the zero inflation policy had to be applied with even more force; the sledgehammer of high interest rates had to hit that much harder. Furthermore, the zero inflation policy meant that the economy was taking a nosedive just as the GST was being introduced, making the economy's adjustment to the hated new tax all the more difficult.

The mishmash of conflicting policies was creating disastrous results all round. For instance, the higher Canadian dollar, which resulted from the interest rate hikes, sent Canadians across the border en masse to buy suddenly cheaper U.S goods. This meant that Canadian producers and retailers, already suffering from the effects of the recession, were left in worse shape as their customers fled south. The government compounded the cross-border shopping problem by its laxity in collecting GST at the border on goods purchased in the U.S. The GST was supposed to apply to goods purchased outside, as well as inside, the country. But Ottawa decided to go easy on collecting it at border points because many Canadians assumed that tax-free cross-border shopping was one of the benefits of free trade, and Ottawa was reluctant to do anything that might diminish the popularity of its free trade initiative.

In no policy area did the Bank's inflation war pose more problems for the government than in its attempt to reduce the deficit. Higher interest rates were the weapon Crow used in his battle against inflation. But raising the interest rate increased the hardship of anyone borrowing money. And no one in the country was borrowing more money than the federal government. The interest costs on the national debt rose from $29.6 million in 1987–88 to $42.5 million in 1990–91.

These mushrooming interest costs meant that the Mulroney government was able to make little headway against the deficit, despite significant cuts in government spending. Contrary to much media rhetoric, the Mulroney government cut federal government spending substantially; Canada under the Conservatives had a tighter budgetary policy than any of the other G7 countries. By the end of the eighties, Ottawa was actually running a fairly tight ship, collecting more in taxes than it was spending, with one exception—the interest payments on the debt. As Michael Wilson well knew, these bulging interest payments—fattened by Crow's inflation war—were a key cause of the Tories' deficit woes.

All the unemployment generated by Crow's inflation war also contributed to the deficit, as we've seen, by reducing income tax revenues and increasing unemployment insurance and welfare costs. Economist Pierre Fortin estimates that $20 billion of the $49 billion deficit of all levels of government in 1992 was due to lower tax revenues resulting from high unemployment, and another $10 billion was caused by higher social assistance costs. In other words, close to two-thirds of the entire deficit was actually caused by the recession, which the Bank of Canada played a major role in creating. And much of the remaining one-third of the deficit was due to the excessively high interest payments, also generated by the Bank of Canada.

But, while Wilson understood this, he was only too pleased to focus instead on the need for more spending cuts. This suited the government politically. The Mulroney Tories were ideologically committed to reducing the role of government and, to some extent, having a large deficit was a great way to drive home the need for more spending cuts. This "beneficial" effect of large deficits was more explicitly

acknowledged in the U.S. by some of the Reagan administration's more extreme anti-government ideologues, who
keenly promoted deficit-creating tax cuts. Paul Volcker commented on this in his memoirs when he described the "novel
theory," prevalent among Reaganites, that "the way to keep
spending down was not by insisting taxes be adequate to pay
for it but by scaring the Congress and the American people
with deficits." According to this view, then, large deficits
were an effective battering ram in the attempt to storm the
citadel of government spending.

In Canada, the Mulroney government never shied away
from using the deficit for such ideological purposes, although
it didn't go to the extent of cutting taxes to further the cause
of deficit hysteria. There is no evidence that the Mulroney
Tories deliberately enlarged the deficit in order to push the
need for spending cuts, as some in the Reagan administration seemed to be advocating. Of course, in Canada this
wasn't even necessary, since John Crow was doing the job for
the Tories, keeping the deficit swollen with his zero inflation
policy.

Crow's actions seemed to grow more unpredictable as
time went on. By the end of 1989, the Bank's interest rate
hikes were starting to slow down the economy. Initially,
Crow responded by easing up a bit, letting the interest rate
drop by an unusually large amount. Wilson explained that
this was an attempt to test the waters, to see if the Bank
could let interest rates drop a bit without setting off inflation. According to John Grant, now a retired director with
Wood Gundy, the investment community took this as a sign
that Crow wasn't serious about achieving price stability, that
it was too difficult a goal and that he lacked the staying
power to tough it out.

The investment community responded by selling off
Canadian dollars, which sent the value of the dollar plum-
meting, dropping a full four cents (U.S.) in just six weeks.

"The Bank put its little piggy in the water and a snapping turtle came along," was the way Wilson described it. This dramatic sell-off of Canadian dollars appeared to be a rebuke to Crow, indicating a lack of confidence in him. A key part of his strategy had been to come out clearly and forcefully for price stability, so that all segments of society would believe he meant business and would therefore adjust their inflationary expectations. Now, here was the investment community telling Crow that they didn't believe him, that his highly prized "credibility" was closer to zero than the inflation rate. Crow, who had come out guns blazing on the inflation front, had tried to present himself as the Clint Eastwood of central banking. Suddenly, he was looking more like Danny DeVito.

The rebuke was to haunt Crow throughout the rest of his term as governor, making him fearful of showing any signs of weakness in his resolve to wrestle inflation to the ground. His immediate response to the market's display of nonconfidence in the winter of 1990 was to come back with greater force than ever. He jacked up interest rates sharply in the spring and summer of 1990—until they were five to six percentage points higher than U.S. rates. This plunged the economy into a deep recession, which turned into the longest period of economic stagnation since the thirties.

John Grant argues that the investment community's rebuke of Crow in 1990 was partly due to the Mulroney government's failure to show strong public support for Crow's drive for price stability. "People thought Brian was a flake," says Grant, and they suspected that, when the going got tough, Mulroney would relieve his government of any commitment to price stability in the interests of getting re-elected. Even Wilson, who was regarded as Bay Street's ally in the cabinet, never appeared to be solidly behind Crow, maintains Grant, and that "gave Crow the appearance of being a lone lunatic."

In fact, the Mulroney government consistently backed Crow; its lukewarm public endorsement of his policies probably had more to do with a desire to distance itself from the political fall-out over high interest rates. Since the general public had a poor understanding of the role of the Bank and its relationship to government anyway, it was just as well for the government to remain silent on the subject and let the Bank go about its business quietly and, apparently, independently.

On the other hand, members of the investment community certainly understood that Ottawa had ultimate control over Crow, and that Wilson could at any time send him a directive ordering him to change his policies—an action that would be considered tantamount to firing him. But the investment community was wildly enthusiastic about the price stability goal and, particularly after his extreme tightening in 1990, it was wildly enthusiastic about Crow, as influential investors were constantly assuring both Wilson and Mulroney. While these influential players often carped at the government for not cutting spending more deeply and more quickly, they were delighted with its monetary policy.

By the summer of 1990, the continuing high level of interest rates was starting to worry even Wilson, and he began questioning Crow on whether rates couldn't drop a little faster. "I just wanted to be sure in my own mind that John was doing it as quickly as was prudent," Wilson recalls. He insists, however, that there was still no disagreement on the ultimate goal of price stability or any question that Crow was in charge of directing monetary policy. "It's like you're driving a car," said Wilson. "I say I want to go to the bathroom; is there any way we could get to a service station? You say, I can't go too fast because the road is slippery. Well, I'm not going to grab the steering wheel. I'm just letting you know that I'd like to get to a service station."

The desire for some relief was building within the ranks

of the Finance department as well. Concerns were expressed inside the department that Crow had so overreacted to the market's rebuke that his behaviour had become erratic. In an attempt to impose some order on the Bank's actions, the department introduced the notion that inflation targets should be established, and that they should be worked out jointly by Finance and the Bank. That collaboration proved to be difficult, however, with the Bank pushing for more stringent targets that would bring inflation quickly to heel, and the department favouring a somewhat more moderate approach.

The final targets, announced jointly by the Bank and Finance in an apparent show of solidarity in February 1991, were the result of anything but an easy collaboration. The targets went back and forth almost two dozen times before an agreement was finally reached. They called for inflation to be reduced to 3 per cent by the end of 1992 and to 2 per cent by the end of 1995. As stringent as this was, Crow ended up overshooting the targets, and inflation fell faster and sharper than had been agreed upon. By the spring of 1994, it had dropped to zero. But much of the country remained mired in a lingering recession, with a stubbornly persistent unemployment problem. Like flowers blooming in a bombed-out war zone, the dream of price stability had come to fruition.

Far more than has been appreciated, John Crow's crusade against inflation was a crucial factor in the devastation of the Canadian economy in the early nineties. This eventually cost him his job when the new Liberal government came to power and decided not to appoint him to a second term, despite vociferous support for him from the financial community. Yet, despite Crow's departure, we are still feeling the lash of his actions in our ongoing problems with debts and deficits. Although monetary policy has loosened somewhat under Crow's successor, Gordon Thiessen, the Bank continues to focus its efforts, above all, on battling inflation. As a result, our real interest rates are still unduly high, hurting our recovery and continuing to exacerbate our deficit problems. This analysis is fundamentally at odds with the prevailing C.D. Howe–*Globe and Mail* view that dominates public discourse, but it is supported by some key studies by academics and even Bay Street analysts.

For instance, the proposition that overly tight monetary policy was the major cause of the recession is supported by the findings of the study by three economists at the University of Toronto's Institute for Policy Analysis, mentioned in the previous chapter. This institute, unlike the many private, quasi-academic think tanks that also call themselves "institutes," is a purely academic research body within the university, unconnected in any way to business, labour, political parties or any other special interest group. It was set up to examine the effects of government policies on the economy, using a sophisticated computer model. Its studies are so technical and dry that they receive little or no public attention. There is certainly no attempt to "market" the findings to the public in the way that has been perfected, for instance, by high-powered public lobbying groups like the C.D. Howe Institute. So if we want a dispassionate assessment of the issues, the U of T institute seems like a good place to look.

The three U of T economists—Thomas Wilson, Peter Dungan and Steve Murphy—set out to determine what had caused the recession. The team wanted to test the popular assumption that something new was at work, that Canada was somehow failing to adapt to the realities of the nineties. In order to gauge the impact of some new "globalization" factor on the recession, they started by first assessing how much of the recession was caused by the usual causes of recession—such as tighter monetary policy, tax increases or a U.S. recession. "If we could 'round up the usual suspects' to see how much they contributed, then we'd know how much was left over," explains Dungan. "We were surprised at how much we could explain. When we added up the pieces, it explained virtually everything." In other words, it turned out that there was no exotic or fearsome new force at work in the world wreaking havoc on Canada's economy. The recession of the early nineties was caused by the same old factors that had caused previous recessions.

If we look more closely at the results of the U of T study, the findings are even more interesting. The study found that the U.S. recession was a factor, but only in making worse an already ongoing recession. "Although the U.S. recession was obviously therefore an important factor worsening the economic performance of its leading trading partner, the U.S. recession alone cannot explain the severity of the 1990–91 recession in Canada, nor the slow growth achieved in 1992."

Instead, the economists identified the "severity of the Bank of Canada's anti-inflation policy," noting that it "significantly reduced real growth in 1990 and 1991, and slowed growth somewhat in 1992." The study showed that even a slightly looser monetary policy would have meant a much less severe recession. For instance, the economists examined what would have happened if the Bank had simply met the 3 per cent inflation target for 1992 that it had agreed to, instead of tightening further to the point of bringing the inflation rate down to 1.7 per cent. The result would have been a much less severe recession, with output approximately $25 billion higher that year, according to their findings. In other words, if Crow had been satisfied to simply bring the inflation rate down to 3 per cent—which is not exactly Latin American–style inflation—our economy would have been more than $25 billion larger than it was in 1992.

The U of T economists also point to one other major cause of the recession—tax increases, including the introduction of the GST. But, interestingly, the study notes that one of the reasons that the tax increases had a depressing effect was that they generated inflation, which the Bank was determined to eliminate. As a result, the Bank intervened with its tough medicine, the study notes. So, once again, the path leads back to John Crow and his overvigilance on the inflation front.

The findings of the U of T economists are similar to the results of an investigation by WEFA Canada, the economic forecasting firm. The WEFA study also rejects the notion that free trade caused the recession, pointing instead to Canada's overly restrictive monetary policy as the key source of the recession. Ernie Stokes, the economist who heads WEFA, explains that tough monetary policy devastated the economy by driving up the dollar and therefore making our goods overpriced in foreign markets.

Like the U of T study, the WEFA study tries to reconstruct what would have happened to the Canadian economy had monetary policy been more moderate. In this case, WEFA examined what would have happened if we had followed the same monetary course as the U.S., which is traditionally what we have done in Canada. The results would have been significantly different, WEFA found. Canada would still have suffered a recession—largely as a result of the U.S. recession—but ours would have been much milder and shorter. Our manufacturing sector would have been much healthier, which would have made an enormous difference, particularly in Ontario. Overall, Canada would have experienced more economic growth and lower unemployment (although higher inflation). WEFA concluded that there would have been about 400,000 more jobs in Canada.

Perhaps what is most interesting in both the U of T and WEFA studies is their conclusions on how tight monetary policy contributed to our deficit problems. Both studies find that the war on inflation has had a significant impact on Canada's debt and deficits. The U of T study shows, for instance, that Ottawa's deficit was $15.11 billion higher in 1992 than it would have been had the Bank of Canada reduced inflation just to 3 per cent—the target it had agreed to—rather than bringing it all the way down to 1.7 per cent. If the Bank had decided to let inflation stay in the 4 per cent range—where it stood before Crow declared war on it in the Hanson lecture—the deficit would have been about $20 billion smaller than it was in 1992, Dungan estimates.

These findings are in line with those of other well-known, mainstream economists. As we've seen, Pierre Fortin concluded that roughly $30 billion of the total deficit for all levels of government in 1992 could be attributed to the recession, which Fortin blames largely on an over-tight monetary policy. Ernie Stokes, head of WEFA Canada and a former Finance department economist in Ottawa, also concluded that Canada's deficit would have been much smaller—by about $25 billion in 1991, for instance—if it had followed the looser monetary policy of the U.S. during the Crow years.

The effects of this tightening of the monetary screws from 1989 to 1992 are still being felt today, Dungan notes, because we are stuck with paying interest on all the extra debt we accumulated as a result of the tight monetary policy of 1989–92. "That's an effect that snowballs," he says. The WEFA study, which only covers the years up to 1991, concluded that, by 1991, the tight-money policy had already driven up the accumulated debt by more than $50 billion. And, while we still suffer from the lingering effects of Crow's extreme tightening, we also suffer from the effects of our ongoing war against inflation. Fortin, for instance, argues that our current monetary policy continues to be too tight, and that any hope of recovery and sensible deficit reduction rests on significantly lowering interest rates. We will explore this idea in more detail later.

So here, then, is the deficit story turned upside down.

The C.D. Howe–*Globe and Mail* version would have us believe that it is ever-growing government spending that is driving up our deficit. The problem, insists *Globe* columnist Peter Cook, is "the exponential growth of government in good times and bad." Yet Ottawa's spending, as a percentage of GDP, hasn't been growing in recent years. Indeed, almost twenty years ago, in 1975–76, the federal government spent 19.7 per cent of GDP on all its programs, compared to just 17.8 per cent of GDP in 1992-93.

But while social spending has not been rising, real interest rates have. Indeed, the rise in real interest rates over the past decade and a half is at the very heart of our deficit dilemma. It is a phenomenon that has been evident worldwide since central banks began tightening monetary policy in the early eighties. But it has been particularly pronounced in Canada since John Crow launched his war on inflation in 1988. As we saw earlier, Canada has had the highest real interest rates among the G7 countries. By the end of December 1994, Canada's real interest rate stood at a devastating 7 per cent.

The effect of this on the deficit is clear. These high interest rates choke the economy and cause high levels of unemployment, which reduce tax revenues and add to social assistance costs. And they also add directly to the deficit by increasing the government's borrowing costs. As *The Financial Post* put it in a headline in December 1994, "Surging rates hurt attack on deficit." So, although social spending has been almost flat for twenty years, interest payments on the debt have more than doubled, rising from 2.3 per cent of GDP in 1975–76 to 5.7 per cent in 1992–93. We will never truly understand our debt and deficit situation so long as we turn a blind eye to the role played by our tight monetary policy and the higher interest rates that have accompanied it.

These high interest rates have been the driving force

behind our deficit, and have masked the effects of the real restraint that we have practised in recent years. Contrary to the media images of overindulgent Canadians living beyond their means, we have been a frugal, thrifty bunch, paying rising taxes and enjoying diminishing services. By the late eighties, with higher taxes and government spending restraint, Ottawa was collecting more tax revenue than it was spending—except for the money it had to pay out to cover the interest payments on the debt. In 1990–91, Ottawa actually collected $10.4 billion more in taxes than it paid out in spending programs, which certainly sounded like the behaviour of a responsible country living within its means. Yet with interest payments of $42.5 billion that year, Ottawa was still running a budget deficit of $32 billion despite all that fiscal prudence. Ottawa was drowning in a sea of interest payments.

To appreciate how much interest payments are contributing to debt growth, it is useful to return to Hideo Mimoto's work. Recall that he calculated that unemployment insurance increases accounted for only 1 per cent of the growth of the debt. By comparison, his calculations showed that the rising cost of interest payments accounted for a staggering 70 per cent of debt growth! This helps explain the baffling phenomenon of recent years: that as we pay ever more taxes and receive ever fewer services, our debt just keeps rising. The more we struggle against the quicksand, the deeper we sink into it. This isn't magic; it's the effect of high real interest rates.

As long as real interest rates are higher than the real rate of our economic growth, our debt burden is growing faster than our ability to pay it, explains economist Michael McCracken. This has been the case since interest rates started climbing more than a decade ago. As Paul Martin noted in his November 1994 statement, "In the early 1980s, the average interest rate on federal debt began to exceed GDP growth for the first time since the War and the gap has since widened. Now interest is compounding at a faster rate than the economy is growing." The situation is going to continue like this as long as interest rates remain higher than the growth rate. Even if we slash social spending and raise the tax burden dramatically, we're still going to have great difficulty keeping up with the debt growth. We'd have to raise almost $20 billion more in taxes than we spend this year just to stabilize the debt at its current high level.

The high real interest rates since the eighties—and particularly since Crow's anti-inflation war began in 1988—have been the driving force behind the deficit. But rather than identifying these high real interest rates as the problem that needs to be attacked, the prevailing wisdom has been that social spending is the problem, and the only solution is massive social cuts. Although those favouring spending cuts wouldn't deny that interest rates are driving the deficit in the way outlined above, they would deny that this is something we should do anything about. Interest rates, we are led to believe, are an untouchable part of the equation; we can cut spending or raise taxes, but we are powerless to do anything about interest rates.

The argument goes like this. First, it is asserted that interest rates are the product of external factors affecting world markets over which Canadians have little control. This is partly true. Indeed, dozens of factors influence world interest rates. The dramatic crash in the Japanese real estate market in 1994, for instance, meant that the world's richest investor community was suddenly poorer by some $10 trillion. This created a scarcity of investment funds worldwide that pushed up interest rates.

But these sorts of developments don't explain why interest rates are higher in Canada than in other nations. So the next part of the argument is that the higher Canadian interest rates are caused by the big Canadian deficit, since investors, fearful that Ottawa will default, demand a higher premium on the money they loan to Canada. This is an intriguing twist that neatly turns the argument upside down; instead of higher interest rates causing the deficit, these higher rates are the product of the deficit. The lesson for Canadians, therefore, is that we will be stuck with these dreadful high interest rates as long as we have a big deficit. "It is remarkable how widespread this view is, in light of the fact that no empirical evidence can be found to support it," says Peter Spiro. He notes that, despite exhaustive investigation of the question in Canada, there is no basis for this common assertion. Economist Pierre Siklos examined the Canadian data and concluded that "no empirical link between deficits and interest rates could be detected." If anything, the data show the opposite to be true: Canadian interest rates have tended to be lower when Canadian deficits have been large, says Spiro. In the early nineties, Canada had extremely high interest rates as well as large deficits and debt. In early 1994, our deficit and debt were still mounting, but our interest rates had fallen somewhat. Thus, it wasn't the deficit that had driven up interest rates in the early nineties. It was John Crow's war on inflation.

But members of the investment community, who profit enormously from the war on inflation, would much rather shift the blame onto the deficit. Indeed, they rarely miss an opportunity to flog the deficit horse. Since developments in the market are difficult to decipher at the best of times, financial analysts are more or less free to give whatever spin they want—especially since no one questions them. So, for instance, they blamed the deficit in March 1994 when interest rates suddenly shot up about five weeks after Martin's first budget. The sudden hike was a "damaging vote of no confidence in Finance Minister Paul Martin's go-slow deficit-reduction strategy," said a front-page article in the *Financial Post* based on a survey of economists and analysts.

But if this were the case, why was the reaction so slow? In

the frantic world of globalized markets—where reactions were usually instantaneous—why had no one been much bothered by Martin's deficit problems in the weeks immediately following his budget? Had Bay Street traders not noticed the budget for five weeks, then suddenly found it lying there on their desks and discovered en masse its horrifying deficit implications? The *Post* quoted one analyst feebly explaining, "There's nothing new; it's just investors are slowly realizing how big the problems really are."

Similarly, when interest rates shot up in December 1994, analysts were quick to pin the blame on the deficit, as well as on the threat of Quebec separation. But prominent Bay Street analyst Ted Carmichael pointed out that even if we manage to deal with the deficit and with the separatist threat, we will still face higher interest rates. In a revealing comment, Carmichael noted: "If we can get the fiscal and political risks behind us, inevitably the Bank's attention will turn to its own central objective of price stability. That will mean more tightening in monetary conditions as we go through 1995 and into 1996." Here then was a fiscal conservative acknowledging that the promise of lower interest rates through deficit reduction is an illusion. The Bank of Canada's zero inflation policy will keep interest rates high, no matter what we do on the deficit front.

No matter how feeble the case, financial commentators seem determined to stick to the view that the deficit is the source of our problems and overgenerous social spending is the source of the deficit. Indeed, the C.D. Howe–*Globe* view is that we shouldn't look at any other possible contributing factors, that we should keep our sights focused exclusively on the need to cut government spending. "Nothing else needs to change," writes Peter Cook. "Politicians simply have to find the will to cut government to manageable proportions."

Why must we keep such blinkers on? Is there not a danger that we are following a false trail? We run ever faster, with axe in hand, in search of programs to hack away at, chanting the mantra that we have no choice in the matter. But perhaps the real source of our problems is not the one we're so keen to track down, slay and dismember. It seems that our problems can be traced—to an astonishing extent—to a particular policy that was imposed on us with virtually no public input, consultation or understanding.

Given the tens of billions of dollars that our tight monetary policy has added to the deficit, how can we leave the subject out of the deficit debate? How can our columnists be so confident in their assertions that all that is needed is further government spending cuts—that, as Peter Cook insists, "Nothing else needs to change"?

All this still leaves us with a great unanswered question: What was it about "price stability" that so inspired John Crow and the experts at the Bank of Canada? Exactly what did they think it offered that could possibly have justified damaging the lives of millions of Canadians who suffered from job losses or the ripple effects of all that unemployment?

The evidence of the benefits of zero inflation must be overwhelming. Right?

But here the story is about to take some twists that make it, to borrow Lewis Carroll's phrase, "curiouser and curiouser!"

CHAPTER FOUR
Jack Selody and the Power of Faith

For the ambitious, the restless or the independent-minded, the Bank of Canada has long been a stifling place. It has done things a certain way and adhered to a certain creed. Its large staff of professional economists and financial analysts have not been encouraged to deviate from the Bank's way of thinking, at least not on anything that mattered. But for those who could adapt to its peculiar, introverted culture, the Bank could be a wonderful home. It provided a secure, tranquil setting, cut off from the hustle and confusion of the outside world—a kind of financial monastery.

Indeed, faith has been virtually a prerequisite for a successful career at the Bank. The central belief espoused by the Bank has been that all its efforts to combat inflation were "laying the foundations" for future economic growth. But was the battle against inflation really laying the foundations for growth, or was it simply laying waste the economy? It was hard to know. As the Bank screwed the oxygen lever tighter and tighter, it was difficult at times to see where all this would lead. Hence the need for faith.

Economist Lars Osberg explains the dilemma this way: "[I]f one observes people digging, and the hole they are digging is getting deeper and deeper, how is one to know whether this is an ordinary hole, or the hole for the foundation of a building? How can one empirically tell the difference? If they are asked what they are doing, and they say 'we are not digging a hole, we are digging the excavation for a big foundation for a beautiful building,' how can an impartial observer know? One can ask 'who will build this building?' but if the answer one receives is 'the market will build the building,' how can one know whether this is justifiable faith in the private sector, or wishful thinking?"

The research department within the Bank was the theological heart of the monastery. Much of the Bank's daily activity involved merely technical operations, like buying and selling government treasury bills, but the research department was the brain-centre of the place. So, while most of the monks quietly went about their mundane daily chores of Bank business, inside the research department the chosen ones were busily working out the big theological issues.

In fact, there was really only one theological issue as far as the Bank was concerned: price stability, and on this issue there was no debate. There could be technical disputes about how best to achieve price stability—should the bank focus on monetary supply targets, interest rates or exchange rates? —but there could be no questioning the importance of achieving price stability. On this issue, the truth was known.

One of the chosen monks was Jack Selody. In many ways, Selody was the perfect monk. He had absorbed the truth. After completing a doctorate in economics at the University of Western Ontario in 1979, Selody had gone straight to work in the Bank's research department, which was then headed by John Crow. Serious-minded and ambitious, Selody had been blessed by entering into a world where there was little to confuse him. He had passed from the ivory tower of classical economics, which held price stability as a central tenet, to the monastic order of the Bank, which held price stability higher still. And John Crow, his first boss, was a formidable character, with a powerful intellect and a strong commitment to price stability.

Even at home, Selody was cloistered from any confusing thoughts. His wife, Heather Robinson, was also an economics graduate who also went on to a job at the Bank of Canada. One of the few women to make it in the male-dominated Bank, Robinson excelled there, co-writing a major document for the Bank about its forecasting model before leaving for a job in the federal Finance department. In Selody's world, all the voices in the choir were singing from the same hymnbook.

If Selody's world seemed calm and tranquil with well-nurtured intellectual beliefs, the world outside was raging. Beyond the walls of the monastery, the Finance department and university courses in classical economics, confusion and terror reigned. It was the early eighties and the economy was in turmoil. The Bank of Canada had sent interest rates skyrocketing in an attempt to wrestle to the ground the apparently chronic inflation that had set in in the mid-seventies.

In this first major round of inflation fighting, the Bank of Canada was taking its cues from the U.S. Federal Reserve Board under the chairmanship of Paul Volcker. Both U.S. and Canadian economies were reeling, choking from lack of oxygen. Businesses found themselves forced to repay loans at rates they couldn't possibly afford, and unable to afford new loans to keep their operations afloat. Homeowners renewing mortgages were confronted with monthly payments that had virtually doubled. Bankruptcies, home defaults, farm closures and unemployment abounded. People were scared in a way that they hadn't been in decades; the possibility of another Great Depression seemed suddenly, shockingly imminent.

Inside the Bank—the operations centre of the anti-inflation war—it was hard for even the devoutest believer not to have the occasional doubt. Could this all be worthwhile?

It was a thought that didn't cross the mind of Bank

staffers very often. Those who had such doubts—and there had been many—generally left the Bank for other pastures. "After you've been here for five years, you start to ask: am I wasting my time, my life on a useless pursuit?" explained one veteran of more than a decade. "Either you believe it matters and you stick around, or you go."

Those who stuck around were therefore a hearty breed of believers convinced that the crusade against inflation was a noble one. It was a crusade with a long and honourable tradition, as almost anyone at the Bank would explain. Just as the king in medieval times was tempted to "debase the coinage" by reducing the amount of gold in the coins of his realm, so are sovereign governments today tempted to debase the value of their debts through inflation. Hence the need for an ever-vigilant central bank to stand on guard for the currency—or, more accurately, for the nation's bondholders. Bank staffers frequently used the king-debasing-the-coinage image as a way to illustrate the importance of their task.

But Selody, a relative newcomer at the Bank, yearned for an image that was a little more up-to-date, a little more relevant to the lives of ordinary Canadians. Wouldn't it be nice if he could establish that all this inflation-fighting would lead to specific benefits that Canadians could understand?

Of course, others had had this thought before. For centuries, economists had pondered the phenomenon of inflation and described its dangers, which they concluded boiled down to a threat to economic efficiency. But most of these arguments—to which we will return later—were rather nebulous. For a discipline that prided itself on being more "scientific" than the other social sciences, economics had mounted a rather vague and unsubstantiated case against inflation. Inside the brain-centre of the Bank of Canada, Selody attempted to plunge boldly into this breach.

He set out to put some numbers—some meat and bones—on the vague concept of the dangers of inflation.

"For years, the Bank had been trying to prove there was a link between inflation and the real effects on the economy," recalls John Parker, an economist who worked in the research department with Selody in the early eighties. But it wasn't an easy link to prove. There was plenty of anecdotal evidence and lots of theoretical arguments to suggest how inflation might harm economic efficiency. But it was far more difficult to make the leap and establish that inflation actually harmed something concrete, like income levels or economic growth rates. And it was even more difficult to then figure out how much of a benefit controlling inflation could deliver.

Selody came up with an interesting way to tackle the problem. Canada had suffered a considerable slowdown in its productivity growth starting in the mid-seventies—at roughly the same time that the high levels of inflation had set in. Since productivity growth was a good measure of economic efficiency, Selody set out to determine if there was a connection between the two. Did the high levels of inflation in the seventies cause the decline in the nation's productivity growth? If he could establish this, he would score a major breakthrough that would strongly bolster the case for price stability, and lead to much happiness within the monastery. Eliminating inflation could then be presented as the key to raising Canada's productivity levels—a goal everyone would support. Teaming up with a colleague in the research department, Peter Jarrett, Selody set out to make his mark in the annals of Bank theology.

The task would not be easy. The economics literature was full of explanations pointing to factors other than inflation to explain the decline of productivity growth throughout the industrialized world in the seventies—the energy crisis, the shift to a service economy, the fact that factories were operating well below their capacities. Jarrett and Selody, however, focused on whether they could establish a relationship between inflation and productivity growth—the only thing that was really useful to them in gathering ammunition for their price stability argument. To do this, they set up a series of complicated mathematical models to test various theories.

Much to their delight, they managed to come up with a long mathematical equation that seemed to make the case they wanted. The amount of inflation experienced from 1976 to 1979 coincided perfectly with the amount of productivity decline that one of their models told them to expect. Jarrett and Selody were ecstatic. "In other words," they wrote, breaking from the arcane mathematical language that otherwise dominates their report, "the increase in inflation through the past decade is sufficient to explain virtually the entire measured slowdown in labour productivity growth!"

The study was published in a prestigious U.S. journal, *Review of Economics and Statistics*, in 1982. Although it caused quite a stir within the Bank, there was also some wariness about it. After all, the study had not proved that inflation affected productivity. The authors had simply created some theoretical models and found that the facts of inflation and productivity growth in the seventies fit with the numbers in one of their models. This didn't prove anything, other than that they had constructed a model to fit the facts. Jarrett and Selody certainly hadn't proved that the productivity slowdown in Canada was *caused* by inflation. Interestingly, they conceded that their models showed it was also possible that both inflation and productivity decline in the seventies were actually caused by a third, entirely different and unknown factor—perhaps the oil price shocks, which many economists believed were responsible. In other words, Jarrett and Selody's findings were also consistent with this standard explanation—an explanation that did nothing to bolster the case for price stability.

Nevertheless, Jarrett and Selody were quick to draw some dramatic conclusions. They argued that their results showed that for every one percentage point decrease in inflation, productivity growth increased by 0.38 per cent. Armed with this rule-of-thumb, they could now argue that reducing inflation had a direct and measurable effect on the economy. Price stability would no longer be just an article of faith. In Jarrett and Selody's hands, it became a proven formula for economic growth.

For those who had been arguing the merits of price stability, the Jarrett and Selody study was a godsend. Here were two fully accredited economists using sophisticated mathematical models to show the real-world benefits that price stability offered. No more fuzzy theories about how inflation might hamper efficiency. Now there were hard facts! And numbers! Not a big round number, that sounded like a vague estimate. But a specific, precise little number— 0.38 per cent! Supporters of price stability were no longer obliged to rely on vague assertions that reducing inflation would help economic growth by some undefined amount. Now they could say precisely how much economic growth there would be: It was all so scientific; it sounded like the law of gravity, or the theory of relativity.

In fact, in the serious economics literature, the study and its findings came under considerable criticism, but this didn't prevent its being used to bolster the case for price stability. It was cited as evidence of the long-lasting benefits of price stability by Bank of Canada officials as well as by the department of Finance. It was also the basis of an astonishing assertion made by one of the Bank's most prominent supporters, economist Peter Howitt.

It is worth taking a close look at what Howitt did with the Jarrett and Selody study, because it sheds some light on what lies behind the case for price stability, on the kind of thinking that has been used to justify this important public policy. Howitt, who teaches in the University of Western Ontario's economics department, is a respected scholar who has been one of the leading voices in Canada supporting price stability. Once again, the story involves the C.D. Howe Institute, which turned to Howitt to write a large portion of a special book it published in 1990 called *Zero Inflation: The Goal of Price Stability*.

In the book, Howitt is clearly anxious to cite Jarrett and Selody's exciting findings about the benefits of price stability, but he is also somewhat cautious. He knows that their study didn't actually prove anything, that their finding involves an enormous, unsubstantiated leap—the kind of leap that careful academics generally feel nervous about making. So while he cites Jarrett and Selody's dramatic conclusion—that each percentage point of inflation reduces productivity growth by 0.38 per cent—Howitt reveals that he regards this finding as purely speculative. "*If this estimate is correct*," he writes, "then the present discounted value of the gain to reducing inflation by one point is enormous [italics added]."

But then Howitt does a very odd thing. Having distanced himself from the speculative finding of Jarrett and Selody, he goes on to do some calculations of his own based on it. Once Howitt has done his own calculations, the numbers involved become truly mind-boggling, and price stability becomes the economic equivalent of the second coming of Christ. "Then, according to this estimate," continues Howitt, "the present value of the gain from reducing inflation permanently by one point equals more than 16 times current GNP[!]" With Canada's GNP running at more than $700 billion a year, Howitt's estimate of the value of a permanent one-percentage-point reduction in inflation is in the neighbourhood of $11 trillion! Imagine if we reduced inflation by two, three or five percentage points! Clearly, this price stability has got some magic stuff in it.

Having lobbed out this truly fantastic, cosmic number, Howitt once again tries to distance himself from it: "*Of course there is no assurance that this estimate is correct; accordingly this conclusion must be treated tentatively* [italics added]." This seems like excellent advice; if there is no assurance that the estimate is correct, clearly we must be very cautious about drawing *any* conclusions from it, let alone those that might be used to justify important public policies. It raises the question of why a serious scholar like Howitt would even toss the preposterous number out into public discourse in the first place.

But then, having again advised caution, Howitt once more throws caution and academic care to the wind: "Nevertheless, in the absence of any other empirical estimates, *one must take seriously* the possibility that this is the order of magnitude of the long-term gain to society from having a lower rate of inflation [italics added]." Really? Why must we take any of this seriously? Just because nobody has come up with a different estimate? Perhaps no one has come up with a different estimate because it isn't possible to do so accurately. Surely, if we acknowledge that there is no assurance that the estimate is correct, there is no reason to entertain it seriously at all. Wouldn't basic logic—not to mention academic prudence—lead us to conclude that we simply don't know the answer?

Howitt doesn't leave it there. He returns to Jarrett and Selody's finding again in his summation. Once again, he refers to his own calculation, based on their finding, that a permanent inflation reduction of one percentage point would amount to a gain of more than sixteen times current GNP. But, he notes, this gain "is so large that one hesitates to place too much weight on it in the absence of corroborating evidence." Having decided that perhaps the number is simply too fantastic to be believed, Howitt then decides to come up with a more "conservative" estimate.

Once again, however, he bases his calculation on Jarrett and Selody's estimate of the 0.38 per cent gain, even though he has already admitted that this is only an "estimate" and that "there is no assurance that the estimate is correct."

Nevertheless, through another set of calculations, Howitt comes up with a new "conservative" estimate of benefits. Instead of his earlier prediction of a sixteen-fold increase in GNP, his "conservative" estimate predicts only a 1.25-fold increase—almost $1 trillion.

This is a breathtaking piece of logic. First, Howitt has set up the extreme position that reducing inflation by one point is worth $11 trillion. Then he counters with a more "conservative" estimate that puts the gain at only about $1 trillion. Having come up with this more "conservative" estimate, apparently in the interests of balance, Howitt now appears quite comfortable with treating the Jarrett and Selody estimate as fact: "Recall that a one point reduction in inflation increases the marginal product of capital by at least three-tenths [0.30] of a percentage point." Yet only a few pages earlier Howitt was pointing out that we didn't know if this estimate was correct. It seems that if it is repeated often enough it starts to sound like fact.

Howitt now seems confident about making some sweeping conclusions: "Thus, *even under these conservative assumptions*, the current discounted value of the gain to society from reducing inflation further below the current 5 per cent level is far greater than the estimate of the cost [italics added]." But wait a minute. Something is wrong here. Both these calculations—the extreme and the "conservative"—are based on an estimate that Howitt himself originally cautioned us may not be correct!

With the positions staked out like this, we are tempted to believe that the truth lies somewhere between the two extremes. This is a phenomenon we often see in the media: where current affairs programs generally present two opposing views, and the audience is left concluding that the truth must lie somewhere in the middle. A report by the Economic Council of Canada, reviewing the benefits of inflation reduction claimed by Jarrett and Selody and by

Howitt, suggested that while the first estimate (16 times GNP) might be high, the second (1.25 times GNP) was likely conservative. But is there any reason to believe either estimate is even remotely accurate? As economists Brian MacLean and Mark Setterfield commented, "We are not convinced. If two people claim to have seen a UFO, with one person claiming that it was large and the other person claiming that it was small, should we assume that the UFO was medium-sized?"

Asked about his reliance on the Jarrett and Selody study, Howitt conceded that the study "probably gives an exaggerated estimate of the productivity gains from price stability." He also noted that his own calculations were only "back of the envelope." Still, he continued to defend his extrapolations.

"It must be tempting to dismiss all this number-fumbling and wonder how it could make sense to go through all the cost of eliminating inflation just to get the uncertain prospect of these benefits, whose size is so hard to quantify," wrote Howitt in response to my questions. "I look at it from the other side and wonder how anyone could risk giving up such huge benefits, which good economic reasoning and common sense say should be there, and whose existence is certainly not ruled out by the evidence."

Howitt's willingness to provide his own estimates of the benefits helped make the case for price stability seem stronger than it is, because it creates the illusion that another source has independently investigated the subject and also found evidence that price stability leads to greater economic growth. However, this isn't the case. It should be remembered that both estimates of economic growth are based on Jarrett and Selody's original—and highly questionable—estimate about productivity growth. If this original estimate is flawed, then both estimates of ultimate economic growth collapse.

So while Selody and Howitt do a nice tag-team effort of promoting price stability, once we get beyond the mutually supportive world of the Bank of Canada and the C.D. Howe Institute, we find the sand castle starts to crumble. John Helliwell, an economist at the University of British Columbia, attacked the Jarrett and Selody estimate at its foundations. Rather than higher inflation slowing down productivity growth, Helliwell argues that both higher inflation and the decline of productivity growth were likely caused by outside factors—a theory that is more consistent with the bulk of the economics literature. And Helliwell makes a clever point when he notes that Canadian government policies that eventually brought down inflation did nothing to stop the decline in Canadian productivity. In the early eighties, Canadian inflation declined significantly—by a lot more than the one percentage point envisioned by Jarrett and Selody. Yet we did not see the multi-zillion-dollar payoff in economic growth that their model predicted for such an inflation reduction. Rather, the productivity decline continued. Helliwell suggests that Jarrett and Selody have got things "probably backwards." He suggests that measures to control inflation may have actually driven productivity further down, not up: "Stronger anti-inflationary policies... could easily have made the productivity declines larger," writes Helliwell. In other words, the UFO was really a fish.

All this might be almost funny if it weren't so serious. At stake here is more than just an obscure academic debate. The positions advanced by Jarrett and Selody, Howitt and the C.D. Howe Institute have played a significant role in shaping public policy in Canada, in that they appeared to provide a solid academic foundation for claims about the benefits of price stability. Thus, they were used by the Bank and by the government to justify John Crow's highly experimental zero inflation policy. The C.D. Howe Institute used its considerable reputation in business, financial and media circles to actively sell the zero inflation goal, supporting its position with books like the one in which Howitt's work figured prominently. What Jarrett and Selody and Howitt appeared to offer was evidence that whatever pain the pursuit of price stability might inflict—recession, unemployment, lower incomes—it would all be worth it in the long run, because the resulting economic gains would be so immense.

But if, as Helliwell suggests, these influential advocates of price stability have gotten things "probably backwards," maybe the pursuit of price stability was all a gigantic mistake. If we consider that the growth estimates of Jarrett and Selody and Howitt are simply too unreliable to be a basis for making policy decisions, we are back at square one, asking the question, Why is moderate inflation so bad? What is the reason we must attack it with a sledgehammer, or a nuclear bomb, whenever it so much as pokes its head above the ground? The whole justification for John Crow's actions—choking the economy with high interest rates—rests on making the case that moderate inflation is extremely harmful to society. So let's look more closely at the question.

Fortunately, the Bank of Canada and the C.D. Howe Institute have provided us with ample material on the evils of inflation. Let's look at the work of another influential pair of tight-money enthusiasts, David Laidler and William Robson. Their book, *The Great Canadian Disinflation*, published by the Howe in 1993, was extremely influential in media and academic circles. So if we want to investigate the merits of price stability, this is surely a good source to consult.

Laidler and Robson do not disappoint us. Right at the outset, they lay out what they see as the costs of inflation. We soon notice that the main thrust of the arguments is the old familiar one—that inflation destroys economic efficiency. We also see why Jarrett and Selody were so keen to put some meat on this carcass; without it, the theoretical arguments seem rather weak. For instance, Laidler and Robson complain, "The bodies responsible for setting accounting standards have found it essentially impossible to produce workable solutions created by the problems of inflation. How does one adapt inventory valuation conventions to a world of generally rising prices? What about the valuation of land held in reserve by real estate developers? In assessing the profitability of a financial institution, how should one treat depreciation in the real value of its bond portfolio?" While one can sympathize with the difficulties inflation apparently creates for individuals governing the accounting profession, it is hard to imagine that these sorts of problems would be considered by the general public as a pressing national concern.

Laidler and Robson also tell us that inflation "means that time and effort that could be producing useful goods and services are devoted instead to changing prices frequently and to communicating information about these changes." So this is what's dragging down our national productivity—the extra time it takes for waiters and store clerks to make price adjustments on menus and supermarket shelves? Laidler and Robson go on to suggest that the really big productivity loss is that talented people end up using their energies to figure out ways to take advantage of inflation. "[I]n an inflationary environment, it pays to devote scarce talent to seeking out and exploiting the profit opportunities that inflation creates. Specialist knowledge of finance, tax accounting, tax law and the like goes for a premium, and able people who have been working in research and development, production engineering and so on are attracted into privately profitable but socially less productive lines of work."

Essentially, Laidler and Robson seem to be concerned that talented individuals, who could be devoting their energies to socially productive work, are instead channelling their efforts towards figuring out tax and financial schemes to profit from inflation. This is an odd line of argument. The diversion of talent into the tax and financial sector is admittedly lamentable, but the phenomenon can hardly be blamed on inflation! Inflation is only one of the many variables assessed by tax and financial planners in devising strategies to allow their clients to achieve the maximum financial gain.

Do Laidler and Robson somehow imagine that, if there were no inflation, the whole business of tax and financial planning would disappear, and tax lawyers, accountants and investment dealers would redirect their energies into, say, finding a cure for cancer, designing shelters for the homeless or creating a Canadian aerospace industry? It is worth noting that, when inflation actually did disappear in the summer of 1994, tax lawyers, accountants, and financial professionals were as busy as ever, engaged in their same old socially unproductive activities. Clearly, it would take a lot more than the absence of inflation to lure these people away from their lucrative business.

Besides, what Laidler and Robson are really complaining about here isn't inflation but capitalism. It's capitalism that encourages talent and energy to be directed, above all, towards the maximization of profit. The whole nature of our capitalist system is based on the notion that the profit motive, rather than social utility, should be the driving force in the economy. Laidler and Robson may find this undesirable and inefficient, but it has little to do with inflation.

Their concern about the misuse of "scarce" talent is also misplaced. Talent is anything but "scarce" these days. With our high unemployment, there is a large surplus of talented people, including engineers and research scientists, who are not doing the socially useful work they are capable of. It's not because they are involved in devising profit-maximizing inflation schemes, but because they have been thrown out of work by the recession. Indeed, in many cases, they have lost their jobs as a result of our central bank's obsession with price stability—the very policy that Laidler and Robson so fervently advocate.

This may seem to be labouring the point, but it is worthy of considerable attention because the advocates of price stability consider it the centrepiece of their argument. Laidler and Robson insist that "the really large potential gains [in reducing inflation]...will stem from improvements in the allocation of scarce talent among diverse occupations and the improved investment and research and development performance that this shift might bring about." They even lift a chunk out of Peter Howitt's chapter in *Zero Inflation* to reinforce the importance of this point. Howitt, too, regards this "diversion of talents from productive activities" as perhaps the most insidious of all the negative effects of inflation. It was this diversion-of-talents factor that prompted Howitt to speculate about the catastrophic effects of inflation on economic growth. Right after he identified it as perhaps the most serious effect of inflation, Howitt proceeded in the next paragraph to make his dramatic speculation that reducing inflation may be worth about $11 trillion.

So can it be possible that this diversion-of-talents factor—a specious argument based on a unique understanding of the tax and financial planning industry—is the reason we must declare an all-out war against inflation? Is this what ultimately lies behind the case for price stability? Is this really all there is to it? For *this*, hundreds of thousands of people have been thrown out of work, tens of thousands of businesses have been bankrupted, countless families have slipped into poverty, a generation of young people has grown up with a sense of hopelessness, and our deficit has soared? Wouldn't it have been simpler just to outlaw the financial planning industry? Surely there is more to it than this!

But it doesn't seem that there is. In a thoughtful essay on inflation, Robert Solow, the U.S. Nobel Prize-winning economist, briefly mentions the diversion-of-talents and other similar arguments about the negative effects of inflation and goes on to say that it is "hard to get excited" about them. "It is hard to believe that they amount to much." He describes these adverse effects of inflation as "no worse than a bad cold."

Solow essentially dismisses the notion that moderate inflation leads to any significant economic inefficiency. Indeed, if we leave theory behind, and look at real-world experiences, we find little evidence to suggest that moderate inflation has had much effect on productivity growth. If we look at inflation rates and productivity growth in the leading industrial countries in recent years, we find that there appears to be no relationship. Pierre Fortin notes that some low-inflation countries experienced high productivity growth between 1960 and 1985, while others had low productivity growth. Similarly, some countries with relatively high inflation experienced low productivity growth, while others didn't. Like Solow, Fortin argues that the alleged benefits of reducing inflation have been grossly exaggerated.

The belief that zero inflation has a significant impact on productivity growth is something of a Canadian phenomenon. Zero inflation has supporters elsewhere, but they don't make extravagant claims that the policy will increase productivity, as many Canadian advocates do. In the United States, for instance, the most ardent supporter of zero inflation, Lee Hoskins, president of the Federal Reserve Bank of Cleveland, doesn't even mention improved productivity growth in his list of benefits. (Interestingly, also, when Hoskins' bank sponsored a conference on zero inflation, most of the leading monetary economists who attended concluded that zero inflation wasn't even a good idea.)

So why are certain people, including those who run the Bank of Canada and the C.D. Howe Institute, so exercised about inflation? Solow notes that, while the costs of inflation may not be large for the economy overall, they can be large for the finances of individuals. Particularly hard hit, he says, are those with wealth, who "see their real wealth eroded," and creditors, who see their loans repaid in less valuable dollars. Thus, as mentioned in the last chapter, there is a redistribution of wealth from creditors to debtors.

Laidler and Robson also mention the fact that inflation redistributes resources but, as we saw in the last chapter, they make it sound as if the only victims of inflation's redistribution are pensioners and single mothers. Solow counters that these vulnerable people can be easily protected from inflation with "a little well-aimed indexing."

Indeed, indexing offers such an apparently simple solution to the concerns expressed by Laidler and Robson that their lack of interest in the subject seems perplexing. Why do they express concern about inflation's effects on pensioners and single mothers, and yet express no concern that Ottawa reduced the indexation protection for single mothers and attempted to reduce it for pensioners as well, until a public outcry forced it to back down in 1985. When asked about the Howe's position on all this, Robson has trouble remembering specifics. Yet surely, if the Howe had been genuinely worried about inflation whittling away the purchasing power of these low-income groups, it would have been up in arms over Ottawa's moves to de-index virtually all federal social benefits—thereby *guaranteeing* that vulnerable groups would be hurt by inflation.

All this leads us to speculate whether inflation-fighters like those at the C.D. Howe Institute aren't perhaps less concerned about the way inflation threatens poor pensioners and more concerned about the way it threatens wealth-holders. If we look at the C.D. Howe's membership list, we notice an absence of groups representing pensioners, single mothers or any other vulnerable group, and a strong presence of wealthy individuals, investment houses, stock-brokerages, accounting and law firms and other businesses that serve the wealthy. It's not overly cynical to suggest that these firms support the Howe and its campaign against inflation because they are concerned about the way inflation erodes the value of their financial holdings and those of their clients. Although they may recognize that it is politically more saleable to carry the banner for pensioners and single mothers in the inflation battle, their primary concern is likely what inflation does to their own finances.

Ironically, to the extent that inflation hurts the poor, Solow says that the damage is not so much from inflation as from the strong measures taken by central banks to curb it. The deliberate tightening of credit through a policy of high interest rates may be wonderfully effective in killing the demon inflation, but it also kills much of the economy, leaving a wide swath of unemployment and recession in its wake. John Smithin, an economist at York University, observes wryly, "[I]t is always possible...by a tight-money policy...to reduce aggregate demand and economic activity up to some point where inflationary pressures...begin to ease. In the limit, after all, if economic activity were to cease entirely and the population starved to death, we could be quite confident that there would be no inflation." The anti-inflation medicine, then, is a bit like a cancer drug that kills cancerous and noncancerous cells alike. The medical profession has wisely withheld such drugs after seeing they fail the most basic cost-benefit analysis: getting rid of your cancer is of limited benefit if you end up dying in the process.

The key difference in the case of inflation-killing medicine is that the injury can be deflected onto others. A heavy dose of inflation-killing medicine can be lethal, but it is not lethal across the board. Some members of society will be hurt by it, such as the unemployed, those who live in fear of unemployment and those whose wages drop due to a loss of bargaining power caused by high unemployment. But others often find themselves more prosperous than ever after the

central bank has imposed a heavy dose of anti-inflation medicine. To them, the medicine perhaps doesn't seem so bad.

And inside the walls of the monastery, shuttered from
ordinary life, things don't look so bad either. In fact, things
look rather lovely inside the Bank of Canada. There is a
spectacular, vaulted atrium full of plants and trees that grow
thick and lush like a moist green jungle. Here, in one of the
coldest cities on the continent, the Bank is warm and shel-
tering. Not even the chilly wind of restraint reaches inside.
Unlike just about every other corner of the economy, the
Bank remains untouched by the recession, unscathed by
John Crow's punishing lash—a lush oasis in a harsh, freezing
landscape. There have been no pay cuts at the Bank, no
downsizing, no restructuring, no need to match Third World
wages in an increasingly competitive world marketplace.
(The one exception has been the Bank's janitors, who lost
their jobs when the Bank decided to privatize its cleaning
services.) The Bank, which prints the nation's money, turns
a handsome profit and is awash in cash.

Everything looks verdant and alive here. There is no suffering, just reports of it far away, beyond the walls. But not to
worry: the economic models worked out by the brain-centre
assure everyone in the monastery that this suffering is greatly
exaggerated. The Bank's research shows that the negative
side effects of killing inflation are actually minor—just as its
research showed that killing inflation would lead to enormous benefits, measured in the trillions of dollars.

It's all very reassuring, for those who believe.

As the din grew louder outside in the late eighties, some
days it seemed you could almost hear it through the walls of
the monastery. Try as they might, those in the brain-centre
could not insulate themselves completely from it. Every day,
the media reported the latest interest rate climb, and fresh
tales of bankruptcies and mortgage foreclosures. Even if

those on the inside knew they were doing what was right—
what the models clearly showed was right—it was impossible
to be unaware that many people on the outside were blindly,
stupidly angry. Sometimes it seemed that what the
monastery needed wasn't just thick walls, but a moat.

From Selody's office inside the Bank, it was fairly easy not
to hear the din. As a senior economist in the "special studies"
section within the research department, Selody was about as
far away from the ugly realities of normal life as it was possible to get. Just as the research department was removed from
the day-to-day operations of the Bank, the "special studies"
section was even removed from the rest of the research
department. Selody's office had a large window overlooking
the stately building of the Supreme Court of Canada, where
the country's top lawyers hustled into the richly decorated
court chamber, prepared to give the performance of their
lives. No signs of unemployment or hard times there either.

For Selody it was all very simple. He and Jarrett had
clearly demonstrated that the benefits of zero inflation were
immense. But although their paper had been greeted warmly
within the Bank and among a small group of monetary
scholars, clearly it hadn't put the debate to rest. Whether
through ignorance or obstinacy, many seemingly intelligent
people—including some economists—continued to argue
that zero inflation could only be achieved at a devastating
price. The angry mob of unemployed workers in the country
seemed to be saying the same thing in a cruder way.

Selody had no intention of responding to the mob, or
even to the doubting intelligentsia. But he did want to clarify things for those who understood the issues, like those
inside the monastery. He had demonstrated the benefits of
price stability. Now he had to debunk the notion that the
costs outweighed the benefits.

This was a more difficult task. It was one thing to try to
make the case that price stability offered benefits; that case

was shaky enough, as we've seen. It was quite another to argue that these alleged benefits were larger than the costs of achieving price stability—costs that were known to be very large. Although there was debate about exactly how large these costs were, there was no debate over whether they existed and were significant. All economists—even those within the monastery—acknowledged that the Bank's anti-inflation medicine inevitably caused recession and unemployment, at least in the short run. There was even a name in economics jargon for all the suffering: the "sacrifice ratio" identified how much of a sacrifice would have to be made (by unidentified people) in order to bring inflation under control.

But, once again, Selody was not deterred. He began by laying out several different estimates of this "sacrifice ratio." The range he presented was limited, confined to estimates produced by the Bank's own researchers and also by Peter Howitt. He ignored the work of a wide range of economists with a more critical perspective on Bank policy. Astonishingly, even given this highly biased sampling of views, the evidence Selody presented amounted to a damning indictment of Bank policy, revealing just how destructive the Bank's anti-inflation policies have been.

The first estimate he provides comes from Howitt, who, as we know, is a strong supporter of the Bank's tough anti-inflation stand. So how much economic hardship does a price stability enthusiast like Howitt think we'll have to endure to achieve the cherished goal? Howitt estimates a "sacrifice ratio" of 4.7 per cent of GDP—roughly $30 billion! Here we have one of the leading advocates of the Bank's tough anti-inflation medicine arguing that, for every percentage point drop in inflation achieved by this medicine, the economy will suffer by about $30 billion!

Selody then reports some lower estimates presented by the Bank of Canada's own staff. But even these are staggeringly high, ranging from about $15 billion to about $22 billion.

Apparently frustrated that these numbers still seem awfully large, Selody does another little calculation of his own to bring the estimate of damage somewhat lower. He argues that, if the Bank makes clear to the public that it intends to adhere rigidly to the goal of zero inflation, it will gain "credibility." The public will believe the Bank means business about squeezing inflation out of the economy and will stop making excessive wage demands. Therefore, the Bank won't have to drive interest rates as high to keep prices down; Canadians themselves will, in a sense, become their own inflation police, moderating their behaviour in order to keep prices down. This "credibility" factor may sound a little nebulous and hard to measure. Not to worry. Selody proceeds to make the unexplained assumption that "credibility" will bring the costs of achieving a one percentage point reduction in inflation down to a "sacrifice ratio" of 1.7 per cent of GDP—still about $11.5 billion.

But while Selody is clearly struggling to get the number as low as he can—although $11.5 billion is not exactly a small price to pay—research by economists outside the Bank suggests that these numbers are ludicrously low, that the true costs of inflation reduction are far higher. Pierre Fortin, for instance, found that the "sacrifice ratio" for a one percentage point decrease in inflation is more likely in the range of 15 to 20 per cent of GDP, or about $105 billion to $140 billion.

It is important to remember that all these estimates of the "sacrifice ratio"—whether Fortin's estimate of $105 billion or Selody's of $11.5 billion or any others in between— represent the amount of lost output for *each percentage point* reduction in inflation. However, the Bank's goal was not to reduce inflation by merely one percentage point, but rather to eventually bring it all the way down to zero. Even if we look at, say, the Bank's short-term aim in 1993 of bringing inflation down from 5 per cent to 2 per cent (a reduction of three percentage points), we see that all these estimates must be multiplied by three.

So, if we use the "sacrifice ratio" estimates of Fortin, we can see that the cost involved in reducing inflation by three percentage points would be simply colossal—somewhere between $315 and $420 billion. With classic academic understatement, Fortin writes, "These results raise the possibility that previous research has vastly underestimated the costs of the traditional recession method of reducing inflation." If we accept the more modest "sacrifice ratio" estimates presented by Selody, we still find that reducing inflation by three percentage points involves staggering losses to the Canadian economy—from $34.5 billion (the best-case scenario put forward by Selody) to $90 billion. Indeed, Selody's paper—"Technical Paper No. 54" of the Bank of Canada—presents what amounts to an overwhelming case against the Bank's policies.

When a rough draft of the paper was sent to the Finance department for review and comment, there was considerable concern. Why was Selody conceding so much about the costs of controlling inflation? Wasn't it better, Finance asked, to say nothing about the bad news and focus instead just on the good news? Finance didn't disagree that the costs were great, but it was concerned about drawing attention to the fact. Although the Bank of Canada operated in its own little world, largely cut off from the public, the Finance department was far more savvy about public relations, about the need to spoon-feed the public with carefully selected information. And information about the terrible costs of the Bank's war on inflation hardly seemed like a suitable chunk to be serving up.

Another fact that the Finance department was keen to suppress was that it had done its own internal studies, which, if anything, contradicted Selody's findings. The Finance studies showed that the benefits of inflation reduction diminished as the inflation rate fell. In other words, there were considerable benefits to the economy in reducing inflation from a relatively high level to a medium level—say, from 12 per cent down to 6 per cent. But it was far less clear how great the benefits were in reducing inflation from, say, 4 per cent to 2 per cent or from 2 per cent to zero. At these lower levels, inflation was not so clearly a problem. Indeed, some economists argued that a low level of inflation, particularly if it was fairly steady, posed no real problems and could even act in some ways as a lubricant to help the economy function.

The Finance studies clearly showed that, at lower levels, it became increasingly difficult to squeeze out the last remaining bits of inflation, so the Bank had to squeeze more vigorously, or to use a popular phrase of central bankers, to "lean harder against the wind." This suggested that the downside of inflation control—unemployment, bankruptcies, recession—became more pronounced, even as the benefits of lower inflation seemed to shrink or even disappear. Thus, the Finance studies amounted to a devastating commentary on the folly of Crow's policy—a policy that required the Bank to carry out a ruthless attack on the economy to eliminate what was perhaps an essentially harmless rate of inflation.

Back at the Bank, Selody was undeterred. He had no fears about publicizing the bad news about the war on inflation, because his whole point was to show that the bad news was outweighed by the good news. Indeed, Selody's paper argued that, despite the immense economic losses caused by the Bank's anti-inflation policies, the battle was still worth fighting. How could this possibly be? a reasonable person might ask. It's simple, if we only remember the groundbreaking work of Jarrett and Selody. Recall that their calculations showed that trillions of dollars' worth of benefits could be realized if we achieved zero inflation. Clearly such trillion-dollar mega-benefits dwarf the loss of only hundreds of billions of dollars!

So we are back where we started—relying once again on the questionable findings of the Jarrett and Selody study—back in Lala Land, dreaming of phantom trillion-dollar benefits that seem to be visible only to true believers. This time Selody fleshes out the numbers with some commentary on economic efficiency, trotting out the familiar diversion-of-talents argument as his central theme. The world of monetary policy and the Bank are increasingly resembling a maze in which all paths lead back to the centre.

So Selody's attempt to downplay the costs of battling inflation turns out to be a weird one. All he did was restate his earlier dubious case for the benefits of zero inflation, concede that there are also enormous costs, then attempt to compare those costs and benefits, and conclude that the benefits outweighed the costs. The only problem, for those without true faith, is that, on close examination, the benefits seem to be about as real as the Loch Ness monster.

If only the same could be said for the costs.

As we delve into the theology that prevails at the monastery, some curious notions emerge. Most striking is the peculiar attitude towards unemployment.

For most people, it is hard to imagine a worse scourge on the economic and social landscape than a high level of unemployment. There is, first and foremost, the obvious problem that unemployment deprives people of a livelihood and results in whole families living in poverty. But it deprives people of much more than mere money: it deprives them of a sense of self-worth, of the feeling of being productive, contributing members of society. There are few costs more negative than these. A recent study reported in the *Lancet* medical journal found evidence that unemployment may actually weaken the body's immune system, suggesting that it has such a profound psychological effect that it produces a physical deterioration in the body.

The profoundly important role that employment plays in our lives is captured well by social psychologist M. Jahoda:

There are latent consequences of employment as a social institution which meet human needs of an enduring kind. First of all is the fact that employment imposes a time structure on the working day. Secondly, employment implies regularly shared experiences and contacts with people outside the family. Thirdly, employment links an individual to goals and purposes which transcend his own. Fourthly, employment defines aspects of status and identity. Finally, employment enforces activity.

It is these "objective" consequences of work in complex industrialized societies which help us to understand the motivation to work beyond earning a living; to understand why work is psychologically supportive, even when conditions are bad; and by the same token, to understand why unemployment is psychologically destructive... Now it is true that the latent or manifest consequences of other social institutions—schools, voluntary work, clubs—can produce one or more of these psychological supports. But I know of none in our society which combines them all and which, in addition, has as compelling a manifest reason as making one's living. Nobody prevents the unemployed from creating their own time structure and social contacts, from sharing goals and purposes with others, or from exercising their skills as best they can. But the psychological input required to do so on a regular basis, entirely under one's own steam, is colossal.

Bank theologians—as well as mainstream economists—see unemployment in a different light. Modern economics focuses on the notion that human beings are rational creatures who are solely motivated by greed and the prospect of material gain. Thus, faced with the prospect of either working to earn income or getting it free from the unemployment insurance office, the one-dimensional creatures of economic theory will choose the freebie.

But, if we look beyond the economics textbooks, we realize that in fact human beings are infinitely more complex than this, and that they require far more than the satisfaction of their greed impulse. While greed is undoubtedly an integral part of the human personality, so are the deep psychological needs for self-affirmation, a sense of self-worth and belonging to a community that Jahoda describes so eloquently, and these are in no way satisfied by an unemployment insurance cheque.

These psychological needs play no part in the economist's model of human behaviour, perhaps because they are too difficult to measure in statistical terms. Unlike financial payments such as UI cheques, which have specific numbers of dollars attached to them, these psychological needs are not quantifiable, and thus they frustrate the desire of economists to measure, calculate and be specific, to render their work "scientific." But are these needs any less real, in terms of human experience, just because economists have trouble fitting them into their "science"? Few people would believe, for instance, that children who have all their physical and material needs satisfied will turn out fine, regardless of whether they get enough parental love and attention to give them a sense of self-worth and self-esteem.

All this is perhaps self-evident. But it is worth mentioning here, at the risk of stating the obvious, because it does not fit into the equations of economists, or into the economic models of the Bank of Canada. Even the most extreme theologians at the Bank would no doubt agree that, on an individual basis, it is bad for a person to be unemployed. But by treating unemployment as a deliberate choice made by rational individuals, they take much of the sting out of it. Rather than being something painful and destructive that most people deeply dislike, unemployment is transformed into a lifestyle of choice. The problem then becomes one of determining how low benefit levels should be set in order to create a work incentive, how many pellets of food are to be placed in front of the rat to get him to respond in the way we want. We are tinkering with nothing more than the human greed impulse.

All this is very useful to anti-inflation crusaders, since their goal often requires them to take actions that result in massive job losses. Their task will be easier to sell if unemployment is presented as a deliberate choice rather than something that is foisted on unwilling victims. They use an elaborate vocabulary that makes unemployment and the Bank's role in causing it sound benign and merely technical. As we've seen, they talk about the "sacrifice ratio," by which they refer to the amount of suffering people will experience when the Bank induces a recession to control inflation. This ratio is measured as a proportion of GDP, making it all sound very scientific, rather than painful and soul-destroying. Also, instead of talking about "unemployment," which has overtones of people being thrown out of work and families suffering, they speak instead of the "slack in labour markets."

Only by creating enough "slack in labour markets"—that is, by throwing enough people out of work—can inflation be controlled, according to Bank theory. A large pool of unemployed people will reduce any inflationary pressure on prices, since there will be fewer people with money to buy goods. All these unemployed people will also serve as a constant, scary reminder to those lucky ones who remain employed: don't be too demanding, accept a pay cut if necessary, remember that there are many people out there who would love to have your job.

It is important, then, to maintain enough "slack" in

labour markets, but just how much is enough? That depends on your vantage point. If you're unemployed or in fear of being unemployed, the less "slack" the better. On the other hand, if you are a Bank economist, whose career has been devoted to controlling inflation, then you will tend to want more "slack," and you will probably not be disturbed by high levels of unemployment. Indeed, those levels may seem fine to you. Gideon Rosenbluth, an economist at the University of British Columbia, suggests that Bank economists and their academic supporters are suffering from a syndrome that he has dubbed "slack denial." To them, high unemployment rates do not represent unnecessary slack. After all, those unemployed people are serving a useful purpose; they are lambs being sacrificed to the god of inflation control.

Selody is fairly explicit about what he considers to be the merits of unemployment. In "Technical Paper No. 54," he writes about the important role unemployment plays in changing people's expectations about inflation. He argues that unemployment "acts as a signal to individuals to change their expectations about future wage and salary increases." He even goes on to suggest that if workers fail to pay attention to these signals by moderating their wage demands, it will be necessary to increase the level of unemployment further, to drive the message home harder. As he puts it, "The more rigid wages and salaries are (that is, the longer it takes individuals to learn about a change in inflation), *the more unemployment is necessary* to convince individuals that it is appropriate to accept smaller increases in money incomes [italics added]." In Selody's view, then, unemployment is needed to reinforce the message that workers must moderate their wage demands. It is the lash that will convince reluctant workers to accept lower wages.

If this sounds like a fairly extreme position, it falls well within the view that prevails in central banking circles. Indeed, this view is basic fare for the elite group of central bankers who meet every month in Basel, Switzerland, at a unique organization called the Bank for International Settlements (BIS). This "bank," which was established by international treaty in the 1920s, has become, among other things, a regular meeting place for the central bankers of the most advanced industrial nations, including Canada. The annual reports of the BIS provide a window into the thoughts of the most important central bankers in the world, who play a major role in managing the world economy by controlling the supply of money. And these central bankers are explicitly enthusiastic about the desirable effects of unemployment. In its 1980 annual report, the BIS argued that the problem with democratic governments is that they have traditionally been reluctant to accept long periods of high unemployment—largely, of course, because high unemployment angers voters, who tend to throw such governments out of office as soon as possible.

The following year, the bankers at the BIS noted with approval that Western governments were being won over to the tight-money doctrines long advocated by the central banking community. Here, for instance, is what the BIS said in its 1981 annual report: "[M]any if not most governments now appear to believe that restrictive demand management offers the main—and perhaps the only—hope of a gradual return to *more satisfactory levels of unemployment* [italics added]." The concept of more satisfactory levels of *unemployment* is truly amazing. It turns on its head the view that unemployment is destructive to the human spirit and to society, and portrays unemployment as a desirable economic tool that we should see a lot more of. The BIS bankers appear to be suffering from a particularly acute strain of "slack denial" that could perhaps be dubbed "slack excitement."

The same enthusiasm for unemployment can be detected in a financial newsletter put out by the privately-owned National Bank of Canada in May 1988, which referred to the "spectre" of full employment. What enthuses all these bankers about unemployment is the disciplinary effect it has on wage demands and therefore inflation. This disciplining of labour has some important ramifications. In the ongoing power struggle between employers and employees, it clearly strengthens the hand of employers. This explains why many business people are supportive of the zero inflation goal, even though the accompanying higher interest rates mean higher costs for their businesses and even perhaps fewer sales in the resulting recession. The upside, however, is that they will be able to count on a weak and docile labour force, which will be more flexible and willing to work for less than before. This is very important, since labour costs account for the bulk of the operating expenses of most businesses.

In this light, it is easy to see why the business community is so keen to reduce unemployment insurance and welfare benefits. These social systems are support mechanisms that prevent workers from feeling too desperate in the face of mounting unemployment; they offer a net underneath frightened workers. Without that net, faced with the possibility of even greater hardship and want for themselves and their families, workers would be more docile still. Selody and others refer to these support systems—these lifelines to desperate workers—as "labour market rigidities."

Perhaps the clearest indication of the importance tight-money supporters attach to unemployment is a neat little concept they call the NAIRU. The NAIRU, which stands for "the Non-Accelerating Inflation Rate of Unemployment," is a measure of the amount of unemployment they consider necessary in order to prevent inflation. The NAIRU thus reflects the notion that a certain level of unemployment isn't just an unfortunate development; rather, it is a necessity, a key tool for controlling inflation. The idea is that there is a "natural" rate of unemployment that keeps inflation in check, and if unemployment drops below this "natural" level, inflation will accelerate. Thus, unemployment must be kept at a sufficiently high rate to keep inflation under control.

Although economists like to portray the NAIRU as a scientific and purely technical measurement, in fact, it is a highly charged concept. U.S. finance professor Edward S. Herman points out that it can be used to suggest that a high level of unemployment is "natural" and inevitable and therefore not something to worry about. "Portraying [unemployment] as part of nature, working implacably and independently of human contrivance, like the law of gravity, reinforces the claims of…analysts that there isn't much society can do about unemployment."

Far from being scientific, the NAIRU, according to economist Lars Osberg of Dalhousie University, can be fixed at almost any level, and "a substantial degree of uncertainty surrounds estimates of its magnitude." Since the NAIRU is essentially a measure of what level of unemployment is considered acceptable and desirable, the level tends to vary with the politics and ideology of the measurer. Economists at the Bank of Canada, whose primary goal is fighting inflation, tend to calculate a fairly high NAIRU; Stephen Poloz, the Bank's research director, recently announced that the Bank had decided the NAIRU for Canada was above 8 per cent. This allows the Bank to argue that an unemployment rate of above 8 per cent, which most people would consider high, is acceptable and even necessary to keep inflation under control.

Perhaps the most interesting aspect of the NAIRU is that it reveals that tight-money advocates recognize there is a trade-off between unemployment and inflation, that if we want to squeeze inflation out of the economy, we pay for it with higher unemployment. This leads to some obvious political questions: Are we paying too high a price to get inflation down? Can the high rate of unemployment generated in the anti-inflation battle be justified? Are the sacrifices required being shared fairly among the population? The tight-money advocates sidestep these compelling questions with a quick sleight of hand. While they're quite willing to admit that their battle to bring inflation down drives unemployment up, they adamantly insist that this is only a temporary phenomenon. After a short period of time, they argue, inflation will be squeezed out of the economy for good, unemployment will drop back down to its "natural" level and enormous economic benefits will follow. This reassuring theory, summed up in their refrain "short-term pain for long-term gain," is once again based largely on faith.

The allegedly temporary nature of the pain is crucial to the argument of Bank theologians and other tight-money enthusiasts. They go to great lengths to measure how long the "temporary" period will last, before we reach "payback"—the point when the benefits outweigh the costs. Once again, the outcome is made to sound very precise and scientific. Selody thus presents us with a number of possible payback periods. Will it be 0.53 years—six months, in the language of ordinary folk—2.5 years, 4.5 years or 5.3 years? Surely his mathematical models can tell us the answer.

Many practical-minded economists are not convinced by this apparent precision. In fact, they argue that even brief doses of anti-inflation medicine can have long-term effects, since bouts of unemployment often leave workers less skilled, demoralized, even devastated and therefore less employable in the future. This phenomenon was noted by a major British employer back in 1886 when he told the Special Committee of the Charity Society, "We have always found, as to the Artisan, that if he happens to be out of work for three months, he is never the same man again."

If this is the case, perhaps the real effect of harsh monetary medicine is to push up the long-term—as well as the short-term—unemployment rate, so that even when the economy recovers, unemployment never falls back down to its pre-recession level. Perhaps the real effect of short-term

pain, then, is not long-term gain but rather long-term *pain*.
Pierre Fortin's research suggests that "a permanent reduction
in the inflation rate can be achieved only at the cost of *a*
permanent increase in the unemployment rate [italics added]."
According to Fortin, the "sacrifice ratio" is ongoing and perhaps unlimited. He suggests that the unemployment costs
are much bigger than the Bank economists say—by a factor
of about 50. This raises the eerie possibility that the "payback," if it comes at all, may be a long, long way down the
road, offering little comfort to those living in the here-and-
now. As the great British economist John Maynard Keynes
once noted: in the long run, we are all dead.

The city of Toronto boasts few buildings that could be
described as looking like a medieval monastery. The closest
thing is probably a lovely, old Anglican church office building in the downtown area, just on the edge of the financial
district. It is partly occupied by the C.D. Howe Institute,
which could be said to be something of a satellite seminary
for the real monastery in Ottawa.

Like the Bank of Canada, the Howe is spacious, bright
and full of plants, which, oddly, give it a feeling of life and
growth and renewal. Its members can easily walk the short
distance from their gleaming Bay Street office towers to the
institute's tastefully renovated Adelaide Street headquarters
to attend seminars on monetary and fiscal policy. Like the
Bank, the institute is strongly committed to price stability,
regardless of the unemployment costs; many institute members could be said to be suffering from aggravated slack denial.

One severe case of that syndrome is Bill Robson, a senior
policy analyst at the institute who specializes in monetary
policy. Like Selody at the Bank, Robson has an almost mis-
sionary zeal for price stability. While Selody keeps himself
well within the secure and comforting walls of the monastery,
Robson is the public face of price stability, arguing the case

in books put out by the institute, as well as in radio and television chat shows. Still in his thirties, Robson is the popularizer of the notion of price stability. Although he himself has no economics degree—he has an MA in international relations from Carleton—Robson is well versed in the field. But his real skill is to take the technical, academic work of Jarrett and Selody, Howitt and others and package it for more general consumption. His material isn't really aimed at ordinary Canadians, but rather at influential people in politics, business and, perhaps most important of all, the media.

Of course, by reaching influential people in the media— editors, editorial writers, columnists, commentators—Robson and the institute are able to affect the opinions of ordinary Canadians. Robson's booklets make fairly dull reading and would have little chance of reaching a mainstream audience through bookstore sales, the booklets are comprehensible to a media person familiar with economic jargon. If media commentators are convinced by the institute's material, they will transmit the message, in a still simpler form, to a broader audience. Even when media analysts don't specifically endorse the arguments of the institute, they pay attention to what the institute is saying, and present its arguments in accessible form to the general public. Indeed, media outlets increasingly treat C.D. Howe statements and "studies" with the same seriousness and attention that they have traditionally treated reports from, say, Statistics Canada or the now-defunct Economic Council of Canada—even though the institute's material generally advocates a point of view.

By the fall of 1994, however, one would have thought that Robson would be feeling a little antsy. For years, he had been one of the most prominent proponents of price stability in the country, outside the walls of the Bank itself. He enjoyed one of the highest public profiles on the issue. The institute was constantly putting out material on the benefits of price stability, and Robson was almost always involved.

It was all very theoretical back in the eighties, when Robson started writing about it; inflation was running at around 5 per cent, and zero inflation was just a distant dream. Zero inflation was something that, in recent world history, had never been achieved or even really attempted. Claims about the benefits of price stability had a dream-like quality to them. Now, embarrassingly, zero inflation had arrived. And where exactly were the multi-trillion-dollar benefits?

Robson didn't squirm even slightly as we discussed it over lunch in an upscale Greek restaurant in downtown Toronto, just a few blocks from the institute. To the extent that the public had bought the argument for zero inflation, the most compelling selling point had been the promise of low interest rates. The Bank had unabashedly dangled them in front of the public as the promised land of zero inflation. "Monetary policy directed towards price stability is a policy oriented in the most fundamental way possible towards low interest rates," the Bank had said in its 1990 annual report. Once inflation was tamed, it was said, there would be no need for high interest rates, so interest rates would fall—a prerequisite for putting the economy back on track. Yet by 1994, inflation had been all but eliminated. Prices were no longer rising; at times they were actually falling, creating *deflation*. And yet interest rates remained high.

Recall that what matters is the *real* interest rate—that is, the interest rate once inflation has been factored out. Despite Canada's success in reducing inflation in the early nineties, our real interest rate remained high. The real interest rate in Canada stood at 5 per cent in 1987, the year John Crow took over as Bank of Canada governor. It rose to 7 per cent by 1990 and never dropped again, rising above 8 per cent periodically. In December 1994, the real interest rate stood at 7 per cent.

Robson conceded that things had not turned out as hoped on the interest rate front. "It would have been nice if [interest] rates had come down in lock-step with inflation," he said. "If I were being defensive about price stability, I'd blame it on the political situation and the concern that inflation is going to recur." But Robson was not prepared to accept that this indicated the zero inflation policy was fundamentally flawed. "Is that enough to make it a bad idea? It's a question of trade-offs. High inflation has its costs. Would we want to give up the experiment for that reason?"

Many Canadians might. The promise of lower interest rates had been front and centre in the campaign to sell price stability to the public. Now Robson was calmly admitting that that "optimistic scenario" hadn't come true. As he said nonchalantly over lunch, "Maybe we'll end up with real interest rates a bit higher." While that might not offend the financial community, who benefit from high real interest rates, it would certainly be bad news for people who borrowed money and for people hoping to find a job.

If Robson seemed unfazed by the failure of price stability to deliver low interest rates, he appeared equally calm about its failure to deliver on the productivity front. Recall that Jarrett and Selody had concluded that eliminating inflation would dramatically increase productivity growth. Yet as inflation fell in the wake of Crow's anti-inflation battle in the late eighties and early nineties, productivity growth fell too. Indeed, productivity growth during Crow's low-inflation reign was actually lower than it had been in the seventies, the decade of double-digit inflation when productivity growth was supposedly seriously damaged. Now, in retrospect, the productivity growth record of the seventies looked pretty good.

It had been the promise of improved productivity growth that had so excited Robson, Laidler and Howitt about the potential benefits of price stability. If we could wipe out inflation, they had argued, we could prevent the diversion of our talented people into the business of figuring out ways to avoid inflation. So, now that we'd achieved price stability, were we witnessing a surge of talent into more productive activities, unleashing an unstoppable momentum of growth potentially worth trillions of dollars?

"I don't think there's been much impact yet," said Robson calmly.

Well, so much for that idea. Good thing we hadn't already spent the trillions of dollars' worth of benefits.

"Inflation could come back," he explained, munching on a bun filled with ricotta cheese and spinach.

So all our talented people were just going to have to remain cooped up in their offices working on strategies for dodging inflation—even when there was no inflation—out of fear that it might return. If this was the case, how was the achievement of price stability helping us?

One of the reasons that Robson was so effective in TV interviews was that nothing fazed him. And he was no different over lunch. He didn't become defensive or angry at the suggestion that a policy that he had strongly pushed for a number of years hadn't delivered the promised benefits. He listened to the questions, conceded a point or two if necessary and then moved on to some other aspect of the subject, utterly unperturbed and unwavering.

Knowing what we now know, was the price stability experiment still worthwhile? Robson felt that it was. "A lot of the benefits wouldn't be things that could be captured in an economic model," he said, noting that someone receiving an unindexed pension was better off with lower inflation. So it was back to pensioners, the baby seals of the inflation debate. But couldn't we solve this problem by requiring all pensions to be indexed, and thereby avoid putting the entire economy through the wringer to bring inflation down? (Recall that Ottawa's main pension program—Old Age Security—is already indexed.) Robson agreed that further indexing would be possible, although he suggested that it would be "difficult to do." So was this all we had to show for our gruelling anti-inflation war—more protection for seniors with unindexed pensions, even though this goal could have been accomplished with a little additional indexing?

While we were on the subject of indexing, Robson went on to say that he'd like to see the indexation of capital gains, so that those receiving them wouldn't have to pay tax on inflationary gains. Certainly that would cheer the financial community, who receive the lion's share of the capital gains in the country.

Indeed, just about everything Robson said would cheer the financial community. Yet there was a quality about Robson that made him seem removed from the high-powered world of Bay Street financial wheeling and dealing. The son of two Toronto academics, Robson had a fresh-faced, unpretentious manner. He rode a bicycle to work from his modest house in an old neighbourhood in east-end Toronto, where he lived with his wife and three young children. Robson would bristle—and it takes a lot to make him bristle—at the notion that his campaign in support of zero inflation was for the benefit of the Bay Street financial community, which, ultimately, paid his salary at the institute. Rather, he said his strong support for eliminating inflation was part of a "libertarian," anti-government streak in his personality. (Inflation was a form of government theft, since it eroded the value of a citizen's assets in order to help make the government's debts more manageable, he explained.) Whether libertarian or lackey, Robson was promoting what Bay Street wanted promoted.

Certainly, there was to be no backing down from promoting the policy just because the benefits hadn't materialized. In January 1994, when it looked as if Ottawa was backing away from price stability, the institute issued a press release with the headline "Bank of Canada's fight for price stability was worth the effort, says C.D. Howe Institute study." The "study," Laidler and Robson's *The Great Canadian Disinflation*, which we've encountered before, is actually little more than a rehash of the traditional arguments for price stability and in fact provides no evidence to support the case that the fight for price stability was worth it. It admits that there have been considerable costs, and acknowledges that the benefits haven't yet materialized. "The really large potential gains—those arising from improved productivity performance—are likely to arrive with the longest delay, and their magnitude is subject to the greatest uncertainty," they write. This is a breathtaking admission. Does that "greatest uncertainty" include the possibility that the gains won't materialize at all, except perhaps in the minds of those who believe in them? And what will cause these great gains? Once again, we're back to the argument that reallocating scarce talent will produce massive productivity gains. But all this, Robson and Laidler note, "will require a lengthy period of proven price stability to set them in motion; how lengthy is impossible to assess before the event." So much for 0.53 years until payback. Now we're faced with an indefinite stretch of time whose length is "impossible to assess." Once it happens, then we'll know!

What we seem to be left with, by Laidler and Robson's admission, are significant costs and no real gains. The only bright sign is their prediction that there will be some sort of gains at some point in the future, although we have no idea when that future might arrive or how big the gains might be when it does. It would be interesting to imagine how successful Robson and Laidler would be selling life insurance with promises like that.

They acknowledge that those with shorter time horizons and less "faith"—their word!—may have trouble accepting all this. Laidler and Robson note that the faithful have challenged the sceptics in recent years with a number of arguments. One of the key arguments of the faithful, say Laidler and Robson, "amounted to an expression of *more confidence* in the benefits to be realized by pressing towards price stability than was displayed by the policy's critics [italics added]." So, in the end, it seems to boil down largely to a question of faith and confidence. There's no evidence of benefits; there's just "more confidence." Indeed, in the world view of Laidler and Robson, confidence amounts to an *argument* for price stability.

Undeterred by the lack of evidence, the "study" concludes that John Crow's anti-inflation battle "has, on the whole, been successful and worth the pain" (whose pain was that again?). Canada, according to the authors, "has learned many valuable lessons" and the experience has made the country "a leader in achieving price stability" and "has also provided a technical experiment in the execution of monetary policy." It's probably safe to assume that many Canadians would willingly forgo the thrill of knowing their country has led the world in experimenting with monetary policy, if only they could have back those lost years.

Robson and Laidler even pin much of the blame on Canadians. "If individuals and businesses had believed the Bank of Canada when it promised to follow a policy of price stability, the transition from high to low inflation might have been less painful," they say. In other words, it was the failure of Canadians to get their inflationary expectations under control, as instructed by the Bank, that caused the problems.

Luckily for all those who had promoted price stability, the media seemed to have forgotten the promises about the benefits of eliminating inflation. Commentators seemed content to blame rapidly rising interest rates on the deficit, the possibility of Quebec separating or uncertainty over the anti-inflation resolve of Gordon Thiessen. But surely these potential factors were foreseeable at the time when zero inflation advocates were making their extravagant claims about how great things would be if we persevered in the inflation fight. Did Jarrett and Selody, Howitt, Robson, Laidler—and John Crow himself—somehow fail to factor these problems into their forecasts? Were all those predictions of trillion-dollar benefits based on the premise that there would be no deficit, no Quebec separatism and that John Crow would be lifetime governor of the Bank? If so, the claims of an inflation-free nirvana seem to rest on even shakier ground than the wildly quaking turf on which they are already resting.

Somehow nobody seemed to raise the question of the *morality* of the immense experiment in monetary policy that Canada had just conducted. It was a question that U.S. economist and Nobel laureate Robert Solow had raised back in the winter of 1975, in anticipation of the inflation-fighting binge that was to take place in the early eighties.

Solow had outlined in detail how the costs of unemployment and lost production were simply much greater than the costs of inflation. "Yes, tight-money and balanced budgets can stop inflation, but only by depressing the economy for a long time, perhaps a very long time..." he wrote. "One must wonder if there is any defensible set of values that would make this policy a bargain."

It was a simple, eloquent point that the media here never got around to raising. But it was very much on the mind of the first governor of the Bank of Canada more than fifty years ago.

CHAPTER FIVE
Death of a Usurer
(and Other Cautionary Tales)

Amid the glitter of the Ottawa dinner party, it was easy to forget about the plight of debt-ridden Prairie farmers thousands of miles away. It was well known to everyone in the room that the Depression had been taking a brutal toll across the country, striking with particular ferocity in the West. But here, in the superbly appointed dining room of Molly and Graham Towers, with the exquisite table settings and fine cuisine served artfully by a silent corps of maids and butlers, all that human pain and suffering and despair seemed far away.

The Towers were probably as close as Canada came to royalty. Both were from prominent, well-to-do families, having grown up in the rarified atmosphere of the confident and cliquey Montreal English community just before World War I. When Graham Towers was appointed governor of the newly created Bank of Canada in 1934, it had seemed appropriate; his mother's family had been in banking for three generations. Here at his dinner party two years later were top figures from the world of politics, business and government. Even Prime Minister Mackenzie King himself was present, evidently enjoying the splendid surroundings and culinary delicacies of the evening. It was an occasion that

smacked of money and power and the bastions of privilege—
a scene that would have stuck in the craw of the Prairie
farmers left with nothing but bushels of virtually worthless
wheat.

The farmers would have been even more enraged had
they witnessed the scene earlier that day at the cabinet
meeting over which Prime Minister King had presided. With
cool detachment, the Liberal cabinet ministers had debated
whether or not to allow debt-ridden Manitoba and
Saskatchewan to default on their loans. Both provinces were
due to make payments to their creditors—those who had
bought their bonds—and yet both now, in the depths of the
Depression, lacked the revenue to make the payments. They
had turned to Ottawa for help.

This was not some idle threat either, some bombastic
exaggeration from a business group trying to get the government's attention. Everyone in that cabinet meeting, on
January 8, 1937, knew that the threat was real. Indeed, the
scenario had already been played out in Alberta. In
December 1935, Ernest Manning, the acting premier in
Alberta's Social Credit government—and father of
Preston—had written to the major Canadian bond dealers
explaining the province's disastrous financial situation and
asking that they accept lower rates of interest on the Alberta
bonds they had purchased. Such a suggestion had been
viewed dimly, to say the least, by the bondholders, who val-
ued above all else stability and security for their investments.

So when a round of interest payments on the Alberta
bonds came due on April 1, 1936, the bondholders were outraged to discover payments substantially below what they
had been promised when they bought the bonds. Alberta
had thus become the first province in Canada's short history
to default on its debts. There would be no more loans to
Alberta, at least until this breach of trust had been cor-
rected. To put it another way, Alberta had hit the debt

wall—not some imaginary debt wall but a real-life debt wall. Alberta's credit had been cut off.

It wasn't that Alberta had been spending too much on social programs. In fact, there was very little that resembled what we would consider a social program—no public health insurance, no family benefits and no significant old age pensions. Worst of all, as the Depression raged through the country with unemployment reaching 25 per cent in 1932, there was no unemployment insurance. Relief for the destitute and the unemployed was provided by local municipalities, and was usually grossly inadequate. As drought hit the Prairie provinces, desperate farm families ended up on relief as well.

The Alberta default situation was fresh in the minds of the federal cabinet ministers as they pondered the fate of Manitoba and Saskatchewan. Alberta had turned to Ottawa for help, only to be rebuffed. Now the pleas of Manitoba and Saskatchewan also seemed to be having little impact. The cabinet—and the business community—remained singularly obsessed with eliminating the deficit and achieving a balanced budget; coming up with more money to loan to the provinces would only retard that process.

A number of cabinet ministers actually favoured default. They argued that allowing Manitoba and Saskatchewan to default might improve the reputation of the federal government in financial circles by showing its willingness to be tough with its own provinces. The prime minister himself was sympathetic to this hard-line point of view. However, others in influential positions were alarmed at the prospect of more provincial defaults, fearing they would set off a wave of defaults, as debt-weary municipalities, school districts and private enterprises followed suit. One could imagine a mushrooming crisis—a kind of domino effect of debt walls—that would leave the international financial community wary of putting money anywhere in Canada. Among those who had these fears was Graham Towers.

Towers was a formidable supporter for the provinces to have on side. Not only was he governor of the Bank of Canada—an institution established after years of pressure for financial reform—but he personally enjoyed enormous respect. He had been appointed to the prestigious post at the age of only thirty-seven, after a meteoric rise through the ranks of the Royal Bank. With his grasp of economics and international finance and his distinguished, intelligent manner, he had created a considerable reputation in business as well as political circles.

Towers's good rapport with the prime minister also didn't hurt in winning King over to the importance of bailing out the provinces. Although Towers had actually been chosen for the bank post by the Conservative government before its defeat in 1935, he quickly impressed the new Liberal prime minister, who respected his sound financial judgment and seemed to take to Towers personally as well. It was perhaps fortuitous that King had attended the Towers' elegant little dinner party just as the provincial debt issue was reaching its climax.

King had clearly been charmed by Towers and his wife, and went to the trouble of sending Molly Towers a handwritten note of thanks, which positively gushed with enthusiasm. "Ever since the delightful evening spent with Mr. Towers and yourself and your charming guests in your beautiful house, I have wanted to tell you how wholly delightful the occasion was." King raved on about the "exquisite appointments" and the "charming conversation in your lovely drawing room after dinner." "All this and much more continue to linger in my thoughts and to present a series of restful and inspiring pictures [which] are going to constitute a series of most cherished memories." The effusiveness of the letter, unusual even by the standards of the time, took Graham and Molly Towers by surprise. They decided that

Molly would respond by thanking King for his thank-you note, only to be further surprised when they then received a follow-up note from the prime minister thanking them once again for the wonderful dinner party.

Towers's determination not to abandon Manitoba and Saskatchewan in their hour of need added weight to the arguments of those in cabinet pushing for the same cause. King decided that the new Bank should investigate just how bad the provinces' finances were, so Towers led a small Bank delegation that quickly reported back the urgent need for federal aid. After several intense weeks, the desperate provinces got the financial help they needed from Ottawa to stave off default.

As the financial struggle continued through the Depression, Graham Towers was making his presence felt. In fact, he was defining for the nation's fledgling central bank what amounted to a central role in the nation's affairs. The Bank of Canada was still so new at this point that no one really had any idea what to expect from it or its governor. Certainly, there was plenty of reason to see it as just another cog in the eastern money establishment, designed to protect the wealth of the privileged. Originally set up by a Conservative government, the Canadian central bank was modelled on the Bank of England, which, since its establishment in 1694, had been a bulwark of conservative sound-money principles.

And Towers, whose great-grandfather had been a founder of the Bank of Montreal, seemed suitably steeped in the most conservative banking traditions. With his dignified manner and appearance, he seemed in many ways to belong more to the rich world of commercial banking than the less glamorous world of the civil service, to which he now ostensibly belonged. His $30,000-a-year salary as governor was well above the salaries of even the most senior Ottawa officials, and in line with what top bankers earned. It allowed the

Towerses to live a very rich life in Depression-era Ottawa, with four maids, a lovely city home in exclusive Rockcliffe and a fabulous, sprawling summer home in Murray Bay, Quebec.

But the Bank was more than just another prop to the establishment. Ironically, it was the product of years of agitation and protest by popular reformers in the farm and labour movements, their political champions in the Progressive Party and the Co-operative Commonwealth Federation (CCF), as well as reformers in the Liberal Party. At the root of all this agitation had been frustration with the private commercial banks, which were seen to be arbitrary and all-powerful in their decisions about who would have access to credit and how high the interest rates on that credit should be. Without access to affordable credit, there was little opportunity for growth and employment, whether in the factory or on the farm.

Now, it was wrong to assume that a central bank would operate like a "people's bank," providing access to credit to all who needed it. Some who had pushed for a central bank had made this assumption, even though this wasn't the way central banks operated elsewhere. But while the expectations on the part of some reformers may have been naive, it was true that a central bank did offer potential for real change. Most interestingly, it took the crucial function of controlling access to credit—that is, controlling the economy's oxygen supply—out of the hands of private bankers and put it into the hands of an institution that was subject, ultimately, to the will of the people. This potential for wresting power from the private banks was what gave the idea of a central bank such appeal to reformers, and made it originally distasteful to private bankers. With the exception of the Royal Bank, the private banks vehemently and relentlessly opposed the establishment of the Bank of Canada, making the reformers all the hungrier for it.

Certainly, in its original design, the Bank of Canada was intended to serve many purposes, including promoting growth and employment in the country. Its mandate, as we saw in Chapter Three, specifically included the goals of influencing production, trade and employment—all the factors that contribute to growth—as well as holding the line against inflation. To a large extent, this broad mandate reflected the goals and attitudes of the reform-minded group of Canadian civil servants who had played a key role in putting the Bank in place.

To call this group "reform-minded" is not to confuse them with activists who had fought for a central bank through involvement in farm and labour movements. This was a small group of men, largely from academic backgrounds, who had been drawn to senior posts in the federal civil service in the thirties, largely out of an excitement about the possibilities of what government could do. Historian J.L. Granatstein has described the motivation of this extraordinary group of civil servants: "[T]hey believed that what they were doing was the most important job in the country...they shared a belief that public service was a civic virtue."

This excitement about the role of government—a concept so out of sync with today's world—was very much a part of the idealism of reform sentiments in the thirties. These reformers had a strong belief in the importance of participating in public issues and debates, and they expressed their commitment by joining civic-minded groups like debating clubs or political science associations, where the emphasis was on discussing serious public issues. Many became involved in the push for a public broadcasting network, in the hope of establishing a permanent vehicle for serious debate in the country. Notions that later became a part of our North American culture—such as the acceptability of personal greed and self-interest—played no part in the public-spirited, reformist mood of the thirties.

In their politics, the reformers were strongly nationalistic and generally liberal. But above all, they were activist in their vision that change and improvement were possible. With the hardship of the Depression as their backdrop, they set out to build a better world. There was a terrible sense that everything had broken down, that the old ways of doing things no longer worked, that the old theories no longer applied. Out of this sense of dislocation came a determination that something had to be done to put things back on track, to create a new order out of the chaos. Social problems had to be faced and resolved, the economy had to be made to work again. The laissez-faire approach that had long dominated economics, relegating crucial decisions to the marketplace, no longer seemed so convincing, now that the economy lay shattered and the barons of business seemed unable or unwilling to put it back together. If business and the invisible hand of the marketplace couldn't tackle the problem, government could. And these public-spirited reformers wanted to be there to make sure that it did.

This dissatisfaction with the old economics found its most persuasive voice in John Maynard Keynes, the British economist who rose to international prominence in the thirties with his radically different prescriptions. Keynes's wry insights cut sharply through the tired old economics of Adam Smith and his disciples, turning the conventional wisdom on its head. Smith, whose teachings had dominated economic thought since the late eighteenth century, had argued that the marketplace should be left to function with a minimum of government interference, thereby unleashing the utmost in human productivity and efficiency.

An important elaboration of this theory, by economist Alfred Marshall writing in the 1890s, was that capitalist economies usually achieve full employment as long as governments don't interfere in the workings of the marketplace. Marshall's idea was that unemployment occurred when the

price of labour became too high; if governments didn't intervene with minimum wage laws or impose other pro-labour
regulations, the price of labour would eventually fall. When
it fell low enough, employers would find it profitable to
rehire the unemployed workers. Whether or not the wage
would be high enough to allow these workers to eat was
another issue. The important point, according to Marshall
and the vast number of economists who found merit—and
still find merit—in his prescription, was that the marketplace had a self-correcting mechanism that allowed it to
work effectively, if left on its own. Without the meddling of
government, full employment was possible most of the time,
thanks to the magic of the marketplace.

The Depression more or less kicked the wind out of
Marshall's theory. Wages fell and yet the slump continued
and got worse. Factories closed, and the ranks of the unemployed just kept growing. Desperate men, offering to work
for food, were lucky to get a hot meal after a day's hard
labour in someone's field. If this was Marshall's idea of full
employment, it left a lot to be desired.

Keynes, who had been a prize-winning student of
Marshall, turned the idea around when he argued that the
problem was lack of spending. Economists had traditionally
focused on the need for capital to be accumulated, so that it
would be available for investment in factories. But they had
paid less attention to the question of whether the public had
sufficient money to buy the products that the factories produced. Keynes argued that this was essential, that the factory
would only operate if there were people out there able to buy
its products. So, when the economy was in a slump, what
was needed was to somehow get money to the people.

The most effective way for people to obtain money was
through employment, so Keynes advocated that money be
spent employing people. If private enterprise was willing to
do that, fine. But if private enterprise wasn't willing or

lacked the resources to do so, then government should step into the breach—even if it meant spending more money than the government actually had at that time. In other words, the government should be prepared to run a deficit if necessary to put people back to work. Only by putting people back to work—by creating demand for the goods that the factories produced—could the slump eventually end. Then, when good times returned and people were working again, taxes could be raised to pay off the debts that had accumulated during the slump.

Keynes brilliantly challenged the whole notion that the key to increasing a nation's wealth lay in accumulating savings and building up pools of capital. Rather, he suggested, wealth was created by people working and generating economic activity. This explained the apparent paradox that wars, which destroyed so much of a country's physical capital and possessions, could often make a country richer. Wars had the effect of putting the country to work; people were needed to manufacture weaponry, to go to battle and then to rebuild the country after the fighting was over. Similarly, earthquakes and floods and other natural disasters could kick-start economic activity and growth. These catastrophes clearly had horrible human costs, and destroyed many things of value, but they also could be a spur to growth, if people were put back to work rebuilding after the devastation. What mattered ultimately for an economy was not accumulating riches and possessions; what mattered was creating a situation where activity flourished and new growth abounded.

This emphasis on promoting growth—so central to the thinking of Keynes as well as to the reformers in Ottawa—called for a strong role for government in managing the economy and masterminding that growth. And one of the key tools that government needed to manage the economy was a central bank, which would oversee the nation's access to credit. Thus, a great deal of the focus of the Ottawa reformers was on establishing a Canadian central bank. Three of the key proponents of such a bank—Clifford Clark, W.A. Mackintosh and A.F.W. Plumptre—were academic economists who had ended up in senior positions in the Finance department. Along with several economists outside the government, notably Clifford Curtis and Frank Knox, they had all written extensively on the desirability of a central bank for Canada. And Clifford Clark, who became deputy finance minister, was instrumental in convincing the government to set up a royal commission to investigate the question.

These academic reformers also played influential roles on the commission, which ended up recommending the establishment of a central bank. Mackintosh, Curtis and Knox wrote the key brief to the commission and Curtis and Knox actually wrote some of the chapters of the commission's report. Plumptre, who had studied under Keynes in England, served as assistant secretary of the commission, and ended up writing most of the rest of the report. Clark, as deputy minister, oversaw the eventual drafting of the act that created the bank. Clark and Mackintosh also played a role in recruiting the original team of Bank staffers, ensuring that the same ideas took root within the Bank.

The central bank that these reformers had fought so vigorously for, designed and staffed was thus very much imbued with their activist, interventionist approach to the economy. They saw the Bank as a key element of the Ottawa apparatus they were creating, which would allow them to make the kind of sweeping changes they believed were necessary and desirable. The notion of the central bank restricting itself to inflation control—as it conceives of its role today—would have been utterly foreign to the thinking of its architects. Just as government today is busy dismantling its institutions and limiting its programs, this powerful and influential group of government bureaucrats in the thirties were working vigorously to increase the scope of Ottawa's powers in the interests of better managing the economy, digging the country out of the Depression and preventing such future debacles.

So it was not surprising that the Bank almost immediately came to play a vital role in the nation's life. It became heavily involved, as we've seen, in helping manage the serious debt problems of the western provinces, working on debt servicing strategies and steering Ottawa away from the temptation of abandoning the indebted provinces to sink into their own quicksand. When Bank officials looked more deeply into the causes of the massive provincial debt, they became convinced that the problems were more fundamental, and had to do with the flawed financing arrangements between Ottawa and the provinces. Pressure from the Bank was instrumental in the establishment of the Rowell-Sirois Royal Commission, which conducted an exhaustive examination into the entire financing structure of government.

The Bank quickly became an integral part of the Ottawa team that was remaking the country. Its research department and facilities were considered the best, with analytical capabilities greater than those of the federal Finance department. And its staff included some impressive and innovative talent, such as Donald Gordon and Sandy Skelton, the rebellious son of Ottawa's most respected mandarin, O.D. Skelton. Sandy Skelton took over the key post of director of research at the Bank, and also acted as director of research for the Rowell-Sirois commission, ensuring the Bank had an inside role on this far-reaching initiative to reorganize government. Gordon and Sandy Skelton, who became key figures in Ottawa policy-making, bore little resemblance to the financial monks who now beaver away in the Bank of Canada monastery. Both men had a rebellious quality that provided the Bank with a very different feel than the devout, humourless atmosphere that prevails there today. Sandy Skelton, widely respected for his abilities, was also known for his eccentric dressing, his late working hours, his hangovers and his one-time role in leading a panty raid on the women's residence at Queen's University, where his father held the prestigious post of dean of arts and sciences.

But the spirit of the new Bank and the important role that it was to play in its early years was perhaps best captured in the personality of Graham Towers himself. In many ways, he seemed to embody the dual role of the Bank's original mandate. A born-and-bred banker, he could be trusted to defend the value of the currency against the corroding effects of inflation. Nonetheless, he got on well with the Ottawa mandarins, and shared their interest in an activist government concerned with fostering growth and employment. Certainly, Towers was more sophisticated in his outlook than traditional bankers, with an interest in new ideas and approaches. He was a prize student of Stephen Leacock, who, as well as being Canada's best-known humorist, was also an innovative, reform-minded economics professor at McGill University. Towers himself ended up teaching commerce part-time at McGill.

At the Royal Bank, he rose quickly through the ranks, showing an unusual grasp of the complex fields of foreign money markets and exchange mechanisms, and even writing a technical book on the subject after only a year at the Royal. While most of the commercial bankers were committed to the status quo and adamantly opposed to the creation of a central bank in Canada, Towers, with his familiarity with foreign systems, found considerable merit in the idea— as did other senior figures at the Royal.

On the personal side, too, Towers was more than just a stodgy banker. He had a gentlemanly and distinguished manner, but he was also known for telling off-colour stories, even in the presence of women, which was considered eccentric in the courtly world he moved in. Indeed, Towers's relationship with women was a subject of considerable speculation.

Tall, handsome and charming, Towers was known around Ottawa for taking a shine to lively, intelligent women. His biographer, Douglas Fullerton, tells a story of Towers getting into an animated dispute on a train with a "woman who was a well-known financial journalist." A male friend travelling with Towers was shocked as the discussion became unusually vehement when "Towers suddenly stood up, as did the woman, and he embraced and kissed her. Presumably it was to apologize for his aggressiveness, to applaud the force of her argument, or to show his admiration for her charms."

There are plenty of tales of Graham Towers as a dashing, irresistible charmer. In one story, a student of his was dining with a small group of friends who, through an unusual connection, happened to be entertaining British stage star Gertrude Lawrence at a swanky supper club on top of the Mount Royal Hotel in Montreal. Towers, who had been sitting alone at a nearby table, recognized some of his students and used that as an excuse to approach the group. The dashing Towers apparently had little interest in discussing commerce with his students and turned his attention to charming the glamorous actress. "Within a few minutes, he and 'Gertie' had disappeared," recalled one of the former students, "leaving us very much let down and with a large bill to pay."

Indeed, Towers's reputation as a rakish charmer was so well-known that Fullerton, a friend as well as his biographer, felt the need to point out that none of these antics impinged on the bank governor's duties: "There is no evidence whatsoever that what Graham Towers did in his private life had any bearing on the manner in which he carried out his daily work." Rather, Fullerton tries to leave us with the impression that Towers was, above all, a man with a keen eye for foreign exchange fluctuations.

Certainly, Towers was a dynamic and influential figure on the national political scene who worked effectively with the reform-minded group that was trying to put a Keynesian stamp on the country. Indeed, he got along well with Keynes himself when they had extensive dealings during and after World War II. Keynes was then working for the British government and the two men tried to develop arrangements for repaying Canada's war loans, as well as extending new ones.

Observers who saw them discussing monetary matters reported that Towers's grasp of issues seemed almost as great as Keynes's—no small feat. Keynes clearly respected Towers, as he demonstrated by making the surprising suggestion that Towers be appointed governor of the Bank of England when Montagu Norman, the long-reigning and distinguished governor, retired in 1943. Towers was considered for the prestigious position by the Bank of England's board—known as its "Court"—but he was ultimately rejected. The fact that he was a Canadian didn't help, but what appeared to have eliminated him was the observation that he was "too Keynesian"—a condition that deeply offended the conservative men who made the key decisions at the Bank of England.

Perhaps what scared the "Court" about Towers was the same quality that was to make him a pivotal—although little remembered—figure in Canada's postwar development: he placed great emphasis on growth and employment. Whether through exposure to Keynesian ideas or through his own reaction against the horrors of the Depression, Towers was strongly committed to putting the country back to work. For the staid financial men who oversaw the Bank of England, what really mattered was upholding the value of the currency—ultimately, preserving the value of existing wealth—and fighting unemployment was merely a sideshow that threatened to get in the way.

Before we return to Towers and the activist years at the Bank of Canada, it might be interesting to take a brief and highly selective tour through the annals of money, banking and debt to see how the same themes recur over time. The opposition to allowing Graham Towers to run the Bank of

England has overtones of the perennial battle between the goal of defending the currency and that of encouraging growth and expansion. This, as we saw in Chapter Three, is essentially a struggle between those who have wealth and those who want a chance to accumulate it, or even just a chance to get enough of it to survive. And the outcome of this ongoing struggle has had a great deal to do with who has reaped which rewards through history. Indeed the way that the balance is tilted in this struggle probably has more to do with how we divvy up the resources of our society than any discrepancy in brains or talent between our citizens.

The death of a usurer was not a pretty one. In the Middle Ages, the practice of usury—that is, lending money at excessively high interest rates—was treated by the Christian Church as a serious sin. Medieval religious writing provided the following list of sinners who would be subjected to a horrifying death: usurers, the covetous, the avaricious, knaves, the prideful, brigands, murderers, quarrelers, the lustful, and all those subject to similar vices, called by St. Paul "works of the flesh." Medieval historian Jacques Le Goff describes a twelfth-century religious tract, aimed at would-be sinners, that illustrated in graphic detail why usury was a bad bet:

> The usurer of Metz, on his deathbed, begs his wife to place a purse full of money near him in his grave. When the grave is open, the toad escapes from the purse. Another toad is on the dead usurer's chest. The first toad takes the pieces of silver from the purse and the second sticks them in the heart of the cadaver...
>
> One usurer, on his deathbed, divides his money into three parts, one for his wife to remarry, another for his children and the third to be put in a sack attached to his neck and buried with him. This last amount is considerable and the usurer's family, wishing to

recover it, opens his grave during the night. They see demons stuffing burning pieces of silver in the usurer's mouth and flee in terror...

Finally, there is the death of Thierry, the usurer of Wurm in the diocese of Cologne. He is sick and, matter having risen to his brain, he becomes mad. His mouth and teeth move incessantly. "What are you eating, Sire?" they ask him. "My money," he answers, and indeed certain people see demons putting silver pieces in his mouth. He has himself taken to the monastery at Klosterrode in the hope of being delivered from the devils. In vain. There, the demons are more numerous than in his own house. Brought back home, he dies, pursued by hellhounds amidst a thousand torments...

The medieval Church had a number of reasons for considering usurers so vile. To begin with, they were selling time— something that belonged only to God. Furthermore, usurers profited without labour, contrary to the Lord's teaching that "You will earn your bread by the sweat of your brow." The ultimate proof of this idleness on the part of usurers, as contemporary writers noted with outrage, was that they could earn income even while they slept. Thus, while usurers were sometimes compared to prostitutes, Thomas of Chobham noted that prostitutes were a cut above. Unlike usurers who could sin in their sleep, prostitutes at least had to *work* for their money.

The line between usury and legitimate commercial practices was never very clear in medieval times. One medieval edict denounced all forms of money-lending for profit, advising the faithful to "lend freely, hoping for nothing thereby." So those with aspirations of an afterlife—and such a preoccupation was not uncommon in the twelfth century—had plenty of reasons for steering clear of the practice of loaning money. Indeed, the Church had harsh words for those who indulged in any sort of commerce: "Seldom or never can a man who is a merchant be pleasing to God."

Of course, usury and other business activities did go on and, usually, were practised by the same people. But the religious sanctions—sometimes backed by legal sanctions—did have a restraining effect on business and enterprise. In the largely feudal, static life of the Middle Ages, this wasn't such a serious problem. But the rise of commercial and trading centres in the late Middle Ages brought a growing need for some kind of systematic way to ensure that merchants and entrepreneurs could gain access to credit.

It could hardly have been more fortuitous, then, that, around the beginning of the thirteenth century, the Biblical notion of "purgatory" was refined and developed into a form that offered some hope for usurers. Up until then, there was really only heaven and hell, and usurers were always destined for the latter. With the expansion of the concept of purgatory—a short-term hell with the possibility of being rerouted to heaven—people who had indulged in sins such as prostitution and usury were given a second chance. (One contemporary report of the new purgatory option indicated that there was even hope for a cloistered nun who, in a moment of confusion, had lost her virginity to a monk.) Suddenly, there were stories of usurers making the transition from purgatory to heaven, often after their widows devoted the rest of their lives to fasting and offering alms to appease God. This loophole opened up new opportunities for the money-lending industry, and therefore for the expansion of trade and commerce as well. As Le Goff notes, "The birth of purgatory is also the dawn of banking."

The development of the purgatory option was by no means the end of the prohibition against usury. Stringent anti-usury laws were passed in England in the fifteenth and sixteenth century, but increasingly, there seemed to be ways

around them. By the seventeenth century, English goldsmiths had emerged as the nation's early bankers. Since merchants and professionals often stored their gold with
goldsmiths, it was easy for the smiths to turn round and lend
it to others—for a price. Eventually, laws established legal
lending rates—usually in the range of 6 to 8 per cent,
although, in practice, the rates were often much higher.
Before long, this became by far the most lucrative part of the
goldsmiths' business.

Of course there was a potential problem. What if someone who had deposited gold for safekeeping returned to the
goldsmith to reclaim his treasure and discovered that it
wasn't there, because it had been loaned to someone else?
Goldsmiths generally got around this problem by keeping a
reserve of gold on hand, hoping that the amount would be
sufficient to cover withdrawal requests. The more confidence the goldsmith inspired, the less likely it would be that
large numbers of nervous depositors would show up on any
given day demanding their gold back. Hence, goldsmiths
with good reputations could get away with loaning out more
of their deposits, thereby increasing their profits.

Among the goldsmiths' clients was the king. In the late
seventeenth century, for instance, Charles II had excessive
needs that were difficult to meet through increases in taxes,
which not only required parliamentary approval but took a
long time to collect. How was one to meet the costs of maintaining an army of 8,700 men, as well as living a lavish and
indulgent lifestyle? Increasingly, the king found himself turning to the goldsmiths, who could provide ready cash without
asking a lot of questions, on the promise of being paid back
later out of tax revenues.

The goldsmiths recognized a good thing and grew close
to the Crown. But, as the king's dependence on them
increased, so did their rates. While the king had paid 8 per
cent interest in the 1660s, he found himself facing interest

rates of more than 12 per cent a decade later, when he was deeper in debt. And, of course, the king got the best rate. For ordinary merchants and traders, the rate was higher, and for those in more difficult financial situations, the rate was higher still—sometimes 33 per cent or more. With such exorbitant rates, the goldsmiths held a virtual stranglehold over trade and commerce. "Hence there was an urgent need to remedy a situation which was most irksome to the commercial world..." notes financial historian A. Andreades, "and to secure for trade that credit which is one of the essential conditions of its expansion."

By the late seventeenth century, the frustration of merchants—and of the Crown—had become acute. William III found himself in even worse financial shape, particularly when he was drawn into a seemingly endless war on the continent against the aggressive and ambitious Louis XIV, as well as being involved in civil wars in Ireland and Scotland. The English army had grown to 83,000 men, and the king's financial situation seemed desperate. The government searched for new things to tax and, in a sweeping tax grab that makes the GST look unimaginative, settled on chimneys, windows, salt and bachelors. A giant lottery was tried, but this produced a backlash among the ticket-buying public when the largest prize ended up going to a group of foreign Huguenots who had settled in England to keep their religion. To raise a loan from the city of London, the king's men had virtually to go door to door begging merchants to contribute. The king had even been obliged to dip into the city's Orphans' Fund, leaving it greatly diminished. But with budgetary needs of more than £5 million—over half of which was earmarked for the war effort—William was still more than £1 million short.

This was lucky for William Paterson and his associates. Paterson was a financier and adventurer who had travelled widely and made a name for himself—and a great deal of money. Among his ambitious schemes, he had worked out a way to supply drinking water to parts of London and had led an expedition to set up a colony in what is now Panama. Although the colony ultimately failed, Paterson was still highly regarded and listened to by the king. He became convinced that he had the answer to the king's increasingly distressing financial situation. Teaming up with a group of successful London merchants and businessmen in the early 1690s, Paterson struck while the iron was hot.

The serious financial problems of the realm could be greatly alleviated, the group contended, by a plan they had devised for establishing a national bank. Paterson and his colleagues outlined their plan: they would put up initial capital of £1.2 million in gold and silver, which they would immediately lend to the Crown to pay for the continuing war. In return, the government would agree to pay the new bank 8 per cent interest plus an annual management fee, amounting to a total of £100,000 a year. This would allow Paterson and his friends to double their initial capital outlay every nine years.

But the deal got richer. The Paterson group also wanted the king to authorize their bank to make simultaneous loans to members of the public, for which the bank would also collect interest. But these loans—also up to £1.2 million—would be different from the loans made to the king. This time, the bank would not actually hand over any gold or silver; it would simply issue "banknotes," essentially paper currency, on which the borrower would pay 8 per cent interest a year. These notes would be of value to the borrower because they would be issued by a bank that was granted authority by the Crown of England. With this royal stamp of approval, the public would treat the banknotes as a bona fide form of currency, just like gold or silver coins.

Technically, the paper banknotes would be redeemable for gold on demand, which is what would be written on the back of the note. Theoretically, then, this meant that the bank would have £1.2 million worth of gold on hand at all times, in case all those holding banknotes wanted to cash them in at the same time. In practice, however, the bank planned to keep only £200,000 or £300,000 worth of gold on hand at any one time. Interestingly, there would be no requirement that the bank keep any particular amount of gold for such purposes; that was up to the bank.

It was an ingenious scheme: the Paterson bank was essentially lending the same £1.2 million twice, and thereby collecting twice the amount of interest on the money. At that rate, Paterson and his friends, who operated out of their headquarters at Grocers' Hall, would double their money every four and a half years.

So, in a sense, everyone would get what they wanted. The king would immediately receive the large stock of gold he so urgently needed to continue his bloody war and preserve England's honour—and at a manageable cost of 8 per cent a year. All he had to do was to allow Paterson and his friends to use his royal name to endorse the pieces of paper they wanted to lend to the public, also at 8 per cent annual interest. Parliamentary approval was required for the deal, but Paterson et al had many friends in Parliament. Indeed, many Parliamentarians had expressed interest in becoming stockholders in the new bank. With everyone's needs satisfied, it seemed like a sensible plan.

There was, however, considerable opposition, particularly from the powerful goldsmiths' lobby. Threatened as they were by the prospect of a major new player in their lucrative usury business, the goldsmiths fought Paterson's group. Without any apparent embarrassment, the goldsmiths even warned merchants of the danger of falling "into the clutches of this harpy of Grocers' Hall." The country gentry were also opposed, partly out of their usual fear of financiers and partly out of their desire to see King William's financial troubles increase, in the hopes that this would herald a return to the throne of their preferred monarch, the former James II. In the end, the king, with key support from the financial community and Parliament, prevailed. Thus was born the Bank of England, a private corporation operating under public authority.

But while the new plan offered an especially attractive deal for the king, for Paterson's group and for the Parliamentarians who invested in it, interestingly enough, it was not a bad deal for the British public either. Essentially, Paterson's plan had the effect of putting more money into circulation. If the bank kept gold reserves of only £200,000 to £300,000 for the £1.2 million it would loan to the public, it was, in effect, creating at least £900,000 worth of new money. As Paterson noted, "this bank will be in effect as nine hundred thousand pounds or a million of *fresh money* brought into the nation [italics added]." This injection of fresh funds into the economy, like a sudden burst of oxygen, would increase the supply of money in the country. The bank would also take deposits from the public and then loan that money out again, with only part of it held in gold reserves. With the supply of credit in the country thus expanding, the goldsmiths' stranglehold over the country would be diminished, interest rates would fall and economic activity would be promoted.

Indeed, the new bank had the potential to go a long way towards solving one of the most vexing problems facing England at that time: the scarcity of gold and silver. This was a perennial problem for England and other nations. From time immemorial, gold and silver had been used as the medium of exchange, the currency used to pay for goods and services both at home and in trade with other nations. There seemed to be a certain logic to this—gold and silver were strong, attractive metals that were rare in the earth's crust; this natural scarcity enhanced their desirability. Thus, people were willing to accept them as payment because of their apparent intrinsic value. It would have taken a much bigger leap of faith, for instance, for people to accept a medium of exchange that had no intrinsic value, like a bauble or a feather or a piece of paper. By the end of the seventeenth century, when Paterson and his cronies came up with the scheme for the Bank of England, gold and silver coins were still virtually the only medium of exchange.

But the scarcity of gold and silver was also a serious drawback, since the economy required large amounts of both to function. If a worker put in a day's labour, there had to be something to pay him with, or else he would be unwilling to perform the same tasks the next day. Similarly, a merchant would only sell his cloth or his grain to someone who could pay him for them. If there weren't enough gold and silver for these purposes, the economy wouldn't be able to function very well: the worker would stop working, the merchant would stop selling, and both would fail to earn a living. In short, the economy would be operating below capacity; it would stagnate and cease to grow.

Economists had long recognized the need for an adequate supply of money. Adam Smith himself emphasized this point repeatedly: "The quantity of money...must in every country...increase as the value of the annual produce increases." This meant that as the nation's economy expanded—through population growth and various forms of development—there had to be more and more coins in circulation; the supply of coins had to grow in step with the growth of the economy.

The only problem was that, in reality, a nation's supply of coins grew according to much more arbitrary factors, like the discovery of a new gold mine, or the plunder of a foreign ship carrying gold. A country could also increase its supply of precious metals through trade—if it sold more goods abroad than it imported, it would end up holding the difference in gold and silver. To a large extent, plunder had been the proven method of increasing England's supply of precious metals, as the sailors on Spanish galleons heading homeward from the new world with cargoes of gold had the misfortune to discover. Still, even with the efficiency of the British naval fleet, keeping the nation's coin supply growing at a sufficiently rapid rate was a constant problem in seventeenth-century England.

So the establishment of the Bank of England in 1694 was a fortunate development. As Paterson had predicted, it did bring interest rates down. Essentially, it did an end-run around the gold and silver problem. If the public treated the banknotes just like gold coins, the effect would be to increase the nation's money supply, thereby allowing the economy to expand closer to its capacity. In fact, the public took well to the banknotes, partly because the value of gold coins had become so unreliable, since goldsmiths had over the years extracted a great deal of the gold from gold coins, filling them instead with other less precious metals. As a result, the true value of any given gold coin was hard to determine, and the public was just as happy to have a banknote with a clearly established value.

If the shortage of gold had been a problem in England, it was a far more acute problem in its colonies across the Atlantic. There were no gold or silver mines in the British colonies and, since the colonial settlers had generally come from modest backgrounds in the old world, few had brought much gold with them. Furthermore, England, grappling with its own shortages, banned the export of gold and silver to the colonies, and obliged the colonials to import manufactured goods only from England and to pay for them in gold. To some extent, the colonials survived by following the example of the mother country and relying on plunder, encouraging pirates to bring their gold and silver booty to colonial shores by offering extremely generous trading terms.

But the acute gold shortage caused serious problems that hampered the growth of the colonies and prompted them to come up with a radical—although generally sensible and effective—solution. As early as 1690, a few years before William Paterson approached the Crown with his banking scheme, the colonies in the new world began printing their own "banknotes." Like those issued by the Bank of England, these notes were pieces of paper, deemed to be of specific value, that were loaned to members of the public, who had to pay interest on them. The notes were legal tender and were traded from hand to hand just like gold and silver coins. Hence they amounted to a form of currency. Unlike the notes from the Bank of England, however, there was no attempt to claim that these paper notes were redeemable for gold or silver, since there was so little of these precious metals around. Instead, the colonial notes were backed by land, by mortgaged real estate or future tax revenues—something of real value that the colonies had in abundance.

Interestingly, one of the early reasons for printing paper money was to finance military expeditions against Canada. The colony of New York, for instance, issued its first paper money in 1709 "for the reduceing of Canada." But the colonial governments soon saw that issuing paper money was useful for more than just financing wars against Canadians. It also put more money into circulation, thereby reducing the cost of borrowing money and invigorating trade and economic activity.

Pennsylvania and New Jersey turned to paper money issues in the 1720s when their economies fell into a serious economic slump. The preamble to the New Jersey loan bill that issued the first round of paper money explained that the move was necessary because "Silver and Gold, formerly current in this Province, is almost entirely Exported to Great Britain." This shortage of gold and silver, the preamble continued, was responsible for "the Miserable Circumstances of the Inhabitants." The results of the loan bill were impressive: the previously depressed economies of Pennsylvania and New Jersey rebounded vigorously. In New Jersey, the interest collected by the government from the banknotes was sufficient to allow the colony to eliminate taxes for almost twenty years. As historian Richard A. Lester explains, "One of the reasons why the colonialists were so enthusiastic for another loan bill that they piled the table of the assembly high with petitions for another loan act in 1767 and 1768 was that such acts did away with all tax levies."

This highlights a significant difference between the early banking systems in England and in its colonies. Both systems overcame the gold and silver scarcity problem by expanding their money supplies, but England did so through a private banking system, while the colonies opted for a public approach. Both economies appeared to benefit from the expanded money supply, but the colonies enjoyed the added benefit of having the interest from the money land in the public treasury, eliminating the need for taxes. In England, on the other hand, the profits went to the "harpy of Grocers' Hall." And the harpy profited enormously. Over the first five decades of its operation, the Bank of England loaned the British government a total of £11,690,000. By 1746, the government hadn't paid off any of this debt. But, in the meantime, it had paid a staggering amount of interest to the Bank—£23,000,000—more than twice the amount it had borrowed.

The effectiveness of the publicly issued paper money experiment in the colonies even won over the British-appointed colonial governors. The governor of New York, for instance, wrote on several occasions to the British Lords of Trade, reporting the beneficial results of the loan bills in encouraging trade and commerce. "I do affirm and believe your Lordships may have observed that since the circulation of those Bills, the Trade of the place has increased at least above half of what it was," the governor wrote in 1718. He also noted that the effect was to open up trade and commercial opportunities to more citizens, and that this explained the opposition from vested interests who had previously monopolized trade and commerce in the colony. As he explained to the Lords of Trade, the "opposition or threatened opposition from men of private views, piques and interests, the true cause of which, whatsoever the pretended one be, is that this...incourages and enables the many to venture their stocks in trade to the prejudice of the few who had so long monopolized it."

These private interests who had monopolized trade had not been inclined to invest their profits in new trade and shipbuilding. As long as money was scarce and interest rates high, it was more profitable for them to lend their money out at rates of 8 per cent or higher. But, as the New York governor explained to the Lords of Trade, this was detrimental to the economic development of the colony. "High interest is in every Country a great discouragement to Trade, and it has been here. The Usurers your Lordships may be sure were not pleased with [the loan bill] Act which in its consequences might reduce the General Interest of money, and they foresaw their money at Six per Cent from whence I promise myself the pleasure to see Trade and Ship Building revive and flourish."

Although the paper money system was widely experimented with in the colonies, it should be remembered that there was little central co-ordination and each colony handled its situation differently. One of the more bizarre experiments, for instance, was in Maryland, where there were three methods of payment: coins (gold and silver), paper money and tobacco. Up until about 1760, tobacco, which the colony produced in abundance, was the principal and preferred form of money. "It was legal tender for all debts and public dues at all times," notes Lester. "The use of paper money, on the other hand, was restricted. It was not legal tender for the payment of dues to the clergy, or of the quit-rents to the lord-proprietary, or of fees to all the Colonial officers. These had to be paid in tobacco."

It was only after a drop in tobacco prices overseas that the colony tried to wean the public off its dependence on the tobacco currency. As the colonial authorities wrote to the British Lords of Trade, "the exceeding Poverty of the People in general, occasion'd by the low price of Tobaco, hath driven the poor Families to make some few course Woolens & Linnens, to Cloath Themselves, without which they must go naked." But breaking the tobacco habit wasn't easy, and the colony's first issue of paper money in 1733 was literally given away in the hope that its circulation would be "as speedy and diffusive as possible." By the late 1740s, the insistence on receiving payment in tobacco was easing throughout the colony. A new law made paper money legal tender for all fees and duties, for those who did not grow tobacco.

Generally, the government-money experiment was very successful in the colonies. Benjamin Franklin, one of the early colonials to support the paper money experiment, observed, "the colonies that have made use of paper money have been and are all in a thriving condition." Even Adam Smith, who was not a fan of government-created paper money, acknowledged the effectiveness of the system in Pennsylvania. He noted that the colony was able to collect enough money from its paper currency to pay for most of its costs of government, rendering taxes largely unnecessary.

The results, however, did vary, depending on how careful the colonial authorities were. Some colonies, such as Massachusetts, Connecticut and Rhode Island, printed too much currency and it quickly lost its value, resulting in high inflation. In others, such as New York, New Jersey and Pennsylvania, authorities were very responsible, and avoided printing too much money. As a result, Lester notes, prices were actually more stable in some of the colonies under the paper currency systems than they were in countries that had relied on gold and silver standards.

Interestingly, the colonials' enthusiasm for their government-money systems was one of the factors that led to their
eventual breakaway from Britain. A major grievance was
that Britain, while generally allowing the colonies to print
paper money for their own domestic use, insisted that debts
owed to the mother country be paid in silver and gold. Thus,
the colonials were not only obliged to pay taxes to the
British without being given representation in the British
parliament, but they were obliged to pay those taxes out of
their extremely limited gold and silver stocks.

When the colonies declared independence from Britain
in 1775, it was not surprising that they opted to pay for the
war by printing paper money. The financial means of the
colonies were still extremely limited. The total amount of
ready money in the country was only about $30 million, the
bulk of it in paper currency. This wasn't enough to run a
country, let alone fight a major war. Furthermore, the outbreak of revolution created commercial chaos, as trade
routes were interrupted and colonies cut off from their usual
markets. So it hardly seemed like an appropriate time to
impose taxes, which were then almost nonexistent. And no
foreign governments, at the outset at least, seemed interested in lending money to the breakaway colonies.

Since the new republic couldn't gain access to any real
money, its best hope for financing the war seemed to be to
create money. Just as the individual colonies had created
money, backed up by land and future tax revenues, so the
new republic printed money, on the expectation that a victory in the war effort would give the money real value. If the
colonies triumphed, they would gain dominion over a land
of ample resources, and the prospects of future prosperity
would be good. Printing paper money was a way of taking
advantage now of that future promise.

The new nation generally took enthusiastically to its
paper money, and in cases where scepticism prevailed, laws

were quickly enacted to force merchants to accept the new bills. It came to be considered unpatriotic to distrust the value of the paper currency. In North Carolina, for instance, anyone who even spoke disrespectfully of the paper money was to be "treated as an enemy of the country." And anyone who dared to counterfeit these patriotic bills—which many did— was to have his "right ear nailed to the pillory and cut off, be whipped with 39 stripes on his bare back; and be branded with a red hot iron on the right cheek with the letter 'C' and on the left with the letter 'M', said brands to be at least one inch in length, and three-quarters of an inch in width."

As the war dragged on, the Continental Congress ended up printing a massive amount of money, and runaway inflation resulted. This has led to much commentary over the years about the irresponsible way that the breakaway government managed the finances of the war effort, and the unfair impact that the resulting inflation had on many citizens. But as historian Ralph Harlow suggests, "To be sure, depreciated paper [money] would inflict irreparable damage on some individuals, but what of it? So too would the war. There is no more valid reason certainly for mourning over financial losses than over casualty lists." Similarly, financial commentator William Hixson argues that focusing on the inflationary impact of the wartime measures misses the more important point: that the breakaway republic—with virtually no gold or silver in its treasury—managed to win a war against the most powerful nation on earth. If inflation was the price that had to be paid for that, surely it was a bargain.

There was a further interesting aspect of this method of war financing: it pushed the financial burden of war onto those with the greatest resources. As Benjamin Franklin noted, inflation amounted to a "tax" on those who held money—a complaint we still hear today from the C.D. Howe Institute. But Franklin would have been at odds with the institute, which sees this form of taxation as a serious problem. To Franklin, the taxing effect of inflation had a positive side. As he wrote, "Thus [inflation] has proved a tax on money, a kind of property very difficult to be taxed by any other mode: and it has fallen more equally than other taxes, as those people paid most who, being richest, had most money passing through their hands."

While those with money reluctantly accepted the situation during the war, they were anxious to correct it after the war was over. They wanted an end to inflation and cheap money, and they pushed for a return to gold and silver. This was soon accomplished: the paper money issued during the war was virtually worthless by this point, leaving the struggling young nation almost entirely reliant once again on gold and silver coins, which were still in extremely short supply. This tight money situation plunged the economy into recession and deflation. The bustling pre-war years gave way to an era of economic stagnation, with foreclosures, bankruptcies, unemployment and widespread suffering.

All this suffering wasn't necessarily bad, however, for those with money or those who were owed money. Deflation favoured creditors, who were now in a position to have their debts repaid in dollars that had a much greater purchasing power than before, making them automatically richer. On the other hand, debtors were in deep trouble, as they were obliged to repay their debts with dollars that were suddenly scarcer and harder to come by. If they failed to come up with the money, they could face imprisonment or, worse still, could be sold into temporary servitude. (It was only several decades later that servitude was abolished for white debtors.)

Thus, the early years of the republic saw a bitter battle taking shape between a strong creditor class and a weak and impoverished class of debtors. Although creditors were more powerful, debtors were more numerous, and this could be dangerous in a democracy. The prominent Virginian James Madison wrote that society was divided into "those who are creditors and those who are debtors" and argued that it was important for the national government to intervene to protect the interests of creditors from "the superior force of an interested and overbearing majority." The danger, Madison argued, was that the debtors might develop "a rage for paper money, for an abolition of debts…or for any other improper or wicked project." The fears of creditors were increased in the early postwar years, when pressure for a return to paper currency pushed seven states in the union to issue their own currencies, just as they had in the pre-war years.

One of the key issues that was to occupy the attention of well-to-do creditors in the decades to come was the handling of the federal government's debt. The creditor class held most of the nation's debt, and it was extremely important to them that the government honour its debt obligations fully. The creditors had acquired much of this debt in the early years after the War of Independence, when a large number of government IOUs and loan certificates were in circulation. The new government had issued these certificates during the war to pay settlers for food, tools and supplies seized from them by the U.S. army under special wartime military powers. Soldiers were even paid with government IOUs. After the war, these IOUs could be used to pay taxes, but increasingly heavily indebted citizens had sold them to creditors and speculators, often for as little as one-tenth of their face value.

The IOUs, then, became concentrated in the hands of a tiny group of wealthy creditors who had bought up most of the nation's outstanding IOUs, or debts. This group of creditors was very keen that the federal government should honour its debts by repaying the IOUs fully—in gold, not in devalued paper money. Since most of the IOUs had been bought at a fraction of their face value, this was a lucrative proposition. Benjamin Rush, a Philadelphia doctor who had signed the Declaration of Independence, commented that anyone urging such a repayment scheme "had a mind like a highway robber." Highway robbers or not, these creditors—the early bondholder class—eventually succeeded in convincing the federal government to do just that.

━━━

In the decades following the War of Independence, the newly emergent creditor class won important concessions from the government. They managed to transfer much of the lucrative business of money creation and banking from the public domain into the private domain. They pushed for, and received, the right to operate private banks, a privilege that had been almost entirely absent in the colonial period. As early as the 1790s, private banks began springing up all over the country. By 1800, there were thirty; by 1836, there were 713.

Furthermore, the creditor class pushed the country back onto a gold-and-silver standard. Banks were allowed to issue banknotes, which could be traded from hand to hand almost like paper currency, but these banknotes had to be backed up by gold reserves held in the banks, representing a certain percentage of the value of the loans. Thus, the amount of credit in the country was automatically restricted by the amount of gold in the country, keeping the supply of money tight and inflation under control.

For many, the emergence of this class of bankers and bondholders represented a dangerous affront to the values of the newly independent nation, as their power and dominance threatened to undermine the very democratic nature of the state. As Thomas Jefferson put it in 1816, "I hope we shall crush in its birth the aristocracy of our monied corporations which dare already to challenge our government to a trial of strength, and bid defiance to the laws of our country." The rise of what became known as "Jacksonian Democracy" was about many things, but at root it was about the fears of ordinary citizens that their country was being taken over by powerful moneyed interests.

The flashpoint in the creditor-debtor struggle was the Bank of the United States, a largely private bank chartered by Congress in 1816, modelled on the Bank of England. Pioneer Americans who had faced great hardship to escape the yoke of entrenched power in the old country reacted angrily to the emergence of the same sort of established interests in their new democracy. The farmers, labourers and small merchants who made up the solid citizenry of the new republic had come to believe that this was their country, and they were damned if they were going to surrender it to a new ruling class.

The Bank of the United States represented just such a class. It quickly became the bank of the wealthy, handling the fortunes of rich families and corporations as well as the deposits of the federal government. Under the direction of the sophisticated financier Nicholas Biddle, who himself came from a wealthy family, the bank became an important force dealing in foreign exchange and domestic financial transactions.

More important, it operated almost like a central bank, playing a major role in controlling access to credit throughout the union. One way it did this was particularly infuriating to the smaller banks, which operated under state charters. Whenever the powerful Bank of the United States got its hands on the banknotes of these smaller banks, it returned the notes and demanded that the smaller banks redeem them immediately in gold, which meant that the banks had to recall some of their outstanding loans in order to maintain the same ratio of loans to gold. This not only reduced the smaller banks' profit potential, but it also reduced the amount of money in circulation, as more and more loans were recalled. Although the number of banknotes in circulation had more than doubled between 1812 and 1817, it declined to its 1812 level within a few years of the establishment of Biddle's bank. The result was the familiar one: with less money in circulation, most people ended up worse off.

So Biddle came to be the scourge not only of the smaller banks but also of the commonfolk of America. He seemed to be almost singlehandedly putting the brakes on growth at a time when the nation was itching to expand and develop. Not only were the established cities of the east growing rapidly with the influx of immigrants and the proliferation of factories and sweatshops, but pioneers were trekking westward into the wilderness. The demands for credit were immense as the new nation tried to wrest control of this vast wilderness from Indian bands and from the grip of nature, to create farms out of forests and build canals and railroads and construct new towns and cities. With a whole continent of virgin territory stretching beyond the established states of the new republic, the growth possibilities were virtually limitless. Access to credit was essential to unleash the full growth potential, to put to use the accumulated stores of capital from the wealthy east to build a new world in the west.

Of course, the risks for capital were great. The young nation was full of entrepreneurs and energy and dreams. As cities were constructed and giant canal and railway projects undertaken, great fortunes were made. But there were also great failures, as ill-conceived projects flopped miserably, losing all the capital invested in them. The local banks that sprang up throughout the new states and territories were a part of this dynamic, entrepreneurial culture, and were inclined to take on risky ventures. Many of these banks, as well as smaller banks in the eastern states, operated in ways that were the antithesis of sound money management and were themselves constantly at risk of going under.

This often led to problems for ordinary people as well as for wealthy creditors. The poorly regulated banking system created tremendous opportunities for abuse. In some cases, the founders of banks extended credit to themselves or to their friends for questionable or even fraudulent purposes. Bank failures were common, with depositors losing all their savings. In some cases, banks were simply irresponsible, extending credit far beyond their resources. When the Farmers Exchange Bank of Rhode Island failed in 1809, for instance, an investigating committee set up by the state legislature discovered that the bank had loaned to the public $580 million worth of banknotes, even though it only had a capital base of $3 million to back up the loans.

Sound or not, the entrepreneurial spirit that had been let loose in the new republic thrived on access to credit. And the Bank of the United States, to which the smaller local banks sometimes turned in their desperate need of capital, became a symbol of the cautious conservatism of the eastern establishment. In his crusade against the bank, Andrew Jackson rallied the forces of the hard-working farmers and labourers and would-be entrepreneurs of America. When Jackson won the confrontation, and the bank was stripped of many of its powers in 1832, it seemed that the people had triumphed over privilege. Although this did not turn out to be the case, the demise of the bank did ease the credit squeeze that had plagued the country. The years that followed were largely boom years, as canals and railroads spread across the continent.

With the outbreak of the Civil War in 1861, the demands for credit became greater than ever. And, just like a century earlier when the colonies battled Britain, the union found itself with very little taxing power to draw on. Similarly, financing the war by selling government bonds was going to be difficult. To entice creditors to put their money into a shaky investment like the war bonds of an apparently disintegrating nation would require a healthy discount. A $100 bond, for instance, might have to be sold for only $60, meaning the government would eventually be obliged to redeem it for the full $100 (plus interest, of course) even though the cash-hungry federal treasury would only now be receiving $60 on the original sale.

One solution was to expand the amount of money available. To do this, it was necessary to give up the gold standard—that is, to allow private banks to issue banknotes without holding gold reserves to back them up. By suspending the gold guarantee requirement on banknotes, Congress would allow banks to lend more money. Some of this money could be loaned directly to the government and some of it loaned to members of the public, who could then loan it to the government by buying government bonds.

So, despite spirited opposition from tight-money enthusiasts, the U.S. abandoned the gold standard. But even that wasn't enough to satisfy the almost insatiable needs of war finance. By the end of 1861, the Union army had already swollen from a scrawny force of 17,000 to more than 200,000. It eventually peaked at 900,000. All those men had to be paid, clothed, fed, equipped with weaponry and supplies and moved around as efficiently as possible. By early 1862, the demands of the war effort were so great that Congress took the bold step of issuing paper money, just as the Continental Congress had a hundred years earlier. Eventually, more than $450 million worth of the paper bills, known as "greenbacks," were printed and put into circulation by the government. And unlike the banknotes of private banks, which charged interest, this government money carried no interest charges. Once again, the demands of war had ushered in an era of easier money.

But the creditor class won an interesting concession from Congress. Although greenbacks were made legal tender and could be used as currency for all private and public dealings in the United States, there was one key exception: creditors would continue to receive their interest payments on government bonds in gold. This incredible concession singled out bondholders as a privileged elite, and led to the protest slogan "the same currency for the ploughholder and the bondholder." It also created a costly financial situation for the government. In the postwar period, for instance, the government was faced with paying out $18 million a year in scarce gold to bondholders, badly depleting its gold reserves.

There were powerful forces within the financial and government elite who never really accepted greenbacks and who were anxious to do away with them as quickly as possible. Secretary of the Treasury Salmon P. Chase, a tight-money advocate, had opposed greenbacks from the beginning, arguing that they were unconstitutional. President Abraham Lincoln apparently responded to this objection by noting, "The rebels are violating the Constitution to destroy the Union. I will violate the Constitution, if necessary, to save the Union, and I suspect, Chase, that our Constitution is going to have a rough time of it before we get done with this row." But Chase never warmed to the greenback and by early 1863—with the civil war still raging—he was pushing for a new law that would further his plan to eventually eliminate what he saw as an unnatural currency.

The plan, embodied in the National Banking Act, was to allow banknotes, issued by private banks, to become the "National Currency." This was odd, since greenbacks were already functioning, to some extent, as a national currency. Although the greenback system could have been improved with better legislation, this was not what was being proposed. Rather, the idea was to extend the system of private banknotes. As we have seen, these notes were different from greenbacks in that they required the payment of interest, thus making money more expensive. This would help preserve the value of money—something the creditor class was always keen on—and would also allow banks and their shareholders to earn interest. Private banks were already using a banknote system, but the National Banking Act greatly increased the practice by giving the new "National Currency" the official stamp of the federal government.

The banknotes were actually to be engraved and printed

by the federal government. Indeed, there seemed to be little real role for the private banks in the whole scheme, besides the collecting of interest. This raises the question of exactly what benefits banknotes offered that greenbacks didn't, at a much smaller cost to the public. It was undoubtedly desirable to have a national currency system, as opposed to a confusing system of private notes issued by a large number of different banks, but there was no apparent reason why banknotes were more desirable as a national currency than greenbacks. Indeed, the only real difference appeared to be that banknotes were a great deal more expensive for the government, and the public. As one outspoken critic of the system, Representative Thaddeus Stevens, said during a Congressional debate, "The government and not the banks should have the profit from creating a medium of exchange."

So the real purpose of the National Banking Act, besides enriching bankers and creditors in general, seems to have been to push aside the greenback and return the country to a tight-money regime. As tight-money advocates had predicted, the printing of greenbacks had set off a significant bout of inflation, with prices rising almost 75 per cent in the first three years of the war. The extra cash in circulation had meant boom times for farmers and manufacturers, whose products were in great demand. Still, despite the popularity of greenbacks with the public, the federal government took steps to reduce the supply of greenbacks in circulation even while the war continued to rage. As private banks printed more banknotes under the new laws, the government issued fewer and fewer greenbacks. Having made up 35 per cent of the money supply in the first half of the war, greenbacks constituted less than 1 per cent in the last half. Chase's plan to eliminate the greenback was well under way by the final year of the war.

Whatever tolerance creditors had had for easy money policies during the war quickly evaporated when the fate of the country no longer hung in the balance. Immediately after the war, creditors and tight-money advocates picked up the pace of their campaign to rid the country of greenbacks. They gained an ally in the top ranks of the administration with the appointment of a highly conservative banker, Hugh McCulloch, as secretary of the Treasury. McCulloch considered greenbacks unconstitutional and set out with determination to rid the country of them after the war. Historian Robert Sharkey notes that this view, widely supported by bankers and creditors, failed to take into consideration the fact that "any tampering with the volume of the greenbacks in the fateful years which followed the end of the war was likely to precipitate a depression. The situation called for the delicacy of a scalpel, but McCulloch brought only the bluntness of a meat axe."

McCulloch had an almost religious fervour about the evil of greenbacks and the sanctity of gold. "By common consent of the nations, gold and silver are the only true measure of value," the new Treasury secretary said in a speech shortly after his appointment. "I myself have no more doubt that these metals were prepared by the Almighty for this purpose, than I have that iron and coal were prepared for the purposes for which they are being used."

The notion that God was on the side of gold was a powerful one that enjoyed wide support. As Sharkey comments, McCulloch and many of his contemporaries "accepted the idea that the Almighty had ordained the use of gold and silver as money. To such people, the study of economics itself was an attempt to ascertain the will of God... Is it any wonder that in speaking or writing of the opinions of those who advocated policies of cheap money... the phrase 'financial heresy' was frequently used?" While gold was considered God's currency, greenbacks were sometimes referred to derisively as "rag-baby" money. In order to rid the country of this impure currency, the government actually carried out a policy of burning greenbacks.

As the supply of greenbacks shrank, money became scarcer and more expensive once again, just as the creditor class wanted. McCulloch's eventual goal was to make greenbacks redeemable at face value for gold, thus eliminating their inflationary potential. When this plan was eventually implemented in 1879, the United States had returned fully to the gold standard; its currency was now linked directly to the amount of gold it possessed in its treasury. The days of easy money were over.

If gold was god-like, so was the national debt, in the eyes of the creditor class. Indeed, creditors, who held large chunks of the debt in the form of bonds, were keen that all debt payments be made in gold, and often suggested that the national honour required nothing less. Supporters of an easier money policy countered that, in cases where the government hadn't expressly stated an intention to pay its debt obligations in gold, it was sufficient to pay it in greenbacks, which were, after all, the legal currency of the nation. The difference was significant: gold was a scarce metal that had increased in value, while the value of greenbacks had been eroded through inflation. The desire to repay a debt in devalued currency is always tempting to the debtor.

On the other hand, many of the bonds representing the nation's debt had originally been purchased with paper currency, often at discounted prices. For the national government to now repay these debts—principal and interest—in more valuable gold was a sweet deal for the bondholders. Even President Andrew Johnson, generally no greenbacker, balked at the richness of this proposition: "[T]he holders of the United States bonds ought not to receive in payment thereof any more than the Government received for them in real money."

All this led to furious, passionate debates in the U.S. Congress, where the numerous supporters of the creditor class took on a pugnacious set of greenbackers, including Ignatius Donnelly and William "Pig Iron" Kelley. The debate raged outside Congress too, with the creditor class turning debt repayment into a moral crusade for virtue. "The demoralization of society progresses steadily under the blighting influence of an irredeemable legal tender paper money [like greenbacks]," James Gallatin, a prominent Wall Street banker, wrote in a contemporary financial magazine. "Religion, virtue and honour decline. Vice becomes fashionable. Gambling prevails in the marts of trade and the financial centres from the very necessities of the case, because the slow process of honesty, prudence, forethought and plodding industry are impracticable in occupations subject to the licentious reign of such paper money." With the national honour apparently on the line, the creditor class emerged triumphant.

The deflationary policies of the postwar decades were highly favourable to creditors and banking interests. Money became so scarce that its value just kept increasing—a wonderful thing for those who had or were owed money, but a disaster for those who had little and owed much. It also rendered the economy stagnant, stunting the growth of business enterprises that relied on access to credit. In a speech to the U.S. Senate, William Sprague of Rhode Island lambasted the government for favouring financial interests over productive forces in the country: "You have contracted your currency nearly four hundred million dollars in three years for the purpose of enhancing its value. What has been the result of it? ...You have prostrated every interest and every industry in consequence of that most suicidal and damnable policy."

Among those hardest hit were farmers, who were on a constant treadmill of debt. Farmers were only paid when they sold their crops at harvest time, but they required money up front at the beginning of the season to pay for seed and equipment. To finance these purchases they were obliged to go into debt, often at interest rates ranging from

18 to 36 per cent.

But this was only the beginning of their troubles. Once the wheat and corn were harvested—a backbreaking task in the late nineteenth century—farmers were obliged to pay high freight rates to transport their crops to nearby grain mills. As historian Lawrence Goodwyn notes, "The farmer in the West felt that something was wrong with a system that made him pay a bushel of corn in freight costs for every bushel he shipped." The worst blow of all, however, was the final price he received for his efforts. As money became scarcer and scarcer, prices just kept falling. A farmer who had received just over $2 for a bushel of wheat in 1866 got only $1 a bushel by 1870. And the price kept dropping over the next thirty years. By 1885, the price of a bushel of wheat had dropped to 80 cents, and to 60 cents in the 1890s. Corn, which sold for 45 cents a bushel in 1870, fetched no more than 10 cents a bushel in Kansas by 1889. But, as farm prices fell dramatically, interest rates kept rising, making it harder and harder for the farmer to pay off his loans. The west became known as the "sod-house frontier," where the farm population wore rags on their feet and lived in houses built of sun-dried slabs of grass.

Conditions were even worse in the south. Farm families typically bought their seed and supplies on credit from a local merchant who charged exorbitant amounts, plus an interest rate in the range of 30 per cent. The farmer was also obliged to put up part of his crop as security for the supplies. As cotton prices fell drastically in the last two decades of the nineteenth century, farmers ended up owing the merchants more than they earned on their cotton sales, and were then obliged to sign over their land as security for future supplies. Eventually, hundreds of thousands of men, women and children in states from Virginia to Texas lost their farms altogether, and ended up working as landless peasants or leaving the land for the big cities.

It was in the midst of all this suffering that a vibrant protest movement emerged in the late 1870s, and produced a powerful undercurrent of dissent in American politics over the next twenty years. Populism, as it became known, was primarily a movement of enraged farmers, struggling to overthrow a system that seemed to work against them in so many ways. Like the supporters of Jacksonian Democracy half a century earlier, the Populists were bitterly opposed to the power of moneyed interests who seemed to be running the country, structuring the financial system in their favour. It struck the Populists as fundamentally wrong that farmers, who worked by the sweat of their brow, should be unable to earn enough money to feed and clothe their families, and to hold on to the family farm.

While the movement was driven by anger and despair, its leaders and thinkers developed a fairly sophisticated analysis of their situation. The Populists understood that at the root of their problems was the government's tight-money policy, so favourable to the nation's creditor class and so unfavourable to its debtors. It was this tight-money policy that kept interest rates high and, at the same time, produced deflation.

The Populists also understood that the tight-money policy was the direct result of the return to the gold standard and the disappearance of greenbacks. As long as the country clung to the notion that gold was the basis of the nation's money supply, there would never be enough money to go around. So one of the key planks of the Populists was that there should once again be a national currency that was not linked to gold, just as there had been during the boom days of the Civil War. The Populists wanted the government to start printing greenbacks again, and to print enough of them so that prices would rise sufficiently for farmers and other workers to earn a decent living. The supply of the nation's currency would no longer be limited by the amount of gold in the national treasury. Instead, it would be linked to the

growth needs of the country. And the democratically elected
government, not the nation's bankers, would determine
what those needs were.

The Populists wanted to bring the entire banking system
under democratic control. Rather than have the bankers
running the country, as they seemed to, the idea was to have
the country supervise and control the bankers. Part of the
problem, the Populists could see, was that the gold standard
made the banking system inherently unstable, because it was
unable to respond quickly to sudden increases in the demand
for credit, such as at harvest time. When local banks ran out
of funds, they turned to bigger regional banks for temporary
loans. The bigger banks, in turn, were often obliged to borrow from even bigger banks in New York City or Chicago.

Even these established old banks, however, were sometimes squeezed for credit and had to turn to Wall Street
financiers like J.P. Morgan. The House of Morgan would then
piece together major loans from wealthy sources—often from
Europe—at, of course, considerable rates of interest. But as all
this high finance was being worked out in New York, London
or Paris, the smaller banks back home tottered on the brink
of collapse, and commerce in faraway parts of Kansas, North
Carolina or Texas could virtually grind to a halt. (Thus, the
big banks and the House of Morgan came to function as
lenders of last resort. However, the inadequacy of this system
in meeting emergency needs was one of the factors that eventually led to the establishment of the Federal Reserve System,
the U.S. central bank, just before World War I.)

The ideas of the Populists spread like wildfire. At the
centre of the movement was a group of self-taught intellectuals who analysed the problems, put out newsletters and
prepared a cadre of lecturers who travelled from town to
town holding meetings to educate the people. In time, these
meetings grew to be important political events, as thousands
of men, women and children travelled long distances from

their farms to hear a day of speakers and to become inspired by the possibility of changing the system.

They also took practical steps to overcome their powerlessness. Across the south and the midwest, the farmers formed co-operatives to buy supplies in bulk and sell them to member farmers at low interest rates. The co-operatives would also buy the farmers' produce, store it in the co-operatives' warehouse and sell it over time. The system worked brilliantly in principle, but it proved difficult to obtain enough credit to carry the co-operatives through to the end of the season, when the produce was sold. In an impressive attempt to get around this problem, the farmers' co-operative in Texas raised part of the money it needed by selling shares to its members, with the poverty-stricken farm families putting up title to their land as security.

Yet even though the Texas Exchange was able to collect more than $200,000 in these collateral pledges of land, the banks refused to lend the co-operative the money it needed. Once again, the member farmers, despite their personal dire financial problems, collectively managed to chip in an astonishing $80,000. Their efforts saved the exchange that year but, faced with a similar rebuff from the banking system the following year, the exchange folded.

Ultimately, the Populists were defeated in their bold attempt to bring a kind of people's democracy to America, to seize financial power from the moneyed interests and spread it more evenly among the citizenry. Although the Populist candidate for president, General James Weaver, won more than a million votes in the 1892 election, only a few years later the Populist movement had largely petered out. However, many of its ideas—such as the need for regulation of the banking system and for progressive taxation—continued to inspire progressive causes decades later.

Although the Populists failed to achieve their crucial financial reforms, conditions for farmers actually improved following their demise. The United States experienced a boom at the turn of the century, largely because of the discovery of gold in California and the Yukon. Indeed, the gold standard could cut both ways. A shortage of gold could produce great hardship, but a sudden abundance of the precious metal could produce an unexpected boom. It was ironic that after the Populists' long and bitter struggle against the gold standard, the plight of farmers would actually improve through the discovery of new deposits of their great nemesis: gold. The resulting boom finally raised prices, including food prices, after thirty years of deflation.

With the coming of World War I in 1914, the U.S. and the other powers of the world went off the gold standard again, and then abandoned it for good in the Depression of the 1930s. The financial crunch of a world war and worldwide depression made a stringent reliance on gold impossible. But, interestingly, despite the problems caused by the gold standard throughout history, its abandonment failed to create a saner monetary system.

The central problem of the gold standard was that it almost inevitably involved a scarcity of money—a situation that favoured those with money. But there are other ways to achieve this. Central banks can effectively create a scarcity of money through high interest rates. Indeed, scarce-money policies—the bane of seventeenth-century English merchants, early colonial settlers, greenbackers and Populists—are still a weapon in the arsenal of central banks today. What has been lost is the popular passion over the issue. What a difference from the days when usurers were condemned to burn in hell, when those who spoke disrespectfully of the paper currency were treated as enemies of the nation and those who counterfeited it were branded with a hot iron, or when farmers and their families rode tens of miles in uncovered wagons to participate in impassioned debates about the nation's financial system!

What has certainly been lost is popular understanding of the importance of the issue and its impact on our lives. The world of money and banking has largely been taken away from ordinary people, who have been convinced that it's simply too complicated to understand, that it's better left to the bankers and brokers and economists regularly called upon for comment by TV current affairs shows. While we naively leave our fate in the hands of these apparently neutral experts—as if financial matters were a value-free science—we seem to have lost sight of a basic truth that was obvious to the simple farmers in the Populist movement. They understood that there was an ongoing battle in the financial world between creditors and debtors, between those determined to fight inflation and those determined to fight stagnation.

And there was no mistaking which side they were on.

CHAPTER SIX
Revenge of the Bondholders

The Populist outrage that swept through the rural United States reverberated north of the border as well. The ideas that had motivated and inspired such a large movement of American farmers filtered northward where, several decades later, they resonated among farmers in rural Canada. Canadian farmers could readily identify with the anger that American farmers felt. They, too, had come to resent the power creditors wielded over their lives. Like their U.S. counterparts, Canadian farmers also organized politically and formed co-operatives to get around the specific problems they faced.

The Canadian farmers' movement never gained the kind of momentum that Populism had in U.S. politics, however, perhaps because the Canadian situation was not as oppressive as that faced by American farmers. Still, the plight of Canadian farmers was real and at times very painful, and they were plagued with the same sense of helplessness in the face of established elites. In a speech to the Dominion Grange and Farmers' Association in 1913, farm activist W.C. Good complained bitterly about the "Big Interests," the "large financial and business magnates," "the idle rich" and the "giant of Special Privilege, who has enslaved and degraded this nation for so long." Good's attack was wide-ranging enough to include even some rich women "who, apparently, have no social or domestic duties, but who spend their lives in touring the world seeking pleasure."

Specific resentment against the banks and financial institutions came later, in the 1920s and '30s, and was particularly strong in the Prairie provinces. The problems the farmers faced were similar to, although less dramatic than, what the Populist farmers had experienced in the U.S. Since farmers had to borrow up front to finance their operations, they were dependent on creditors, and extremely vulnerable to high interest rates. In Alberta, which became a hotbed of farm protest in the twenties and thirties, farmers faced interest charges of about 8 per cent a year on farm mortgages, and up to 10 per cent on their machinery and equipment—rates that made it difficult for farm families to get by. When the Depression hit, their survival became much more precarious, as farm prices soon dropped to one-third of what they had been in the late twenties.

Although the farmers' protest movement in Alberta is usually associated with the election in 1935 of a Social Credit government—and the province's move to the political right—in fact, the early farmers' movement was quite radical and left-leaning. The Non-Partisan League, which represented both farm and labour interests starting in 1917, called for public ownership of banks, railways, natural resources, flour mills, farm machinery manufacturers and insurance companies. Through such public ownership, the farmers envisioned escaping the helpless situation they found themselves in, where the price of everything they needed to carry on their farming operations was controlled by others. The Non-Partisan League became an important force within the larger United Farmers of Alberta, which in 1921 won the first election it contested and became the government of Alberta for the next fourteen years.

Once in power, however, the United Farmers of Alberta seemed to grow less responsive to the concerns of farmers. By 1932, farmers were furious that their supposedly farm-oriented government stood by and watched as mortgage companies foreclosed on family farms. At a United Farmers party convention that year, farmer delegates demanded that the premier, J.E. Brownlee, declare a moratorium on such foreclosures. But Brownlee waffled, and ultimately refused to do so, on the grounds that it would destroy the province's credit rating. The enraged farmers concluded that the premier had more concern for the province's credit rating than he had for people's homes and livelihoods. The foreclosures continued, and the promises of Social Credit leader William Aberhart to alleviate the plight of farmers began to find a receptive audience in the province.

Aberhart himself originally came across as something of a leftist. Before his election in 1935, he championed the poor and attacked power and privilege, and was widely opposed by business in the province. In a dramatic move in its first year in office, Aberhart's government passed a law retroactively cancelling all interest owing on farm mortgages for the previous four years. The *Financial Post* promptly labelled the law "an unprecedented attack on private capital." The move was widely supported within the province, however, where mortgage companies were extremely unpopular. But Aberhart's reformist zeal also soon waned and he began moving his party to the right. In the end, it became not only authoritarian, but also friendly to the big business interests it had once denounced, with particularly close relations to the multinational oil industry.

Meanwhile, elements in the farm movement had linked up with the labour movement to try to put their concerns on the agenda with a new national political party, the Co-operative Commonwealth Federation, or CCF. The CCF's bold "Regina Manifesto" called for a number of financial and

monetary reforms, including the development of co-operative credit and banking institutions, lower interest rates and
a "drastic increase" in taxes on large incomes. Indeed, the
manifesto is so radical that it is astonishing to recall that this
party later transformed itself into the mild-mannered NDP.
Expressing a vision of reform that would send Bob Rae, Mike
Harcourt and Roy Romanow running for cover, the manifesto advocated what amounted to a fundamental rejection
of capitalism: "Industry should be organized for the service of
man and not for private profit."

The emergence of the farm protest movement may have
helped push Conservative prime minister R.B. Bennett into
establishing a central bank. A central bank was certainly a
less radical alternative than the more sweeping kinds of
financial and economic reforms being advocated, apparently
with some popular support. The heavy-handedness of the
private banks in cutting off credit to those burned by the
Depression had certainly sparked widespread anger, even
beyond the farm and labour movements. This resentment
against the banks was particularly strong in the West, where
it fuelled a sense of regional alienation, since all the major
banks were headquartered in the East.

Even the prime minister felt the need to respond to the
public mood by chastising the banks. In a 1933 letter to the
Canadian Bankers' Association, Bennett, a former bank
shareholder, struck an unusually critical tone: "I desire to
record formally with you my disapproval of the general conduct of the Banks in Canada in forcing to the wall customers
who are unable to meet their liabilities at this time."
Reminding the banks that their federal charters would
shortly be up for renewal by Parliament, he continued, "I
write this letter in order that the banks may be informed
that it is idle to expect any member of Parliament, any
Canadian citizen for that matter, to justify some of the acts
of the banks in driving their customers to the wall who are

unable to liquidate their liabilities under existing economic conditions."

Increasingly, agitation for financial reform focused on the need for a central bank. All the major farm and labour groups, as well as parts of the small business and academic communities, had come to see a central bank as the solution to the nation's financial problems. In theory, this made sense. Rather than allowing a private financial elite to control the nation's access to credit, a central bank offered the exciting possibility of handing that power to an institution ultimately controlled by a democratically elected government.

On the other hand, a central bank—particularly one modelled on the Bank of England—posed no real threat to the financial elite. So, when the Bennett government appointed a commission to investigate the desirability of a central bank, it was no accident that two of its five commissioners were distinguished British professionals who admired the Bank of England. (Two Canadian private bankers and Premier Brownlee of Alberta were the other members.) While the commission supported the notion of a central bank for Canada, with the two private bankers dissenting, it recommended that the bank be privately owned, just as in Britain. The public's ability to use the bank to take control of the reins of finance would be limited if the shares of the bank were sold to private interests, the buyers presumably being influential financial investors. Bennett was easily persuaded that this was the route to go. So, after years of farmers' agitation for financial reform, the final prize was a central bank that was to be owned by members of the same hated financial elite.

Those advocating private ownership of the Bank insisted that this was necessary to guarantee its independence from political interference—a theme that still echoes today in debates about the Bank's role. But "political interference" is just another way of saying control by democratically elected

governments. Why is it so desirable to remove ultimate control from the Canadian public? In the ongoing struggle
between creditors and debtors—a perpetual part of the
financial landscape of any country—why would it be considered advantageous for control of the banks to rest largely in
the hands of the creditor class? After the Liberals won power
in 1935, the government took over ownership of the Bank,
bringing it into the public domain, but the push to insulate
it from the "political interference" of Canadian voters by no
means disappeared.

Still, as we've seen, the Bank had been skilfully designed
by bureaucrats intent on giving it a broader purpose than
simply serving the financial elite's desire for inflation control. In a carefully worded section that Deputy Minister
Clifford Clark had persuaded Bennett to include as a preamble to its mandate, the Bank was called upon "to regulate
credit and currency in the best interests of the economic life
of the nation...to mitigate by its influence fluctuations in
the general level of production, trade, prices and employment...and generally to promote the economic and financial welfare of the Dominion."

And in Graham Towers the Bank had an innovative
thinker who, unlike many in banking and financial circles,
was wary of deflation as well as inflation. As early as 1932,
when Towers was assistant to the general manager of the
Royal Bank, he had written a detailed memo explaining the
dangers in the U.S. tight-money policy, which was creating
serious deflation south of the border. Towers warned that
Canada risked being dragged in the same direction.
According to Robert Bryce, a former deputy finance minister
who has written a financial history of the period, Towers
urged Bennett to adopt policies that would allow Canada to
experience some inflation. But Bennett wouldn't listen.
"The carefully conceived proposal of Towers did not persuade Bennett," observes Bryce. "The debtor mentality—the

concern to protect the country's credit rating—was so widespread in Canada that it reached right up through the Finance Department to the prime minister."

Indeed, the obsession with the deficit—under both the Conservative and Liberal governments—remained the central focus of the government through the Depression. Even though the Bank largely pursued an easy-money policy with low interest rates, there was so much slack in the economy that it wasn't sufficient to stimulate an upturn. The constant cutbacks in spending by Ottawa, and its insistence that the provinces, too, cut their spending, only seemed to exacerbate the problem.

It wasn't until World War II began in 1939 that the plight of the unemployed began to improve significantly. With the country at war, Ottawa changed its priorities overnight. The goal of a balanced budget was put on hold, as the government dramatically escalated its spending, mobilizing an army, navy and air force and handing out contracts for the manufacture of war supplies and equipment. Suddenly, after a decade of depression and joblessness, the country was back to work. A new attitude prevailed in Ottawa: if something was needed for the war, money would be found to pay for it.

As Ottawa swung into full gear to fight the war, Towers and the Bank of Canada came to play a central role in the war financing effort. The Bank was intimately involved in the overhaul of the tax system, as personal income and corporate taxes were raised dramatically and an excess profits tax was imposed, partly to show the Canadian public that the outrageous war profiteering of World War I would not be tolerated this time. The Bank was also involved in designing Ottawa's wartime anti-inflation board, with the Bank's senior deputy governor, Donald Gordon, serving as its chairman. And Towers himself ended up heading Ottawa's massive campaign to sell victory war bonds.

Despite the horrors of war in Europe, in many ways things were dramatically better back home. With the country back at work and dedicated to the task of defeating Hitler, an energy and hopefulness returned, wiping out the gloom of the long Depression years. There was still much deprivation and shortages of many basic goods, but the great gulf that had existed between the employed and the unemployed in Canadian life was now gone. Keynes certainly seemed to have been vindicated.

With the war still raging in the early forties, the mandarins in Ottawa began to worry about what would happen when it finally ended, and hundreds of thousands of Canadian soldiers came flooding home. There was a strong conviction that, if Ottawa did nothing, Canadians would return to the same desolate conditions that had persisted during the Depression. This reinforced the feeling among top bureaucrats that there was a tremendous need to strengthen and enlarge the role of government. The talented crowd that had flocked to Ottawa in the thirties was more than ever convinced that a strong public sector was needed to complement the private sector. Key players at the Bank of Canada, including Graham Towers, shared this view.

The most influential opponent of this expanded role for government was C.D. Howe, after whom the institute is named. A dominant figure in Canadian politics from the mid-thirties to the late fifties, Howe served during the war as minister of munitions and supply and later as minister of trade and commerce. In cabinet, he was a tireless champion of unfettered free enterprise throughout his long career, arguing that what the market needed most was to be left alone.

However, most of the influential players in Ottawa— including those at the Bank of Canada—were now headed in the opposite direction, in their determination to avoid a return to the desperate times of the Depression. Among the more radical proposals being advanced within government circles came one from Leonard Marsh, an academic who was serving as research director of a government committee considering plans for postwar reconstruction. Marsh, who had been an important figure in the League for Social Reconstruction, the intellectual wing of the CCF, wrote a far-reaching report calling for the establishment of a universal social security system for Canada.

Marsh was a former student of William Beveridge, the British economist who prepared the well-known Beveridge report for the British government in 1942, calling for a universal social insurance scheme. But Marsh's report was, if anything, more visionary. While Beveridge had focused on consolidating existing British programs into a comprehensive package, Marsh was attempting to create out of virtually nothing a plan for a comprehensive social welfare system in Canada. Perhaps because it was so far-reaching, the report ended up having minimal impact on immediate postwar planning. Still, Marsh's strong recommendation for a universal family allowance quickly became a high priority on the Canadian political agenda.

Interestingly, the Bank of Canada provided some important support for the family allowance proposal. Towers lent his personal backing to the idea, partly because he saw it as a way to stem upward pressure on wages. He submitted a detailed memo to the government endorsing the proposal. The memo, prepared by the Bank's research chief, J.R. Beattie, quoted from the Beveridge report about the desirability of family allowances as the centrepiece in a broad social security system. Against C.D. Howe's strong opposition, the government introduced family allowances in 1944, the legislation sweeping through Parliament without further resistance. The allowance, paid each month for each child, was large enough to contribute significantly to the family's income, particularly in homes with a lot of children. Had such a program been in place in the thirties, the Depression would have been considerably less brutal for hundreds of thousands of Canadian families.

Another burning memory of the Depression—the long lines of the unemployed—pushed Ottawa to focus on ways to maintain the high wartime employment levels. Indeed, a government white paper set out "a high and stable level of employment and income" as a national objective. Ironically, the white paper was produced by W.A. Mackintosh, a senior adviser to C.D. Howe. Howe had reluctantly agreed to the white paper, apparently because it also advocated tax breaks for business and generally espoused a free market philosophy. Most in government circles, however, agreed that Ottawa should do whatever it could to avoid a return to the dreaded unemployment levels of the thirties. Indeed, part of the appeal of family allowances, as well as housing assistance and veterans' grants, was the notion that placing money directly in people's hands would stimulate the economy and put people back to work.

Over at the Bank, priority was given to maintaining high employment levels. As Douglas Fullerton notes, "The spectre of post-war unemployment was never far from Towers' mind, and it influenced his views on policy." Although the Bank was later to set aside this priority in its overriding obsession with controlling inflation, Towers saw the maintenance of high employment levels as a crucial national goal.

Towers's concern about maintaining employment after the war was one of the key factors that led him to resist the traditional tight-money approach to conducting monetary policy. He rejected the use of high interest rates as a weapon against inflation. Fullerton observes, "What is clear from the story of the post-war years, and indeed of earlier years, is that Towers at no time showed much faith in higher interest rates as a way to counter inflation." In fact, Towers stressed that interest rates had to be kept low, arguing that great weight must be given to encouraging employment and "the most rapid possible transition to civilian activity" of those leaving the armed forces.

Towers also argued that low interest rates were essential for sound business and government finances, noting that unstable interest rates would make it difficult for business to make long-term plans. Furthermore, he cautioned that a rise in interest rates on future government bond issues would cause the value of existing bonds to drop (since their lower rates of interest would make them worth less). As a result, people would lose confidence in holding on to their bonds and in buying bonds in the future. And, in a useful insight that received far too little attention, he noted that high interest rates would also make it far harder for government to cope with its debt problems.

In his commitment to low interest rates, Towers went so far as to signal clearly his intention to maintain this policy into the future. In the Bank's 1943 annual report, he publicly committed the Bank to an easy-money policy in the postwar years:

> There can be little doubt that the easy money policy which has been pursued since 1935 assisted in promoting recovery from the depression and facilitated the adjustments which have been required during the war period. Indication that the Bank intends to continue this easy money policy should be helpful in making plans for the future.

Towers was as good as his word, and the Bank's low interest rate policy greatly assisted the maintenance of high employment through the early postwar decades. It also made it feasible for Ottawa to pay off much of its enormous war debt. In fairness, it should be noted that demobilization after the war reduced government spending levels significantly, making it easier to deal with postwar debt. Furthermore, inflation was not the problem that it later became in the 1970s.

Still, even when inflation did heat up from time to time in the postwar period, Towers resisted demands to deal with the problem with higher interest rates. This was not because Towers was indifferent to inflation. He was in fact concerned about containing—although not eliminating—inflation. But he felt that there were effective methods of inflation control that could be used without resorting to high interest rates. He argued instead for price and exchange controls, higher taxes or "moral suasion," whereby the Bank of Canada would use its influence to persuade the private banks to restrict some types of lending. This had the effect of restricting credit in certain overheated markets—by imposing ceilings on loans, for instance. Through this sort of targeted approach, the Bank could deal with potential inflationary hotspots without submitting the entire economy to a punishing round of interest rate hikes. (A somewhat similar approach was advocated by some Bank critics years later, when the overheated real estate market in Ontario in the late eighties threatened to set off a round of inflation. Rather than respond with the full force of higher interest rates, as under Crow's zero inflation policy, critics urged the imposition of restrictions on certain real estate loans or a speculation tax on real estate profits.)

Perhaps it was easy for Towers to take these stands, given the climate of the times: the United States and Britain were also generally pursuing low-interest-rate policies, making it easy for Canada to follow suit. Still, Towers's well-articulated position on the need for low interest rates seemed to have been a matter of conviction, and he took that position even when there were significant internal pressures for higher rates. When the government's dire shortage of cash in 1943 and '44 prompted suggestions that the Bank should raise interest rates to attract money, Towers strongly resisted.

Astonishingly, despite the wonderful successes of the early

postwar years in producing high levels of employment, some economists later attacked Towers for not using high interest rates as a lever to fight inflation. One such critique came from Edward Neufeld, an academic economist who later became a senior executive at the Royal Bank. Neufeld faulted Towers for his "[p]reoccupation with thoughts of deflation and overemphasis on the problems of debt management."

Towers was unrepentant. Before his retirement in 1954, he responded to his critics by arguing that a tighter monetary policy would have caused business uncertainty, reduced government infrastructure investment and therefore would have made it much more difficult to achieve high levels of employment. Besides, he noted, higher interest rates would have done little to restrain inflation, which was largely caused by the general rise in world prices. Towers went on to say that he had rejected a tight money policy because he felt that the benefits of beating back inflation did not equal the negative effects higher interest rates would have had on economic recovery. In other words, Towers believed that the benefits of taming inflation didn't justify the costs—a position that indicates he didn't have the benefit of the research later done by the Bank on the miracle-power of zero inflation.

It would be wrong to see Towers as some kind of radical Populist. He was a conservative who believed in balanced budgets, free enterprise and the merits of a private banking system. But, unlike others who have directed monetary policy, Towers's conservatism included a strong commitment to growth and employment, and a belief that government and the central bank had a vital role to play in achieving these goals. Towers conducted himself—as the Bank's mandate instructed him to—in a way that attempted to balance inflation control with the pursuit of high levels of growth and employment. Ultimately, for Towers, creating an economy where everyone could earn a living and participate in the community was part of the moral duty of government. As he eloquently put it just weeks before the end of the war,

> After the demonstration the war is providing of what
> a determined state and a determined people with a
> single objective can do to provide employment and
> raise the national output, it is impossible to contem-
> plate a situation in which mass unemployment exists
> because the state and the people fail to adopt with
> equal determination a peacetime objective of maxi-
> mizing the national output for use, or because they
> lack in imagination the means necessary to accom-
> plish this objective... If we fail this time to build a
> better country and a better world, once peace is ours,
> it will not be because of lack of knowledge but
> because of lack of purpose. The spirit of community
> and the sense of national purpose which have pre-
> vailed among us recently have given us a glimpse of a
> promised land. Shall we be strong enough to hold on
> to this? to substitute for the will to victory some other
> driving force, some other inner compulsion?

It was a glimpse of a promised land—a glimpse that has all
but disappeared within the cloisters of the monastery.

Towers's prescription prevailed throughout the early postwar
decades—decades that now seem like a golden age. After
the bleak, spiritless days of the Depression, the country was
back to work. Virtually everyone who wanted to work could
find a job. Credit was available for businesses to expand to
meet the explosive postwar demand for new housing and
cars and all the things that people had done without during
a decade and a half of depression and war.

Even the enormous overhang of debt from those difficult
years didn't stand in the way. With the economy booming
and the country back at work, tax revenues poured into the

federal treasury, whittling down the debt. Provincial coffers also benefited from the infusion of cash from the booming economy and a fully employed workforce. After hitting the "debt wall" in the depths of the Depression, the Prairie provinces were once again back on their feet financially, their credit ratings on financial markets restored.

Yet the memory of the Depression continued to haunt the country. No one wanted to risk slipping back into those bleak, hopeless days, and there was widespread support for government taking an active role to prevent that from happening. After the successes of the great war effort, government came to be viewed in a very different light—as a strong, responsible, capable force that could effectively use modern knowledge and planning skills to oversee the well-being of the entire country. There was wide support for broad, new social programs—from unemployment insurance to family allowances to old age pensions to medicare—to protect Canadians from the capriciousness of the marketplace. Canada was on its way to becoming a more inclusive and egalitarian society, in which almost everyone had a job and had access to education and health care and the basics of life.

In many ways, the golden era of the late forties to the early seventies represented a kind of historic compromise between powerful financial interests and the working population. With low interest rates and affordable credit, there was enough money around to fuel a booming economy with employment for all; oxygen was pumping through the nation's body, bringing it to life. That also meant slightly higher inflation than had historically been the case under the tight-money days of the gold standard. Still, interest rates were held to a level where those with capital could make a comfortable return on their money. It wasn't the kind of profiteering that had been possible at times in the past when a scarcity of money had driven up real interest rates dramatically, giving wealth-holders fantastic rates of return. Rather, it was a compromise of sorts that gave both lenders and borrowers a chance to prosper.

It was, however, a fragile compromise that survived largely because of the general prosperity, when the leaping growth rates of the postwar boom produced enough bounty for all. That began to change in the early seventies, as storm clouds appeared on the economic horizon. Just as the postwar boom began losing its steam, the oil crisis set off a dramatic round of inflation. Interest rates rose, too, to compensate bondholders for the erosion of the value of their money, but they weren't rising enough to keep pace with inflation. Indeed, as we saw earlier, throughout much of the decade, bondholders were actually receiving negative rates of return; that is, they were actually losing money on their investments. The rich were no longer getting richer, making the compromise more and more fragile.

In the United States, frustration was building on Wall Street with the leadership at the Federal Reserve, the U.S. central bank. Throughout the seventies, the Fed, as it was known, had done a half-hearted job of reining in inflation. Arthur Burns, an academic economist who had served as Fed chairman in the early seventies, talked tough on inflation, but seemed unwilling to follow through with the kind of recession-inducing medicine that many on Wall Street believed was needed to cure inflation. Burns was suspected of backing off from this kind of tightening for fear of jeopardizing the re-election chances of Richard Nixon, who had appointed him Fed chairman. The Carter administration replaced Burns with William Miller, a former businessman whom Wall Street regarded as far too soft on inflation. Wall Street's acute dissatisfaction with the inflation situation eventually pushed Carter to transfer Miller to the post of Treasury secretary and hand over the crucial job of chairing the Fed to a more rigorous inflation foe, Paul Volcker.

In many ways, Volcker was an unlikely candidate for the

job. While most senior government appointees were drawn from the ranks of the private sector, Volcker had spent his career in government, holding key posts in the Treasury department. Volcker didn't even look the part. In his rumpled suits, he lacked the polished appearance associated with the world of senior banking. But Volcker had developed a reputation for shrewdness and toughness over the years, holding his own impressively under the intense grilling of congressional committees. He was credited with playing a key role in moving the world to floating exchange rates in the early seventies—a reform that, while not universally popular on Wall Street, had shown Volcker to be a highly able and effective operator, even something of an innovative leader. In many ways, he seemed like the sort of person who might have the guts to take on inflation.

And Volcker did not disappoint. When he took over the Fed in the late summer of 1979, inflation had become so deeply ingrained in the public psyche that it seemed like a permanent fixture. Even when interest rates rose in pursuit of rising inflation, somehow people just kept borrowing at the higher rates. The public had come to believe that inflation would keep rising, so the higher interest rates didn't seem so intimidating. And inside the Fed, staff economists who were used to working under William Miller seemed more concerned by the possibility of provoking a recession than by the risk of ever-rising inflation. Volcker knew it would take some wrenching and dramatic action to break the cycle.

Only a month after taking office, he got some of the inspiration he needed while on a trip to Europe to attend the annual meeting of the International Monetary Fund. The inspiration didn't come from the meeting but from a brief stopover in Hamburg, where he met with West German chancellor Helmut Schmidt and Otmar Emminger, the stern president of Germany's central bank, the Bundesbank. The Germans, who had experienced the true horrors of hyperinflation after World War I, when consumers had to carry wheelbarrows full of money to pay for their groceries, were understandably ever vigilant on the inflation front. The visit with Emminger and Schmidt shored up Volcker's resolve that severe action had to be taken.

The sense of crisis and encouragement from the German anti-inflationists emboldened Volcker to experiment with a new approach. Until then, the Fed had set interest rates in a fairly arbitrary way. Central banking was considered almost an art—the art of figuring out how much inflationary momentum there was in the economy. If the bank figured there was too much inflationary pressure building, it raised interest rates in an effort to slow things down. On the other hand, if things were slowing too much, the bank would lower interest rates, thereby making credit more widely accessible and providing a stimulus for the economy. The only problem was: how did one figure out how much inflationary momentum there was out there? The whole exercise was highly arbitrary. And although the Fed constantly monitored all the available signals, read the financial press carefully and interviewed people in different sectors of the economy, in the end it was a judgment call by the Fed chairman. This put tremendous responsibility on the chairman to make highly subjective decisions that determined the fate of the economy.

For years, economist Milton Friedman from the University of Chicago had been trying to push a different idea: that the whole matter of controlling inflation could be approached in a much more systematic way. Reviving an ancient theory about the nature of money, Friedman argued that inflation was the result of too much money floating around the economy. Therefore, he argued, controlling inflation was simply a question of controlling the supply of money in the economy. The Fed should stop trying to magically divine what economic conditions were, and start systematically studying the quantity of money in circulation.

For Friedman, this was more than just an effective means of managing the country's monetary policy. It was also the key to a healthy economy: if the money supply grew in line with the long-term growth rates of the economy, then the economic fundamentals would be right, and growth and prosperity would follow. Thus he argued that getting the money supply right should be a primary goal of economic policy.

Friedman had long been considered a brilliant but somewhat eccentric scholar whose ideas fell outside the modified Keynesianism that became widely accepted after the war. But Friedman's persistence in pushing his theories—at congressional hearings, and academic and political forums—eventually paid off in the economic breakdown of the seventies. Certainly, the old method of trying to balance inflation and unemployment didn't seem to be working as effectively as it once had. In the past, there had seemed to be a trade-off: higher unemployment meant lower inflation, and vice versa. Now there was both high unemployment and high inflation. The impasse led to a willingness to consider new solutions, even radical, slightly off-base ones. Among those who were willing to give Friedman's theories a try was Paul Volcker.

Part of the appeal, according to Volcker, was that the new system would effectively tie the Fed's hands when it came to inflicting pain on the economy. This might seem like an odd sort of appeal—rendering oneself deliberately powerless. In the weird world of central banking, however, it had a certain logic. If the goal was to control inflation, then one had to be prepared to inflict pain on the public in order to slow the economy and bring down rising prices. But inflicting pain was not something most people liked to do, particularly people in public life. "After all, no one likes to risk recession, and that is when the political flak ordinarily hits," noted Volcker.

It was much better, then, to be in a position where decisions about inflicting pain were beyond one's control. In a sense, this is what Friedman's system—known as "monetarism"—offered. The Fed would simply establish set amounts or "targets" of how much money there should be in circulation, and then focus on achieving these targets. To do this, the Fed would still have to raise interest rates, but at least there would be a rationale for doing so; there would be targets—carefully worked out by experts—that would provide a technical justification for these high interest rates. Thus, the Fed would to some extent be a passive agent, simply responding to the dictates of the targets.

This not only allowed the Fed to duck some of the political heat during a recession, but it also made it more likely that the Fed would be able to stay the course no matter how much heat there turned out to be. As Volcker put it, "[W]e would find it difficult to back off even if our decisions led to painfully high interest rates." This willingness to let interest rates climb if necessary had considerable support among the powerful group of regional bankers who sat on the Open Market Committee, the Fed's key decision-making body. A majority on the committee actually supported the position that there should be no effective limits on how high interest rates might go—a position that scared even Volcker.

So, after years of baying in the wilderness, Milton Friedman finally saw his long-ignored theories become official policy in the world's biggest economy. Volcker was hoping that his official announcement of the change, coupled as it was with much talk about slaying the inflationary dragon, would be enough to break the inflationary psychology that gripped the land. This was crucial, since as long as people believed that prices would just keep rising, they would demand ever-larger wage and salary increases, and thereby continue to drive prices higher still. The job of controlling inflation would be infinitely easier if people believed that the Fed was serious about ending inflation, no matter what the cost.

But as the Fed implemented its new system of monetary targets, a strange thing happened. As expected, interest rates rose; indeed, they rose uncomfortably high. The commercial banks' prime lending rate climbed to an unprecedented 15.25 per cent. Volcker watched in horror, his hand sitting uncomfortably on the lever controlling the country's oxygen supply. But there was more bad news. Not only were interest rates punishingly high, but, despite them, inflation kept rising! By February 1980, it had reached 14.9 per cent. Volcker had apparently failed to inflict even a slight wound in the impenetrable flesh of the inflationary dragon.

Amid a growing atmosphere of crisis, Volcker and the White House came up with a package deal to further tighten the screws. In a big White House ceremony, President Carter announced the introduction of controls on credit, such as credit cards and consumer loans. Although the controls were not all that stringent and only had the effect of raising the cost of credit slightly, Carter's message apparently reverberated among the public in a way that Volcker's hadn't. Carter seemed to be saying that there was a national emergency, that people must stop borrowing. The economy plummeted abruptly in response, producing a sharp economic downturn which helped defeat Carter in the November 1980 election. But within a few months, inflation and high interest rates were once again dominating the economic landscape.

That false start in the inflation war only convinced Volcker and his colleagues that they had no choice but to be tougher the next time they made a foray against inflation. They would have to "lean harder against the wind." With the election of Ronald Reagan, that became a more complicated task. Along with his hostility to big government, one of the central tenets of Reagan's crude political philosophy was the need to restrain inflation. And, during his years on the fringes of the Republican right, he had been tutored on the subject by Milton Friedman himself. As president, Reagan continued to listen to Friedman's advice on an informal basis.

But while this lined up nicely with Volcker's plans, there was a conflicting side to the Reagan dogma. In Reagan's somewhat bizarre view, low inflation and sound money policies were equated with a rosy economic scenario: low inflation would bring economic growth. Although many economists also believed in this as a long-run scenario, none believed it would be the effortless' transition that Reagan seemed to assume. Even the most determined anti-inflationists acknowledged that bringing double-digit inflation down to manageable levels would be a painful process. Short-term pain for long-term gain was the way they liked to put it. But Reagan, who publicly paraded his optimism about the world and the economy, would have none of that naysaying. His presidency was to bring about the rebirth of American greatness after the Carter years in the wilderness. The last thing Reagan would acknowledge was that a horrible recession was in the offing if Volcker proceeded with his plans.

What followed was confusion. Volcker went about his solemn task of trying to prepare the public for the brutality that lay ahead. "Let us not be beguiled into thinking there are quick and painless solutions," Volcker grimly told a banquet audience in New York. Meanwhile, Ronald Reagan was as cheery and upbeat as Volcker was gloomy. Reagan promised to usher in an era of tremendous growth, and claimed that already there were signs of a turnaround. "There is a kind of glow out there among the people," he told a TV audience early in his presidency. To spur on this new growth, Reagan offered up his dramatic tax cuts, which were especially generous at the upper end. That certainly helped put a glow on some people's faces—particularly those of the very well-to-do—but it also left more cash out there circulating in the economy, making Volcker's job of tightening the inflation screws all the harder. With Volcker directing the economy towards a bruising crash and Reagan trying to spirit it into a new euphoria, the country, according to U.S. writer William Greider, increasingly resembled a "car with two drivers."

But the bruising crash came, just as Volcker had warned. As the Fed tightened the screws throughout 1981, the U.S. economy went into a tailspin. Interest rates shot up to unheard-of levels, making it impossible for many businesses to stay alive. Any business that depended on credit or on consumers having access to credit was virtually dead in the water. The home-building industry, for instance, all but shut down as the soaring cost of mortgages made new homes unaffordable for the vast majority of the population. Manufacturing interests, resource developers and small businesses were all badly hit, as was labour in general. One of the few industries that survived intact—even flourished—was the banking and financial sector.

Volcker's brutal therapy had an enormous impact on Canada as well. Our heavy reliance on the American market for our exports made it inevitable that we would suffer from their recession. In addition, Volcker's action greatly influenced our monetary policy. With our closely integrated economies, we had to be careful about letting our financial situation—our interest rates and inflation—get too far out of line with theirs.

In fact, Canada had been struggling on its own to contain inflation throughout the seventies. And the same sorts of tension existed between the central bank and the government as inflation and unemployment began to climb in the early seventies. Initially, the Trudeau government had been primarily concerned about the unemployment problem. Believing that the economy needed more stimulus, the cabinet decided to lower taxes significantly. The 1973 and 1974 Liberal budgets, under Finance Minister John Turner, were full of tax breaks designed to keep money in circulation and keep the economy buoyant. Over at the Bank of Canada, this strategy was regarded with alarm; it meant more money out there fuelling inflation, and would eventually oblige the Bank to clamp down harder on the overheated economy.

Then Bank of Canada governor Gerald Bouey faced the same dilemma as Volcker had faced. With inflation escalating at a worrisome pace, the task of bringing it under control was going to be grim. And that was not an easy message to sell—either to the public or to politicians. Bouey wanted something that would make the message more saleable, something he could point to to explain why he was obliged to jack up interest rates so high, something that would prevent him from having to take full personal responsibility for crushing the economy.

Just as in the U.S., monetary targets seemed to offer the answer, the perfect impersonal tool that promised to provide a technical justification for imposing brutally high interest rates. Research done at the Bank of Canada in the early seventies, and promoted by deputy governor George Freeman, convinced Bank officials that targets would be effective. With that research to back him up, Bouey adopted targets for the Bank in 1975—four years before Volcker succumbed to the appeal of the doctrines popularized by Milton Friedman. Bouey's announcement of the targets was praised by Friedman as "a marvelous speech... It is the best speech I have ever heard a central banker give."

In fact, the targets did little to mollify the public, which was apparently less interested in justifications for high interest rates, and more interested in seeing interest rates fall. The targets were more popular with economists and financial analysts, who eagerly devoured every bit of data about the money supply. Bond traders waited patiently every Thursday for the money numbers to be released, and then pored over them painstakingly in search of any clue to the Bank's plans on interest rates. It was all so complicated that it gave monetary policy a real scientific feel. Experts debated which measure of the money supply should be used for the targets. Would it be M1 (currency and chequing account deposits) or M2 (all the money in M1 plus savings accounts and time deposits at banks) or M3 (all the money in M2 plus exotica like $100,000 non-personal term deposit certificates)? If all that wasn't complicated and pseudoscientific enough, a new category was developed by the Fed called "shift-adjusted M-1B." With names like that, it sure sounded as if the experts knew what they were doing.

But while monetary targets excited segments of the academic and financial communities, they proved to have a fatal flaw: they didn't work. Both in Canada, where they were applied gradually, and in the U.S., where a more abrupt approach was taken, the targets simply proved unreliable as a way of assessing the inflationary momentum in the economy. The problem was partly that it was difficult to get an accurate measure of the money supply, given the wide variety of financial and banking options available.

The bottom line was that inflation continued to rage. At times, it seemed that the inflationary psychology was too deeply ingrained to be broken, as some people in desperation signed up for mortgages with ludicrously high interest rates of 17 and 18 per cent, because they feared rates would go higher still. By the early eighties, both countries had abandoned the targeting system, leaving central bankers once again forced to admit that they were relying on little more than intuition as they decided whether to take a sledgehammer to the economy.

For Bouey, taking that sledgehammer to the Canadian economy was a deeply disturbing experience. In his public appearances as the nation's central banker, he felt obliged to maintain a stern-faced toughness at all times, lest the financial markets sense any sign of weakness, any fading of resolve in the inflation war. In reality, Bouey was anything but happy. A modest man with a self-deprecating sense of humour, he had never forgotten the deprivation and despair he had witnessed first-hand in small-town Saskatchewan growing up during the Depression. He had gone on to be a prizewinning economics student at Queen's in the late forties, when the department was still dominated by the men who had helped design an activist role for the federal government and the central bank in the thirties. One of Bouey's mentors at Queen's was W.A. Mackintosh, who had written the Liberal government's white paper establishing high employment as a national objective for the postwar years.

Bouey had seen the storm coming, and had taken precautions—more so than the Fed had. The monetary targets may have been a political scapegoat for him, but they had also been a systematic method of gradually tightening the screws in a way that he felt offered the hope of avoiding severe tightening later. Now, with the failure of that method hopelessly evident, he decided to follow the U.S. car—the one with two drivers veering wildly out of control. Following the U.S. lead, he cranked up interest rates—the prime hit an incomprehensible 22.5 per cent in the summer of 1981—until the economy finally wheezed and gasped into submission, bringing inflation down with it.

By the fall of 1981, the economy was in the grip of the worst recession in almost fifty years. The situation never got as bad as the thirties, partly because by this point Canada had in place a substantial social welfare system that propped up the unemployed and kept a regular stream of money pumping into the economy, preventing further contraction. Still, with unemployment reaching 11 per cent, the suffering was immense, as jobs disappeared, businesses went bankrupt and the hopes and dreams of hundreds of thousands of Canadians were dashed. In November, a crowd estimated at close to 100,000 gathered on Parliament Hill to protest the high interest rates and the crushing of the economy. Across the street, the Bank of Canada remained a shuttered fortress.

The devastation sparked the beginning of a new protest movement that was to sputter along throughout the eighties and into the nineties, trying to mount an attack on—or at least a defence against—the massive power shift that was taking place in the country. Since the Depression, there had been a consensus that full employment should be the nation's top priority. That deeply held conviction had been part of the problem for Bouey in the seventies as he tried, unsuccessfully, to convince politicians of the need for restraint while they continued to focus on the need to keep the country employed.

But now, in the economic chaos of the early eighties, that consensus was breaking down. For those who owned or controlled financial capital, the seventies had been a watershed. They had seen their financial security eroded, as the government attempted to maintain employment levels. No longer did there seem to be an ever-growing economy with enough to go around for all. Now it looked as if something had to give. It was going to be "us" or "them." The country was in the midst of a game of musical chairs and the music was soon going to stop. When it did, a lot of people would be left standing.

As divisions in the country deepened, the newly forming protest movement found its most eloquent voice in an unexpected place—the upper echelons of the Catholic Church. Despite the formidable opposition of G. Emmett Cardinal Carter, Archbishop of Toronto, a majority of the country's bishops backed a surprisingly strong statement attacking "the scourge of unemployment." The statement amounted to an explicit rejection of the traditional approach of dealing with poverty and suffering solely through Christian works of charity.

Invoking the social justice tradition of the Church, the bishops decried the failure of Canadian policies to respect the "dignity of human work in God's plan for Creation... It is through the activity of work that people are able to exercise their creative spirit, realize their human dignity, and share in creation." Abandoning any pretense of staying out of politics, the bishops urged that the fight against unemployment be made the country's top priority, and took direct aim at a monetary policy focused on inflation control. "First, unemployment, rather than inflation, should be recognized as the number one problem to be tackled in overcoming the present crisis."

The bishops enjoyed a brief flurry of attention. For several days after the release of their statement in December 1982, they made the front pages of newspapers across the country and figured prominently in national radio and television coverage. Bishop Remi De Roo of Victoria, an instigator of the original statement, emerged as a minor national hero and champion of the underdog—a role that was later reinforced when De Roo got into a public war of words with arch-capitalist Conrad Black. Labour leaders loudly endorsed the bishops' statement, as did community groups and leaders from other churches. Editorial writers and columnists across the country were generally supportive, while letters to newspapers and callers to phone-ins shows revealed a high level of public approval. Reporters used the statement to grill cabinet ministers coming out of the House of Commons. Trudeau, on a trip to the Far East, was asked pointed questions about it at a press conference in Thailand. It seemed as if the tide was finally turning, that the bishops' statement had touched a raw nerve of public anger over unemployment and that that anger could no longer be contained.

But the moment would soon pass. Not that the ideas and the feelings disappeared. They remained very much a part of the Canadian mindset, and they would resurface many times during the succeeding years in protests against free trade and social cutbacks. And they were still apparently present during the 1993 federal election campaign when the majority of Canadians told pollsters that unemployment was their number one concern.

But, more and more, the momentum for full employment was fading as a political force in the country. Whereas the Trudeau cabinet had felt concerned enough in the seventies to try to tackle unemployment, that concern was eventually replaced by a new attitude, which held that full employment was simply unattainable or, in a nastier version of the same approach, that the unemployed were to blame for their plight. Certainly the idea that achieving full employment should be the government's top priority fell increasingly out of favour among those actually running the country.

In the seclusion of a private meeting room in Ottawa's Chateau Laurier Hotel, a nearly violent altercation between John Crow and a national labour leader revealed just how far off the political agenda the goal of full employment had moved by the spring of 1989. Crow had requested the meeting with the executive committee of the Canadian Labour Market and Productivity Centre, a government-sponsored group designed to bring together business and labour, after the centre had produced a report critical of Crow's high interest rates. This was more than the usual slap from labour that Crow was used to, since the group also included business heavyweights Tom d'Aquino, president of the Business Council on National Issues, ITT Canada president Tom Savage and IPSCO president Roger Phillips.

As Crow addressed the group in an almost professorial style, it became clear that, in his view, the real goal of the Bank of Canada was to protect the value of investors' financial assets. "People do care about the value of their assets, and they should care," he said. "And in my view it's the most important thing that monetary policy can do is to make sure that people can maintain the value of their assets... And it's our job to provide that confidence." This wasn't at all to the liking of labour leaders at the meeting, including Shirley Carr, who was then head of the Canadian Labour Congress. "I feel like I've just been lectured to, and had a sledgehammer thrown at me," she protested. Crow's harangue on monetary policy also angered John Fryer, head of the National Union of Provincial Government Employees.

Fryer was outraged that Crow seemed indifferent to the effects his policies were having on the country's working population. With emotion rising in his voice, Fryer told Crow, "[W]e think your preoccupation with inflation is keeping [the] unemployment rate higher than it need be… The people I represent come from a different reality than you do. They're hurting."

To the son of a janitor from the roughest part of London, these sounded like fighting words. Crow was accustomed to broadsides from labour, but he wasn't used to this sort of attack, which made him sound like some silver-spoon-in-the-mouth child of the elite. In a rare show of emotion about his past, Crow threw his humble origins onto the table: "I was also brought [up] in England, Mr. Fryer. I was brought up in the East End of London; don't try to lecture me about class. OK. Just remember."

With the two men apparently on the verge of a fist fight, Shirley Carr intervened to restore order. But the bad feeling persisted, as Crow dismissed suggestions that he should focus his efforts on trying to alleviate unemployment and recession. "People hurting, people with lousy jobs; what am I going to do about it?" Crow shrugged. This was certainly a far cry from Graham Towers's description of how much "a determined state and a determined people with a single objective can do to provide employment and raise the national output."

But Crow's position at the meeting sent the same message that he was to deliver often in speeches and testimony:

that it was not his job to worry about unemployment and recession. His job was only to focus on controlling inflation. He acknowledged that this interpretation of his role diverged from what was set out in the Bank of Canada Act. As he told an audience at the University of Pretoria in South Africa in 1993, "In Canada, the preamble to the Bank of Canada Act does suggest a lot of different economic goals. But...the practical focus is unambiguously on price stability."

Crow didn't see this as a dereliction of duty. Rather, he insisted, it was all that was possible; he was constrained by the limited tools he had at his disposal. "Since monetary policy involves the use of a single tool, providing liquidity to the financial system, one might well ask how monetary policy could be expected to achieve more than one economic objective," he said in Pretoria. He went on to suggest that the only way that monetary policy could hope to contribute to broader economic goals—including raising employment—was by keeping inflation under control. In the long run, this would raise employment more than could happen under a regime of high inflation, according to Crow.

Thus, Crow created an essentially circular argument in an apparent attempt to remove himself from the hotseat over unemployment. It wasn't that he was rejecting the goals of encouraging employment and growth. It was simply that, given the tools he had available, the best way he could contribute to these fine goals was by doing the one thing that he was already doing—controlling inflation. (It was never quite clear how this would contribute to raising employment, particularly since its immediate impact was to drive employment down.)

Nonetheless, it was an ingenious little argument, which he repeated at every opportunity, and it provided him with a teflon coating. How could you attack a guy for doing his best, when he just didn't have the means at his disposal to do all the things you wanted him to do? But while this was effective as a debating tactic, driving his opponents dizzy with frustration, the argument was essentially lame. Clearly, the one tool Crow had at his disposal—"providing liquidity to the financial system"—had an enormous potential to influence many aspects of the economy, not just the rate of inflation. The amount of liquidity—or cash—in the system was absolutely crucial in determining whether businesses would have access to credit, whether they'd be able to function and prosper and hire employees, and whether consumers would be able to afford to buy the goods that they produced.

As we've seen, it wasn't just that Crow's war on inflation risked damaging the economy. It was worse: throwing the economy into recession was the *vehicle* for fighting inflation. By reducing the liquidity—that is, by cutting back the availability of credit through higher interest rates—the Bank was able to slow down the whole economy, which, among other things, slowed down inflation. Pierre Fortin described it as "the recession method" of inflation control.

At the very least, then, Crow should have acknowledged that the Bank could not carry out its high-interest-rate war against inflation without inflicting collateral damage on other aspects of the economy. Yet somehow all this collateral damage was absent from his description of how monetary policy worked. His refusal to deal with this damaging aspect of his policy was a bit like the head of a chemical company insisting that his firm was only capable of producing chemical products, so it couldn't possibly do anything about the pollutants it was dumping in the river.

For Crow, the problem lay not with his policies, but with the original preamble to the Bank Act, which had defined the Bank's goals too broadly. Hence, what was needed was to change the mandate, narrowing it to an exclusive focus on fighting inflation. This was a brash idea, to say the least. And in the context of a brutal recession, it was nothing short of audacious. Rather than being on the defensive for his unpopular policies, Crow was advocating that the Canadian constitution be changed to incorporate them. The "recession method" of inflation control was, in effect, to become the supreme law of the land. Astonishingly, this became part of the Mulroney government's political agenda.

It is interesting to look at the sources of pressure for this change. It would be an understatement to say that there was no pressure coming from members of the public who, had they been consulted, would almost certainly have opposed a plan to make it easier for the Bank to ignore the goal of encouraging employment. But while the public remained uninformed and outside the debate, the C.D. Howe Institute was more than willing to step into the breach. Indeed, much of the impetus for the change appears to have originated from within the institute.

In May 1991, economist David Laidler, an Adjunct Scholar at the institute, whom we encountered in Chapter Four, wrote a booklet that became instrumental in the move to redesign the mandate of the Bank. Laidler's booklet, published by the Howe in the trough of the recession, was highly enthusiastic about the performance of the Bank throughout this period of high interest rates and tight money. The problem, in Laidler's view, was not with the Bank, but with the public's failure to understand what good things the Bank was doing. "The Bank is performing well, but is widely perceived not to be." Therefore, Laidler reasoned, the answer lay in making a few changes that would satisfy the public.

Laidler made clear that these changes should not be substantive, that they should not change the way the Bank actually operated. Essentially, the adjustments were to be cosmetic, designed to satisfy the public without altering the Bank's ability to conduct its all-out war on inflation. "[S]uch changes in governance would probably have little effect on the conduct of monetary policy, but they would give that policy some badly needed political legitimacy." In other words, don't change the Bank, just give it a new look so the public will think it has been changed.

Above all, Laidler wanted to alter the Bank's mandate, to restrict it to an exclusive focus on fighting inflation. Laidler argued that the old mandate, which included the goal of encouraging employment and growth, was outdated: "These are wrong goals for the 1990s. The target of price-level stability is both appropriate and feasible, and the Bank's mandate should be updated accordingly." But once again, the problem was not altering the Bank's behaviour; the Bank was already ignoring its mandate on the employment front and single-mindedly pursuing price stability. The problem was in changing the mandate to reflect this single purpose goal, so that the Bank could be removed from public criticism. If the Bank were doing exactly what its mandate said it should be doing, there could be no reason to attack it; it would thus acquire "political legitimacy."

Crow was enthusiastic about Laidler's argument and went on to embellish it, arguing that such a change would make the Bank more "accountable." This notion of greater accountability had a nice democratic ring to it. But if we look closer at what Crow meant, we see that the purpose was, once again, to silence public criticism rather than to make changes that would address the substance of the criticism. As Crow argued on many occasions, if the Bank's mandate were limited to price stability, then the Bank could be made more accountable. If it failed to meet certain specified inflation targets, for instance, it would have to answer to Parliament about this failure. This is a weird concept of increased accountability. Crow was arguing that the Bank should be made strictly accountable, but for only one aspect of the economy—even though its actions impinged on all aspects of the economy. According to this scenario, the Bank would henceforth escape any responsibility for what really mattered: the overall health of the economy.

Laidler's argument for limiting the Bank's role was quickly picked up inside the government as well. A month after the booklet's release, the parliamentary finance committee, controlled by the majority Conservatives, decided to set up a subcommittee to consider whether the Bank's mandate should be changed. A key stimulus to the establishment of the subcommittee was "provided by the very important monograph written by Professor David Laidler and published by the C.D. Howe Institute," the subcommittee noted in a later report.

And, as the government worked out the final package of its proposals for constitutional reform that summer, Laidler's suggestion for reforming the Bank's mandate surprisingly ended up there as well. Among the twenty-eight proposals released by the government in September 1991 was Proposal No. 17, which advocated changing the Bank of Canada's mandate in the way Laidler had recommended. The similarity between the proposals was striking, as the subcommittee noted: "The solutions proposed [by the Government] were similar in direction, if not in detail, to Laidler's suggestions." The inclusion of Proposal No. 17 was curious, since public discussion during the national unity debate had not focused on the Bank of Canada or the need to reform its mandate.

When the subcommittee held hearings in the fall of 1991, there was support for the proposal from experts in the Bank of Canada, including Crow, as well as from academic economists and members of the banking and financial world. But the majority of the twenty-five witnesses, including academic economists and experts on central banks in other countries, opposed the plan to change the Bank's mandate. Drawing on these views, the subcommittee concluded that narrowing the mandate would be a mistake. "First and most general, controlling inflation is not the only legitimate goal of monetary policy...monetary policy has the capacity to influence economic activity in the short run and cannot therefore shun responsibility for responding to events that may throw the economy far off its potential growth path and output... Also, how price stability is attained and maintained has implications for the real economy that monetary authorities should not be permitted to ignore."

It was a defeat for those trying to entrench the all-out inflation war in the constitution. But it was a revealing episode that showed just how far many—inside the Bank and in the government as well as in financial and academic circles—wanted to go in freeing monetary authorities from any concerns about the impact of their policies on unemployment.

In keeping with the discreet nature of the Bank of Canada, John Crow's farewell parties in January 1994 were very private affairs. There was an elegant reception for 115 at Montreal's exclusive St. James Club and, the following night, a dinner for 135 at Toronto's posh National Club. The guest list for these events reads like a *Who's Who* of the financial world, featuring the major players from all the chartered banks, trust companies and investment houses. While the Canadian financial community had never really warmed to Crow personally, it had staunchly backed him and his war on inflation. (Crow had been held in even higher regard in international financial circles, where foreign investors were thrilled by his willingness to push up interest rates and the value of the Canadian dollar. His stature in international banking circles was reflected in the fact that in September 1993 he had been selected by the central bankers of the world's most advanced nations to head the prestigious G-10, the Bank for International Settlement's powerful inner fraternity, which effectively oversees the world's monetary system at secretive meetings in Basel, Switzerland.)

Members of the Canadian public, who paid for the two farewell parties through their taxes, were not invited or even informed of the events. Only later did a press report surface after a reporter obtained documents about the events through a freedom-of-information request.

The press report focused on the fact that almost $30,000 of taxpayers' money was spent on a series of farewell events for Crow, despite the governor's familiar lectures about the need for government restraint. Politicians from both the Reform Party and the NDP joined in the accusations of wasteful government spending. But there was another aspect to the parties that received less attention—the special relationship they reveal between the Bank and the powerful financial communities in Canada's two biggest cities.

A select group of less than three hundred individuals from the financial world were considered by the Bank to be appropriate guests at these events. Why? Certainly, members of the financial community have an interest in influencing the Bank on behalf of their wealthy clients. And the Bank, as the agent in marketing government bonds, is interested in knowing what wealth-holders are thinking and what they are planning to do with their money.

But there is another community out there—the broader Canadian community that doesn't sell bonds or necessarily even know someone who owns one. This broader community is affected just as powerfully by the actions of the Bank as are bondholders and bond sellers. The point is not that the entire country should have been invited to John Crow's farewell parties. The point is rather that, in its close relationship with the financial community, the Bank perhaps comes to share some of the same preoccupations of those in the financial world, and loses sight of the often conflicting interests of those in the broader community.

When the story about the farewell parties surfaced in the press, Bank spokesman Guy Theriault rushed to point out that the Bank had paid for the parties only because there hadn't been time to arrange for the Toronto and Montreal financial communities to pick up some of the costs, as had been the case when Gerald Bouey had retired as governor in 1987. The implication was that, had the financial communities paid, there would have been no issue. But surely the question is not, why should taxpayers be stuck paying for this?—although this is, of course, a good question—but, why are these people so close that they are all partying together? Why is the financial community so pleased with Crow that they are paying tribute to his governorship? Would it have been possible to find a labour union anywhere in the country that would have held a party to honour Crow, no matter who paid the bill?

Perhaps these sound like quibbling questions. Perhaps it is simply a given the banking and the financial community go hand in hand. But there is also an assumption at the very foundation of our political system that public institutions like the Bank of Canada should operate in the best interests of the country as a whole, not just in the narrow interests of one particular group.

On the same day that a report about the Crow farewell parties appeared on the front page of the *Globe and Mail*, another article only a few inches away described the brutal impact of the recession on young people. The story it told was as grim and bleak as the Crow parties were lavish and indulgent: "The recession has had such a disastrous effect on the job prospects of young Canadians that it may actually have created a lost generation," the article began. Certainly no members of the lost generation were at the Crow farewell parties. And yet, ultimately, Crow had as great an impact on their lives as he'd had on the lives of the bankers and bond dealers crowded around the punch bowl, fêting their hero in the luxurious private clubs.

The *Globe* made no attempt to link the two articles, even though they were both, in a sense, about the legacy of John Crow.

CHAPTER SEVEN

The Executioners' Song

In the early weeks of October 1994, the cherub-like face of Bill Robson became a regular sight on television screens across the country. As the federal government tried to sell the nation a new package of social spending cuts, the media had eagerly seized on Robson as the perfect guy to come on TV talk shows and explain why all this cutting was necessary.

Robson, of course, is the C.D. Howe expert on monetary policy whom we've already encountered a number of times. Unlike many commentators on both sides of the political spectrum, Robson is never shrill, aggressive or mean. He expresses himself calmly and carefully, and always comes across as sincere, well-meaning and knowledgeable. He appears as a wrinkle-less font of wisdom, a young man who can speak to all generations about the need for restraint. He certainly doesn't look like someone who, in effect, represents the most powerful interests on Bay Street. This, of course, is why he's so effective.

As Ottawa prepared to take a run at social programs in the fall of 1994, Robson and the C.D. Howe Institute were anxious to become major players in the political battle that was bound to ensue. This was a moment not to be missed.

For years, the Howe had been complaining relentlessly about the need to cut government spending. It had produced volume after volume proclaiming the need to "reform" unemployment insurance and welfare and pensions and health care and education—reforms that were always geared to reducing these programs, cutting their scope and size and cost. But, although Ottawa had certainly done lots of cutting over the previous decade, somehow the social safety net remained stubbornly resilient, with the Canadian public resistant to the drastic kinds of cuts that the Howe had in mind. When the issue of overhauling Canada's social safety net surfaced briefly during the federal election campaign in the fall of 1993, Conservative Kim Campbell distanced herself as much as possible from what promised to be a political minefield.

But by the autumn of 1994, the resistance to social cuts appeared to be waning. The public was weary from yet another round of deficit pornography, complete with graphs depicting mountains of debt and the voluptuous curves of debt-to-GDP ratios. The slick, unpopular Conservative government, with its close ties to Bay Street, had been replaced with the more friendly looking, home-style Chrétien government, which spoke the same language of deficit and restraint but enjoyed the trust of the public. The Liberals had even placed Lloyd Axworthy, traditionally regarded as a progressive in the left wing of the party, in charge of overhauling the social safety net. If any Liberal was trusted by social welfare advocates, it was Axworthy.

At the Howe, there was a feeling that the time had finally arrived. A major social policy review, which had seemed unthinkable only a year earlier, had now been completed. The elusive social policy beast had been hunted down, captured and held still for thorough inspection. If ever the beast was to be carved up, the moment was now. For months, the Howe's analysts had been gearing up for

Axworthy's announcement, ready to pounce with their extreme solutions. As soon as he made his move, they would make theirs.

In the first week of October, the government showed its hand. Axworthy's vague proposals largely followed the policy direction that the Howe had long been advocating: severe cutbacks in unemployment insurance, an emphasis on making the unemployed work for their cheques and a move to shift the costs of higher education onto the individual student. Axworthy's attempt to put a bright face on his reform—dressing it up with talk of fighting child poverty—was quickly overwhelmed by the government's central agenda. An internal memo, leaked to the press the day of Axworthy's announcement, revealed that the Chrétien government was committed to cutting $7.5 billion out of social spending. Axworthy denied that any prearranged amount had been set, but his words had a hollow ring. Two weeks later, Paul Martin confirmed that the government was determined to stick to its plans to reduce the deficit to 3 per cent of GDP by 1996–97, and that somewhere between $6 billion and $9 billion was going to have to be cut; $7.5 billion certainly sounded like a likely compromise.

But the Howe would have none of it. With the social policy beast all tied up and ready for the kill, there was no way that the institute was going to let it slink away again with nothing but a big chunk of flesh cut out of its side. Summoning the media to a press conference, the Howe produced a twenty-eight-page document called *The Courage to Act*, which boldly laid out two choices for the government. Ottawa could either opt for the Howe's "radical" solution, which would require it to make cuts of about $18.5 billion, including cuts to traditionally sacrosanct areas like health care and pensions. Or, if it lacked the courage, the government could opt for the institute's "moderate" package: only $17 billion in cuts. Front and centre was Robson, making it all sound benign and helpful.

There was a certain audacity to the Howe's approach. Essentially, it was attempting to dictate that the government make gigantic social spending cuts in order to eliminate the deficit. The cuts were deeper than any we'd ever seen, and the goal—the complete elimination of the deficit—was far more ambitious than what the Liberals had campaigned on. While the ill-fated Tories had pledged to eliminate the deficit, the Liberals had consistently committed themselves to the more moderate goal of reducing it to 3 per cent of GDP in three years.

A year later, however, the Howe had decided that it wasn't satisfied with the Liberal promise. The 3 per cent goal "is not enough," it declared, apparently quite comfortable with overruling what the majority of Canadians seemed to find acceptable. Having set out its two options, the Howe then graciously declared, "Neither package is written in stone." Lest that sounded as if it was prepared to compromise, the institute made clear that it wasn't. "[F]lexibility in choosing among the options is possible," it noted. But the "bottom line" was "budget balance"; in other words, the deficit had to go. On that issue, the institute would tolerate no dissent. Considering that the institute represented absolutely no one but its own members, this seemed somewhat bossy, to say the least.

But not even this was enough to satisfy some deficit extremists, as the public debate quickly turned into a contest of deficit one-upmanship. Andrew Coyne, a *Globe and Mail* columnist and son of former Bank of Canada governor James Coyne, dismissed Martin's goals as "trivial," and advocated a position that went considerably beyond even the C.D. Howe's most extreme solution. Coyne wanted to slash government spending by 20 per cent over four years—roughly $24 billion.

As the chants for deeper and deeper cuts developed into

a collective howl, what was striking was the lack of apparent concern about the fall-out from all this cutting. The Howe blithely advocated the slashing of billions of dollars from every area of social spending—from unemployment insurance to welfare to health care to pensions—as if nothing more than a bunch of numbers were at stake, as if there would be little impact on the lives of countless Canadians. Yet it abruptly abandoned that cool detachment when the subject turned to something that affected the lives of C.D. Howe members—registered retirement savings plans. In fact, the Axworthy proposals didn't even mention RRSPs, one of the favourite tax breaks of upper income earners. Still, the very thought that the government might be contemplating reducing this generous tax break in the interests of deficit reduction clearly upset the analysts at the Howe. Such a move would be "unconscionable," the analysts fumed.

But perhaps the most astonishing thing about *The Courage to Act* was the complete absence of any mention of the role that our zero inflation policy played in driving up the deficit. This was particularly intriguing since the report was co-authored by Robson, who was thoroughly familiar with monetary policy and its effects.

Robson had in fact conceded in other publications that a strong anti-inflation policy has the effect of driving up unemployment and reducing economic output. Indeed, he had written that this phenomenon is one of the "best established in economics… The existence and, to some extent, the magnitude of these effects are uncontroversial." And unemployment and loss of output are important factors in driving up deficits and debt, since they reduce tax revenues and raise social assistance costs—a phenomenon widely acknowledged by economists. Even a strong anti-inflation fighter like John Grant, a former director of Wood Gundy, notes that the battle against inflation has played a key role in driving up the debt, which he regards as an unfortunate aspect of the zero inflation policy. The C.D. Howe Institute prefers to see no connection at all.

Nowhere in *The Courage to Act*, therefore, was there even a hint that the zero inflation policy pursued by the Bank since 1988 might have in any way contributed to our debt and deficit problems. Instead, Robson and Tom Kierans managed to deflect the entire deficit problem away from zero inflation and onto the "social policy deficit."

This omission has important implications. If the Howe were to acknowledge that the zero inflation policy played a significant role in driving up the debt, it would be obliged to acknowledge that the beneficiaries of the zero inflation policy—the bondholders and bond dealers so well represented among the institute's members—should at least bear some part of the burden of deficit reduction. But instead of acknowledging the "zero inflation deficit," they shift the entire blame onto social policy. The debt becomes the exclusive responsibility of people receiving social benefits, and the cuts should therefore come exclusively out of their pockets. As for all those investors who reaped enormous rewards from the anti-inflation war, they are completely off the hook. They are suddenly invisible in the ongoing deficit drama, having taken their money and disappeared. All we see now are the unemployed hordes with their hands out.

But as Robson's face filled TV screens across the country throughout the month of October, none of this was ever really mentioned. Instead, the debate raged on about how deeply social spending had to be cut. Would it be the moderate solution proposed by Axworthy and Martin, or the more severe solutions proposed by the man with the angelic face? Or would it be the still more extreme solution being advocated in the columns of Canada's national newspaper? Amid these strident demands for social spending cuts, the possibility that the problem lay elsewhere—in our decision to battle inflation with high interest rates—remained out of sight.

Whenever anyone suggested lowering interest rates rather than slashing every social program in sight, Robson simply batted the subject down like a bothersome fly. "I wish it were that easy," shrugged Robson pleasantly during one debate on "CBC Newsworld," in response to a suggestion from economist Michael McCracken that the Bank of Canada lower interest rates.

In his friendly voice, Robson went on to say that lower interest rates had been tried before: "This isn't anything new that Mike's suggesting. I mean, Latin America is a case study." McCracken guffawed loudly in the background, and tried to protest the absurdity of the comparison, but Robson just kept talking and deftly changed the subject to the impressive social spending cuts taking place in Alberta and Saskatchewan. As a result, the national television audience never got to hear McCracken explain just how ludicrous Robson's response was. With Canada's inflation rate running at 1.7 per cent, Robson was drawing a comparison to countries where inflation had been known to reach up to 1,000 per cent a year in the eighties. It would be like saying we shouldn't have a police force because the case of Haiti proves that police can get out of control.

But, lest anyone get the idea that a little inflation might not be a disastrous thing, the Bank of Canada stepped in to squelch that dangerous thought from developing. Governor Gordon Thiessen, who had kept a low profile since replacing John Crow earlier in the year, emerged into the limelight in mid-October with a speech in Halifax warning about the dangers of big deficits and declaring his unwavering determination to keep the lid on inflation. "Our commitment to our inflation targets is without reservation. There are too many benefits from price stability for the bank to take any risks in letting inflation get away on us again."

Thiessen's words were greeted with enthusiasm on Bay Street. Leo de Bever, chief economist at Nomura Canada

Inc., told the *Financial Post* that this proved what those who knew Thiessen had known all along, that "he wasn't really a patsy." Indeed, de Bever had good reason to applaud Thiessen for sticking firmly to the anti-inflation track. De Bever's employer, Nomura Canada, represented Japanese investors who had bought billions of dollars' worth of Canadian bonds when the Canadian dollar was high. A decision to loosen monetary policy would cause the dollar to drop further and result in big losses for de Bever's clients. Only a patsy would allow that sort of thing to happen.

So as the deficit continued to dominate public discourse throughout the fall, the idea of lowering interest rates somehow remained on the sidelines. As far as the public heard, dealing with the debt by reducing interest rates was a kooky idea that had failed in Latin America, and in any event had been ruled out definitively here by the Bank of Canada governor. But was it really such a kooky idea?

One person who thought it wasn't was Pierre Fortin, a highly respected economist, as his election to the prestigious post of president of the Canadian Economics Association attested. For several years, Fortin, a rigorous-minded academic, had been alarmed as he watched the Bank's single-minded pursuit of zero inflation. In his view, the research carried out by the Bank was simply inadequate to justify such a bold policy direction. Fortin's own research, as we saw in Chapter Four, strongly suggested that the costs to the economy in terms of unemployment and lost economic growth were far higher than the Bank was willing to concede. Fortin had written a number of academic articles saying so and had become an annoying thorn in the Bank's flesh.

As the storm over the deficit raged in the early fall of 1994, Fortin had just completed a lengthy, technical study that proposed a wholly different solution from the slashing advocated by Ottawa and the C.D. Howe Institute. Fortin's study, which had been partially funded by the federal

Finance department, concluded that the country's deficit problems were almost entirely the result of the recession. "[T]he present slump is entirely responsible for the fact that the deficit-to-GDP ratio is currently exceeding the 3 per cent benchmark. This is a crucial, yet widely ignored aspect of the present budget quandary." Fortin went on to debunk the popular notion that the Canadian economy had now recovered from the recession of the early nineties. "[T]he solution to the 'mystery of the jobless recovery' is that there has been no job creation because there has been no true recovery," he argued.

Fortin's solution was straightforward. The only way out of the economic quagmire of spiralling debt was to pull ourselves out of the recession, and the only way to do this was through a deliberate policy of lowering interest rates. This would stimulate growth, thereby raising tax revenues and reducing social expenditures. Fortin anticipated the yelping that would be heard from the Howe and the Bay Street brokerage houses, and, in a methodical way, he dealt with their arguments. He dismissed the notion that lower interest rates would set off inflation; there was far too much slack in the economy for inflation to be a serious risk. Indeed, all this slack provided an unusual opportunity to stimulate growth without fuelling inflation, he argued. "[T]he potential for non-inflationary growth in Canada is extraordinary."

The real obstacle to lower interest rates wasn't the sort of problem that was bandied about on TV current affairs shows, and presented as insurmountable. The real problem, he insisted, was something that rarely surfaced in the debate: the strong opposition that would come from foreign investors. These foreigners would see their bond holdings drop in value if lower interest rates caused the Canadian dollar to fall. Although foreign investors were largely absent from the Canadian political scene, they were amply represented in the debate here by their brokers on Bay Street and

by analysts at the C.D. Howe Institute. Naturally, these eloquent Canadian spokespersons were going to make it sound
as if anything that hurt their clients' interests would hurt the
entire Canadian economy.

Fortin said that this was simply untrue; there would be no
harm done to the Canadian economy. The only harm would
be to foreign investors, and it would not be very great.
Besides, these foreign investors had already been generously
compensated by Canada. They had made magnificent profits
on Canadian bonds in the early nineties. And they continued to buy our bonds—not because they were trying to help
Canada out, but because Canada was a safe and profitable
place to park their money. Sometimes there was an extra
bonus from the exchange, sometimes there was a loss. Still,
overall, the prospects for foreign investors to earn handsome
returns on Canadian bonds had been and continued to be
excellent. Of course, Bay Street dealers would squawk and
squeal and insist on the policy that provided their foreign
clients with the handsomest return possible, but such a policy was very damaging to the Canadian economy. Fortin
concluded with a position that didn't seem very radical,
except perhaps on Bay Street: he argued that Canadian policy "should be more concerned with the welfare of
Canadians than with the welfare of foreign investors."

But what if foreign investors then decided to stop buying
Canadian bonds in the future? Fortin said this wouldn't happen. He noted that lower Canadian interest rates would
result in a lower Canadian dollar. But a low dollar would
actually make our new bonds attractive, he explained, since
investors would then have a chance to make a handsome
gain on the exchange if the Canadian dollar rose—as it
probably would—by the time they cashed in these bonds.

Fortin, who had traditionally considered himself on the
conservative end of the political spectrum, argued that there
should be a freeze on government spending for at least two

years in the interests of debt management. But he argued that the consequences of the deep cuts that the government was contemplating—let alone what the C.D. Howe Institute and Andrew Coyne were advocating—would be "horrendous."

Fortin's views remained marginalized, however. The debate focused almost exclusively on how deep the spending cuts would have to be. Astonishingly, the whole subject of our zero inflation policy, and how it was driving up our deficit, was left utterly out of the mainstream discussion, despite massive evidence that it was, if anything, the major contributor to our deficit woes.

Having convinced ourselves instead that our social programs were the culprits, we remained hell-bent on tracking them down and slaughtering them. Yet, in our hot pursuit, we had failed to notice the real culprits sitting tanned and relaxed by the side of the road, urging on the chase! Indeed, as the debate raged on, the proponents of zero inflation on Bay Street, at the Howe and at the Bank of Canada kept up a steady and relentless pressure for spending cuts. It now seemed like only a question of time before their target—billions of dollars' worth of Canada's social programs—would be trussed and ready for the slaughter.

For the powerful gentlemen who sat on the Legislative Council of Upper Canada, it was simply out of the question. The proposition that every child in the province of Upper Canada should go to school was a republican-type notion that was not applicable in the British North American colony. Not only was the concept shamelessly American, but it was simply beyond the financial means of the province.

By the time the Legislative Council gave a firm "no" in 1836, the issue had been festering for some time. The concept of universal schooling was favoured by the Legislative Assembly, the province's popularly elected body. But the idea had been repeatedly vetoed by the Legislative Council, the upper body of religious, professional and business leaders appointed by the British Crown to effectively rule the province.

The elite gentlemen of the Council felt comfortable with their decision; they were operating in the tradition firmly established decades earlier by the colony's first lieutenant-governor, John Graves Simcoe. The aristocratic Simcoe, born to privilege back in England, was determined to foster and maintain a proper British form of civilization in the Canadian colony. Key to this was education, but only for a small, select group—for the "Children of the Principal People of this Country," as Simcoe wrote. Rather than squandering resources on ordinary boys—no one was seriously considering the possibility of educating girls at this point—Simcoe favoured the establishment of a small number of excellent schools where the sons of the elite would receive a classical education to prepare them for their eventual role in running the colony. As for those outside the elite, Simcoe was content to let them fend for themselves. As he put it, "[S]uch education as may be necessary for people in the lower degrees of life...may at present be provided for them by their connections and relations."

For decades after his departure in 1796, the education system of Upper Canada closely resembled Simcoe's vision. Modelled on the British system, a handful of "grammar" schools were set up to educate the sons of well-to-do families in the colony. Although the schools were partially subsidized through provincial revenues, they were only really accessible to those who could afford the tuition, and who could do without their sons' labour on the farm. By the mid-1830s, with the colony's population approaching 240,000, there were still only about 300 boys attending these grammar schools. (In addition, three private schools, specializing primarily in Latin and Greek, catered to the elite.)

Within the elected Assembly, the elitism of the education

system had always been a sore point. By 1816, the Assembly had succeeded in pushing through a bill that, in principle, provided for elementary schooling for all boys. But the funding for these "common" schools was minimal. As a result, they were often housed in churches, town halls or even abandoned taverns. They had nothing but the most primitive education tools—maps, books and blackboards were considered unaffordable luxuries in the public system—and teachers were paid one-quarter of what teachers in the elite "grammar" schools received. In fact, even that salary was considered excessive, and the pay of common school teachers was later cut so deeply that in some districts they were receiving a mere pittance—a fraction of what a craftsman, for instance, would earn. It was not unusual for a common school teacher to be a transient who could find no other work. And while common schools were theoretically accessible to all, in fact, only about half the male children attended.

So it was with high expectations that the Assembly sent educator Charles Duncombe to the United States in 1835 with the double assignment of studying the U.S. lunatic asylums as well as its education system. Duncombe came back particularly impressed by the school system in New York, and proposed that Upper Canada adopt a similar system. This would mean greatly extending and improving the existing common school system, and providing for adequate funding through local taxation.

But the learned gentlemen on the Legislative Council felt things had gone far enough in the direction of public education. The cost of such a system would be exorbitant. The popular notion of universal schooling was rejected, and would not be fully put into law in Upper Canada for another thirty-five years.

More than a century and a half later, this nineteenth-century debate over universal schooling has a kind of quirky old-world charm that conjures up images of prissy men in wigs and clerical collars fulminating against the vulgarities of the common people. Certainly no one ever talks any more about restricting education to "the principal people of this country," or relegating the education of "people in the lower degrees of life" to their relatives. Yet increasingly, whether intentionally or not, we seem to be contemplating policies that risk taking us back to that sort of elitism.

Of course, it is never presented this way. On the contrary, it is generally portrayed as being motivated by a desire to help out those at the bottom. The Axworthy reform proposals, for instance, advocated revamping higher education in a way that ostensibly would be more progressive. The plan, adapted from a scheme that has been pushed heavily both in *Globe and Mail* editorials and in a booklet produced by the C.D. Howe Institute, involves providing a larger, more accessible pool of funds for student loans. The loans would be repayable after graduation and the repayment schedule would in some way be based on the income of the graduate, giving the appearance of progressiveness. Although the details provided are sketchy, the progressiveness appears to be limited to the speed with which the loans are to be repaid; a lower income means a longer time to pay off the debt, not a lower debt. All this is done in the name of making higher education more broadly accessible.

But what is likely to have a bigger effect on the future accessibility of higher education is the increasing transfer of education costs to students. This is already putting education beyond the reach of ordinary people. The essence of the Axworthy–*Globe and Mail*–C.D. Howe scheme is to let students' tuition costs rise dramatically, and then compensate for the increase by offering greater access to loans so that students can afford the higher cost. The C.D. Howe publication that promoted the new scheme suggested that tuition might rise to something like $60,000 for a four-year arts degree. The simple, obvious fact is that students of modest means, who already face plenty of obstacles in attending university, would face a massive new barrier: a far higher overall price tag. The prospect of loading up tens of thousands of dollars of debt by the age of twenty-one or twenty-two would be daunting for anyone, but particularly those from lower-income backgrounds.

Indeed, with costs like this, universities would inevitably become much more the preserve of the wealthy, and would also likely become more strictly practical places, training grounds for high-priced jobs. Students would be intent on ensuring that they emerged from university with degrees that generated large incomes, such as medicine, law, engineering or accounting. This trend, which in itself is not new, would be far more pronounced under the proposed scheme, with so much more personal debt at stake. Students motivated by a love of philosophy or literature or political science or history would have trouble justifying to themselves this kind of expenditure without some clear idea that it would pay off in a higher income later on.

Proponents of the new scheme argue that it would be fairer. Thomas Courchene, author of a C.D. Howe book that enthusiastically supports it, points out that our current system provides enormous public subsidies to students, particularly those in the high-cost professions, where the tuition fees in no way cover the cost of the education provided. Courchene notes that this is unfair, particularly since these professionals—doctors, dentists, engineers—end up in careers with large incomes. This is a good point; we do publicly subsidize the education of these future members of the elite so that they can provide services to us at fees that provide enormous personal gain to themselves. But is the solution to transform our universities even more into training grounds for these high-income earners? Education would thus become little more than a consumer good, for which the student would be obliged to pay handsomely, knowing a handsome return was likely at the end.

Lost in all this is the notion of universities as performing some kind of useful social function, as being places encouraging creative and independent thought, and even social and cultural criticism. The record of universities on this front has of course been spotty; often universities have simply regurgitated the prevailing wisdom of the day. In many cases, however, they have offered more, challenging students to analyse the fundamentals of their thought and of the dominant ideas of their time. As we move into an era of increasing cultural regimentation, of greater domination by media outlets concentrated in fewer and fewer hands, it seems unfortunate, if not dangerous, to be veering away from the concept of the university as an active and open centre of independent, critical thinking.

The proponents of the new system would no doubt insist that this was not their intent, and undoubtedly, in many cases, it isn't. But would it not be the result? With a higher and higher price tag on a university education, the pressure to focus on studies with income-generating potential would be immense. And is this the only solution to the valid problem Courchene raises? If we think that the elite is not paying a fair share of the costs, do we not have other means at our disposal to extract payment from them? How about a more progressive tax system, to catch some of this excess income at the other end, when people actually start earning it? Or what about a less generous system of compensation for professionals in regulated monopolies, such as medicine or law? Surely driving the cost of university up to unaffordable levels isn't the only solution to the problem of ensuring that the rich pay their fair share.

It is worth asking exactly where the savings would come from under the proposed system. Costs that were previously met by the government would be transferred to students. But aren't students, ultimately, just taxpayers, either currently or in the future? What is the difference to them whether they pay higher taxes or pay off the debt of a crushing student loan? This is an aspect of cutting government spending that we often fail to appreciate: if we want a service, such as education, we must pay for it. Whether we pay for it privately, through tuition, or publicly, through the tax system, we still pay for it. It is sometimes argued that a private system would be cheaper because it is innately more efficient, but there is little reason to believe this, beyond pure ideological conviction. Operating a private school might be cheaper, because it can choose to reject difficult, potentially expensive applicants—children with handicaps or cultural problems, for example. But if we want to include such children in an education system, a privately operated system is unlikely to offer any significant savings.

There would likely be savings from the kind of reforms proposed by Axworthy, but the savings wouldn't come from increased efficiency or from transferring the costs to the student-consumer. Rather, the savings would come from the fact that fewer students would attend university. The dramatically higher cost of tuition would deter many young people from going to university, discouraging all but the children of the well-to-do, or exceptionally motivated children from low-income families. Thus society would pay less for education because fewer people would be educated. For those in the upper income brackets—just as for those who sat on the Legislative Council in Simcoe's day—this may have a certain appeal. It is less costly for the rich to pay for their own education than to pay into a collective system that subsidizes the education of all members of society.

But is this solution appealing to the rest of us? Just because some rich people may prefer to pay privately for their own education—and health care, for that matter—does this fit with the goals of the non-rich? If we allow the cost of education and health care to become unaffordable to segments of society, what will we have really achieved? All we'll have done is made our society less egalitarian; services that used to be available to all will become available only to some. This seems a questionable achievement, particularly in an era of the so-called information revolution when we are constantly reminded that education is the key to prospects of high-wage employment.

Surely one of the reasons we are a richer, more advanced society than we were in Simcoe's day has to do with the way we've transformed our education system. Education is clearly a gateway to opportunity; it opens up possibilities to enrich us as individuals and as a society, financially and otherwise. By opening it up to all, we have made ourselves into a collectively richer society—a society that is, among other things, better equipped to compete with the rest of the world. We've also guaranteed a certain measure of equality that was simply absent in the days of Simcoe.

The Axworthy reforms would set us off in the opposite direction, towards a new-style elitism. Higher education would almost inevitably become the preserve of privilege, an expensive training ground for those who would go on to run the country and reap large financial rewards in the process. Simcoe justified this sort of elitism on the grounds that the education of the lower classes wasn't necessary. Today we simply say that we can no longer afford it.

A gloominess seemed to have taken over the minds of media pundits and commentators across the country. Canada's debt overhang had apparently filled them with such despair they could barely muster a cheery word any more.

"[I]t has become dismally apparent that our crushing debt is about the only thing that we have in common in Canada these days..." wrote *Maclean's* columnist Deirdre McMurdy. "The unavoidable question, as Canada struggles to modernize its social policy framework and to pay down its debt, is why bother?" Had it come to this then? Was there no choice but to hurl ourselves collectively off the cliff, committing a kind of national suicide? Had debt really driven us that far?

"There is little doubt that the extravagant social-policy framework we constructed in the affluent 1950s and 1960s no longer meets Canada's needs—or its means," McMurdy wrote. Exactly what she meant by this was left unclear. In what way did our "extravagant" social policy framework no longer meet our needs? Whose needs? Was she talking about the needs of media columnists or the needs of unemployed workers who relied on their UI cheques to feed their children?

McMurdy noted that we were in the process of "adapting our welfare state to a bleaker economic reality"; in other words, we were about to make our social programs less generous to fit with the harsher times. That sounded very modern and adaptable of us, but it masked the reality that some of us were likely to be hurt more than others in the course of adapting.

This was vividly illustrated by a publication put out, oddly enough, by the Fraser Institute, the Vancouver-based think tank financed by business. The publication included data showing how much each income group benefited from government spending programs. The results were clear: the lower the income group, the greater the benefit from government spending. Indeed, those on lower incomes clearly received more in government benefits than they contributed through their taxes.

But, about halfway up the income ladder, the picture changed. For families receiving $45,000 and up, the benefits of government spending were outweighed by the tax burden, so that those in higher income groups ended up contributing more through their taxes than they received in government benefits. This was most dramatically the case for those in the top income group, who, according to the Fraser Institute, contributed $34,000 more than they received in benefits.

These data illustrated what social scientists have long known, that social programs play a key role in redistributing resources from the haves to the have-nots. The private marketplace distributes resources in a highly unequal manner, with great concentrations of wealth at the top and poverty at the bottom; social programs reduce those extremes of inequality. So, if our social programs are "extravagant," this simply means that we are doing a fair bit of redistribution. In fact, compared to many other Western countries, our redistribution is modest. But the point is that when we reduce our social spending, we are almost sure to affect the amount of redistribution we're doing as a society. In effect, we're leaving the distribution of resources more in the hands of the private marketplace—despite its notorious record for distributing income in a highly inequitable manner.

Interestingly, excessive inequality used to be a concern even among conservatives. The late U.S. economist Henry C. Simons, a founder of the well-known "Chicago school" of conservative thought, was a strong believer in the free enterprise system, but he argued that it generated far too much inequality. "Surely there is something unlovely, to modern as against medieval minds, about marked inequality," wrote Simons. "[R]eduction of inequality is per se immensely important." Thus, despite his conservative credentials, Simons strongly advocated a progressive tax system—a position rarely found these days in the ranks of economists.

If cutting social programs is likely to hit lower income groups hardest, it would seem to be an inappropriate strategy for deficit reduction. The strategy becomes particularly inappropriate when we recall that social programs have not been the cause of our deficit problems. As we have seen, responsibility for the deficit lies more with the Bank of Canada and its tight-money policies, which have been highly favourable to members of the financial community and generally punitive to workers, who have suffered from the resulting recessions.

For us to now take a big chunk out of social programs seems to be punishing a group that is not only innocent of the charges levelled against it, but has already, in effect, been punished.

Let's look more closely at all this in an attempt to follow where the money is going. We'll start with the contention that the tight-money policy has been disproportionately beneficial to the rich. A study prepared in the economics department of Dalhousie University found that the Bank of Canada's fight against inflation in the eighties resulted in "a significant transfer of share of total wealth from the less wealthy to more wealthy households, from the young to the old, from females to males, from singles to the married." The study only covered the years up to 1987. The following years, as we know, saw a much tougher anti-inflation campaign and, therefore, probably a continuation of this trend towards greater inequality.

Certainly, as we saw in Chapter Three, the benefits of higher interest rates have been heavily skewed to the more affluent. It is sometimes argued that it is hard to measure who benefits from higher interest rates, because much interest income ends up held by pension plans. While this is true, it is unlikely that this substantially changes the pattern of inequality. To begin with, when high interest rates generate a surplus in pension plans, the benefits are frequently (and perfectly legally) taken out of the plan by the employer. Furthermore, the wealthy tend to have much better pension plans than the less wealthy. This is certainly the case with private plans and RRSPs, but it is also the case with employee pension plans. More than half the workforce is not even covered by these workplace plans, and those who are tend to be in the higher ranks of the employed—executives, on-staff professionals, teachers, bureaucrats and higher-paid blue-collar workers. On the other hand, low-wage, non-unionized jobs rarely provide pension plans. And as we slip even lower down the income scale—to welfare recipients and homeless people—we are even less likely to encounter anything in the way of a pension plan.

Yet the flip side of high interest rates, as we have seen, is a squeeze on employment. Here we encounter the same regressive pattern: increases in unemployment hit low-income earners harder than those with larger incomes. The largest increases in unemployment during the recession of the early nineties in Ontario, for instance, took place among blue-collar, poorly educated men. Across Canada, the unemployment rate among those with only a grade-school education was in almost every province at least double the rate among university graduates. So a tight-money policy reinforces inequality in two ways—its high interest rates disproportionately reward the rich, and the resulting unemployment disproportionately punishes the poor.

But, probably most significantly, the tight-money policy threatens equality by driving up the deficit. The response to this deficit growth has not been to impose extra taxes on those who have benefited from the high interest rates; on the contrary, the response has been to cut social programs. Yet, as the Fraser Institute's data demonstrate, social programs are far more important to those in the bottom half of society, and cutting social programs inevitably hits these people harder. Thus, tight-money policies, having already reinforced a pattern of inequality, deliver another cruel blow to lower-income people by reducing the support programs that are so important in their lives.

Of course, we get little sense of all this in the endless commentary on the need for spending cuts. Instead, social programs are presented as being like a worthless old shoe, worn and outdated and of little use any more. A number of commentators seemed determined to dispel the popular notion that social programs were important to Canadians, that they bound us together and gave us a sense of identity as a nation. Thus, David Bercuson argued in the *Financial Post* that we already had a national identity long before we had social programs. Diane Francis, in a column in the *Post*, even tried to make the case that our social programs were less generous than U.S. social programs, so what were we so proud of anyway? But Deirdre McMurdy perhaps went furthest in showing disdain for social programs and the notion that they counted for anything in our lives. Turning everything upside down, she argued that social programs were no longer the binding agent that held the country together; the honorary role of national unifier now belonged to the debt. What better way to prepare Canadians for the destruction of their cherished programs than to denigrate them, stomp on them and deny that they ever meant anything to us anyway.

Ironically, the same week that McMurdy insisted that all the social cuts were part of "adapting our welfare state to a bleaker economic reality," the press was full of stories suggesting that, for some, the new economic reality wasn't all that bleak. Corporate profits, it was reported, were rebounding magnificently; the Royal Bank was heading for a year-end profit of more than $1 billion, setting a record in Canadian banking history that was posing public-relations problems for the bank. (The other banks were soon to find themselves in the same embarrassing position, having to explain publicly why they were reaping extraordinary profits at a time when much of the population still remained unaware that the "recovery" was well under way.) And BCE Inc., Canada's largest conglomerate, was also on its way to topping the $1 billion profit mark, for the second year in a row. And Frank Stronach, owner of auto parts manufacturer Magna, was reported to have an annual take-home pay of $13 million. Clearly, bleak economic times were not an across-the-board phenomenon.

But the stunning rebound in corporate profits did nothing to discourage the push for stripping our social programs.

None of the commentators even raised the prospect of tapping into these flush corporate coffers for some badly needed funds to reduce the deficit. This omission is intriguing; surely if deficit reduction was to become the national crusade that the commentators suggested it should be, an increased contribution from the richest members of society wasn't too much to ask in these difficult times. Perhaps it just never occurred to the commentators that, if the banks chipped in more, the unemployed would have to chip in less. Instead, it turned out, the banks were busy devising ways to chip in less themselves: they were trying to convince Revenue Canada to allow them to take advantage of a gaping tax loophole so that they could write off some $300 million worth of "research" that they had carried out in setting up their in-house computer systems.

Elite commentators often suggest that tax increases would lead to a tax revolt. It is true that Canadians don't want their taxes raised. When the polling firm Environics asks people to choose between paying higher taxes and receiving fewer services, most of them choose fewer services. As Michel Belanger, then chairman of Canadian Forest Products Ltd., told Finance Minister Paul Martin at a public meeting prior to the Liberal government's first budget, "There's a real consensus against a rise of taxes as a solution to the deficit problem... We must find solutions on the expenditure side."

In fact, Belanger was only partly right, and his mistake is a common one made by elite commentators. As Belanger insisted, there *is* a consensus against tax increases, but it's not against all tax increases. While ordinary Canadians are against paying higher taxes themselves, they do not oppose—indeed they strongly favour—higher taxes for higher-income Canadians. They strongly favour, for instance, higher taxes for high-income people such as Michel Belanger.

Indeed, the public's desire for higher taxes on the rich is a strong theme in Canadian opinion polling. Donna Dasko, vice-president of Environics, describes the sentiment for higher taxes on the rich as so basic as to be a "law of polling." "People always want higher taxes on the rich." She points to an Environics survey done after the Mulroney government's budget of April 1989. The survey, which attempted to measure how fair Canadians considered the budget's tax increases, showed that 73 per cent felt wealthy Canadians were paying too little tax while 68 per cent felt low-income Canadians were paying too much. An Angus Reid poll from April 1993 also showed that 78 per cent of Canadians supported a tax increase on large, profitable corporations.

Given the apparent strength of the desire to tax the rich, it is surprising that this sentiment receives so little attention among commentators. Indeed, they appear at times to be anxious to dismiss or deny it. Thus, Mary Janigan's "debt handbook," which we encountered in Chapter One, virtually rules out the possibility of raising some taxes as a way to reduce the deficit. The handbook, which was published in *Maclean's*, lists in detail all possible areas for cutting government spending, but provides no similar list of tax breaks that could be eliminated. Indeed, Janigan dismisses the possibility of tax increases: "The public will not tolerate more taxes." But this, as we've seen, is not strictly true. It would be more accurate to say that elite opinion—including the *Globe and Mail*, the *Financial Post*, the BCNI and the C.D. Howe Institute—will not tolerate more taxes. The public, on the other hand, has apparently been yearning for more taxes *for the rich* for quite a while, and saying this to anyone who bothers to ask.

Certainly, there is room for some tax increases. For instance, an inheritance tax on large estates has long been a good idea, and is a particularly good one now, with trillions of dollars passing from one generation to the next over the coming decades. And it is hard to imagine how we would be worse off as a nation if we were to impose a windfall profits tax that would hit the banks. (If the banks were to pack up and leave in a huff, we could surely find some other enterprising Canadians willing to take up this low-risk, high-profit line of business.)

Indeed, there is plenty of room to increase certain taxes to reduce the deficit, and these sorts of changes should be made anyway, in the interests of creating a fairer tax system. But while tax changes can help out, the deficit problem should be dealt with at its roots. As we've seen, the problem is not that we are spending more than we are paying in taxes. On the contrary, our tax revenues are more than adequate to pay for our government programs—when we are not mired in recession. As Pierre Fortin argues, we should focus instead on finally shaking off the recession by stimulating growth through lower interest rates. This formula, as we've discussed, would bring in more tax revenues, lower our social assistance costs and reduce interest payments on the debt—the only area of government spending that is growing out of control, or growing at all for that matter.

But while this solution would attack the problem at its roots, it would also, as we've seen, step on the toes of some extremely powerful interests, including foreign investors and their influential Bay Street representatives. While the political problems of doing so are not insurmountable in a democracy, it is certainly a lot easier to simply take a chunk of flesh out of the hides of the unemployed.

For aristocrats in seventeenth-century Britain, wealth was tied up in land. But for lawyers, physicians, merchants and other well-to-do members of the emerging new elite of professionals and traders, there was an annoying problem: where to store the little hoards of wealth they were accumulating. A farm or a field or a flock of sheep might be safe investments, but they were not very liquid; they couldn't be sold for cash at an hour's notice. And simply storing gold coins under a mattress or inside a snuff box wasn't very safe or rewarding. So, for the rising new elite, the creation of the British national debt at the end of the seventeenth century couldn't have been more timely. At last, there was somewhere to store one's money—and earn interest.

While the national debt proved a godsend to this new class of investors, it also, nevertheless, provoked concern and outrage among this same investor class, as well as among just about all other educated segments of society. It is perhaps reassuring for us to realize that deficit mania among the elite is nothing new. The plaintive cries of the C.D. Howe Institute, the *Globe and Mail* and the Business Council on National Issues over our mounting debt come from a long and honourable tradition of those convinced that death-by-deficit is at hand.

Here, for instance, is the renowned English economist and philosopher David Hume writing in 1776, bemoaning the size of the British national debt.

Our late delusions have much exceeded anything known in history, not even excepting those of the crusades. For I suppose there is no mathematical, still less an arithmetical, demonstration that the road to the Holy Land was not the road to paradise, as there is that *the endless increase of national debts is the direct road to national ruin. But having now completely reached that goal,* it is needless at present to reflect on the past. It will be found in the present year, 1776, that all the revenues of this island north of Trent and west of Reading are mortgaged or anticipated forever. Could the small remainder be in a worse condition were those provinces seized by Austria and Prussia? ... No imagination can figure a situation which will induce our creditors to relinquish their claims, or the public to seize their revenues. So egregious indeed has been our folly that we have even lost all title to compassion in the numberless calamities that are awaiting us [italics added].

Wow. Hume was convinced that the British debt load in 1776—when Britain was poised to enter the most prosperous century of its history—had rendered Britain so powerless in the face of its creditors that it might as well have been conquered by Austria and Prussia. But Hume was a respected economist and, were he around today, would no doubt be a regular guest on shows like "Prime Time News" or "Canada AM." His view that a heavy debt load is roughly equivalent to being conquered by a foreign power seems only slightly more extreme than the regular commentaries we hear today.

And Hume's comments fit well within the debt-mongering tradition. The nineteenth-century historian Lord Macaulay, in his massive history of England, noted that the sense of calamity over the debt was constant and unrelenting.

Such was the origin of that debt which has since become the greatest prodigy that ever perplexed the sagacity and confounded the pride of statesmen and philosophers. At every stage in the growth of that debt the nation has sent up the same cry of anguish and despair. At every stage in the growth of that debt it has been seriously asserted by wise men that bankruptcy and ruin were at hand. Yet still the debt went on growing and still bankruptcy and ruin were as remote as ever. When the great contest with Louis the fourteenth was finally terminated...the nation owed about fifty millions; and that debt was considered, not merely by the rude multitude, not only by the foxhunting squires and coffeehouse orators, but by acute and profound thinkers, as an encumbrance

which would permanently cripple the body politic...
Then came the war of the Austrian succession; and
the debt rose to eighty millions. Pamphleteers, histo-
rians, and orators pronounced that now, at all events,
our case was desperate... Soon war again broke forth,
and...the debt swelled to a hundred and forty millions. As soon as the first intoxication of victory was
over, men of theory and men of business almost
unanimously pronounced that the fatal day had now
really arrived...

But Macaulay, with the sweeping view of a historian, noted
something that appears to have been lost on the gloomy
decriers of debt: that as the debt grew, so did the nation!
Macaulay wrote that, when the debt hit £50 million and
cries of hysteria went up all over, "trade flourished; wealth
increased; the nation became richer and richer." That pattern repeated itself over and over, Macaulay noted. In
response to Hume's gloomy assessment in 1776, Macaulay
commented that "this great philosopher...had only to open
his eyes, and to see improvements all around him, cities
increasing, cultivation extending...artificial rivers joining
the chief inland seats of industry to the chief seaports, streets
better lighted, houses better furnished, richer wares exposed
to sale in statelier shops."

After the wars that sprang from the French Revolution
left England with a debt of £800 million, Macaulay wryly
commented, "We can hardly wonder that the cry of despair
should have been louder than ever. But again that cry was
found to have been as unreasonable as ever...in every
county we saw wastes recently turned into gardens; in every
city we saw new streets, and squares, and markets, more brilliant lamps, more abundant supplies of water... Soon the
island was intersected by railways."

What Macaulay was perceptively noting was that the

burden of debt is relative. As the economy grew, so did the society's ability to pay for a larger debt. As he noted, "a debt of eighty millions was less to the England which was governed by Pelham than a debt of fifty million had been to the England which was governed by Oxford." Macaulay's observations of history also allow us to see another pattern: that debt was part of the process of growth. At least part of the debt was incurred financing the growth of the burgeoning nation's infrastructure, transforming Britain from a primitive medieval country into a modern industrial state. It all cost money: the "artificial rivers joining the chief inland seats of industry to the chief seaports," the "streets, and squares, and markets, more brilliant lamps, more abundant supplies of water... the island... intersected by railways." Of course, much of the debt was spent fighting wars. As deplorable as wars are—and Britain certainly engaged in its fair share of brutal bloodshed—they, too, fuelled growth, as armies had to be employed, and outfitted and equipped with battle gear and weapons. And the territorial acquisitions of war also created new trading and investment opportunities for British merchants and manufacturers.

And, of course, the build-up of public debt paralleled a similar rise in private debt, as the nation moved from a primarily agrarian economy to an industrial one. Just as the nation needed to build roads and canals and railways to adapt to the changing world, so newly created corporations took on debt to build factories and warehouses, to purchase equipment and to hire employees. In both the private and public spheres, debt was essential to the process of growth. Debt was the means of ensuring that hoards of wealth didn't remain hidden under mattresses or tucked away in snuff boxes, that the savings of physicians and lawyers and merchants would be lent to someone who would put them to productive use.

As discussed earlier, those with wealth to lend extracted a

price—in the form of interest payments—from their debtors. This was the price of opportunity, it was the price the have-nots had to pay for the privilege of using the resources of the haves. Whether or not the have-nots were given a fighting chance to succeed largely depended on what the price of opportunity was. In the great divide between creditors and debtors, between the haves and the have-nots, between insiders and outsiders, the interest rate was the determinant of destiny. For society to function, it was obviously important that some kind of reasonable balance be struck between the competing interests of creditors and debtors.

In the 1970s, as we saw, the balance arguably swung too far in the direction of debtors, with creditors often seeing their capital whittled away through inflation. But the reaction since then has been too fiercely in their favour. Since the early eighties, central banks throughout the developed world have adopted a much tougher stand against inflation. This has shifted the power balance sharply in favour of creditors, who have enjoyed unusually high real rates of interest. Debtors—the have-nots of society—have suffered considerably under the new power shift, losing access to credit and struggling to regain ground in the economic crunch and rising tide of unemployment. Pierre Fortin suggests that much of the high and persistent unemployment seen in the developed world over the last decade and a half can be attributed to "the drive to eradicate inflation led by central banks beginning in the mid-1970s."

Nowhere has this been more true than in Canada, where John Crow took the crusade against inflation to new extremes. Under Crow, the power balance shifted definitively. Gone was any lingering notion that the role of the Bank was to maintain a delicate balance between encouraging growth and fighting inflation. Instead, the Bank opted to focus exclusively on fighting inflation, and in doing so, came down heavily in favour of those with financial assets to protect, and against the interests of those whose primary need was employment.

Perhaps the most stunning aspect of all this is the fact that it is a political struggle that remains largely off the public stage. Whether we, as a society, focus our attack on inflation or on unemployment has enormous ramifications in terms of who benefits and who loses, and what kind of society we live in. And yet this all-important political choice remains obscured; even the notion that there *is* a choice is rarely discussed. Rather, we are led to believe that there is no trade-off between inflation and unemployment, between the interests of creditors and debtors. We are led to believe that the decision to focus exclusively on fighting inflation is simply in the best interests of all of us. Thus, a crucial political contest—one that has reverberated throughout history—has been all but obliterated from contemporary public debate.

So, despite the fact that even price stability enthusiasts concede the cost of eliminating inflation is considerable, there has been surprisingly little discussion about whether or not this should be our goal. Jack Selody has written extensively in obscure publications about the costs and benefits of achieving price stability, and concluded that this should be the Bank's exclusive focus. But would the Canadian public necessarily agree with him? Canadians are largely unaware that there are two possible paths—focusing exclusively on fighting inflation or broadening the focus to include fighting unemployment as well—let alone that people like Selody may be influencing which path we are following.

While the choice of paths remains outside the public debate, the ramifications of this choice, which has been made for us, have an ongoing impact on our lives. We will have to live with the consequences of recession and unemployment, and the repercussions of an ever-mounting debt. A highly effective campaign is now under way to use this debt to justify dismantling what is arguably the most admirable aspect of our society—our ability to collectively create strong public institutions and programs that serve us all.

In the sun-dappled offices of the C.D. Howe Institute, John Crow sits among the ferns. From the mighty heights of presiding over one of the world's most powerful and secretive private fraternities nestled in the Swiss Alps, it has come to this: a modest office inside the Howe's Toronto headquarters, with a desk that he shares with others who occasionally make guest appearances there. As a "fellow in residence," the former Bank of Canada governor is spending some time at the institute contributing his knowledge in the area of international finance.

Crow is also working these days as a "consultant" for the Canadian subsidiary of a large, diversified U.S. insurance company, American International Group, Inc. The company's Canadian operations are heavily focused on underwriting commercial and property insurance—stimulating work, no doubt, although perhaps lacking the cachet of controlling the world economy.

Crow's presence at the institute will undoubtedly help strengthen the Howe's resolve to keep up the fight for inflation and deficit control—not that there were any signs that the Howe's spirits were flagging on these fronts. And the Howe, with its congenial atmosphere of like-minded people, could prove to be like a second home for Crow. Certainly, there would be few places more warmly receptive to a seasoned general of the inflation wars than this institute, so generously funded by the Toronto investment community.

One can sense the baby hippo lurking just off stage, waiting to be brought on for her cameo appearance. It will, of course, be a brutal scene: the little hippo's execution. But no doubt we'll all feel better once the deed is done. So, before time runs out and we're all buried alive under a mountain of debt, let's search our souls and see if we can't come up with some resolve as a nation. The danger is that we will fail to muster the needed determination, and will let that infuriating little creature waddle off, her continued existence taunting us forever with the knowledge that we lacked, to borrow a phrase, the courage to act.

Notes

CHAPTER ONE

Page   *They Shoot Hippos, Don't They?*

1 **The hippo story**, Eric Malling, "New Zealand Special," *W5*, CTV, aired Feb. 28, 1993.

2 **Vancouver *Sun* columnist**, Jamie Lamb, "The New Zealand Syndrome: exposing core of our rotten economy," *Vancouver Sun*, Oct. 15, 1993.

8 **In some communities**, Mabel Wilson, Oakville Historical Society, Oakville, Ont.; interview.

9 **In a column**, Rick Salutin, "Don't privatize the CBC, publicize it," *Globe and Mail*, Dec. 9, 1994.

14 **Malling has even been known**, Eric Malling in a speech in January 1993. Copy provided by Malling.

19 **The institute taped**, Bruce Little, "Debt crisis looms, study warns," *Globe and Mail*, Feb. 16, 1993.

19 **Furthermore, the transcript**, Irene K. Ip, William B.P. Robson, *Avoiding a Crisis: Proceedings of a Workshop of Canada's Fiscal Outlook, Jan. 27, 1993* (Toronto: C. D. Howe Institute, 1993).

21 **"It is simply not true**, Jonathan Boston, Victoria University, Wellington, New Zealand. Interview.

23 **Interestingly, it consistently**, Murray Dobbin, "The Remaking of New Zealand," transcript of CBC Radio "Ideas" program, aired Oct. 12, 1994.

25 A study by two economists, Isabelle Joumard and Helmut Reisen, "Real Exchange Rate Overshooting and the Persistent Trade Effects: the Case of New Zealand," reprinted from *World Economy*, Vol. 15, No. 3, May 1992, OECD *Reprint Series*, No. 43 (Paris: Organization for Economic Co-operation and Development, 1992).

25 **A 1993 report**, Sylvia Ann Hewlett, *Child Neglect in Rich Nations* (New York: United Nations Children's Fund, 1993).

26 **A 1993 study**, Pat Colgate and Joselyn Stroombergen, *A Promise to Pay: New Zealand's Overseas Debt and Country Risk* (Wellington, N.Z.: New Zealand Institute of Economic Research, 1993).

28 **With the deficit show likely to air**, A Special Report With CTV, "Tough Choices," *Maclean's*, Sept. 27, 1993.

31 **While Janigan is**, Mary Janigan, "A Debt Handbook," *Maclean's*, Sept. 27, 1993.

32 **The handbook, called,** Harold Chorney, John Hotson, Mario Seccareccia, *The Deficit Made Me Do It!* (Ottawa: Canadian Centre for Policy Alternatives, May 1992).

33 **An Angus Reid poll**, Eric Beauchesne, "Deficit concern growing, poll finds," *Ottawa Citizen*, May 5, 1993.

34 **This fits with the results**, All Environics poll results reported here are from Donna Dasko, vice president of Environics, Toronto; interview.

36 **The deep concern over unemployment**, Peter Cheney, "They waited in The Line," *Toronto Star*, Jan. 11, 1995.

37 **In a revealing comment**, Edward Greenspon, "Finance ministers emerge optimistic on major changes," *Globe and Mail*, Dec. 2, 1993.

39 **Dalton Camp, a former top-level Conservative**, Dalton Camp, "Analyzing the fibs," *Toronto Star*, Feb. 27, 1994.

39 **Although mainstream commentators**, Peter Cook, "Good, good, interest rates are going up," *Globe and Mail*, Dec. 16, 1994.

CHAPTER TWO
Scissorhands Meets the Deficit Slayer

41 **As Tom Kierans,** Jonathan Ferguson, "The real tragedy of tizzy over rates: loss of sovereignty," *Toronto Star*, March 23, 1994.

42 **Indeed, to put Canada's creditworthiness,** Moody's *Sovereign Ratings: Global Outlook* (New York: Moody's Investors Services, May 1994).

44 **In an attempt to clarify,** Moody's *Special Commentary: Moody's Examines Canada's Fiscal and Foreign Currency Debts* (New York: Moody's Investors Services, June 1993).

46 **Indeed, they have been a boon to Canadians,** in Manitoba, for instance, the cheap power generated by massive hydro projects has been a substantial subsidy to both businesses and consumers. Two economists at the University of Winnipeg, Michael Benarroch and Hugh Grant, examined the Manitoba debt situation and concluded that the publicly owned utility has allowed Manitoba residents to benefit from "inexpensive, below-market electricity rates," with savings amounting to some $600 million a year—more than the province's annual deficit. As the authors conclude: "[i]f hydro-electric power was sold at market values [in Manitoba], annual government deficits would disappear and [a] significant budgetary surplus would result." In other words, Manitoba Hydro's debt represents a subsidy to Manitobans. If it didn't exist, they would have to pay a great deal more for their power.

See Michael Benarroch, Hugh Grant, "Measurement Issues in the Deficit Debate," paper presented at the second annual Economic Policy Conference, Laurentian University, Sudbury, Ont. Feb. 25-26, 1994.

48 **"No revolution but,** John Geddes, "No revolution but first shot at deficit," Budget '94 Pullout section, *Financial Post*, Feb. 23, 1994.

48 **Inside an upbeat,** Lisa Grogan-Green, "Optimism about budget attack on deficit feeds rally," *ibid.*

52 **As the *Financial Post* said,** *Financial Post*, Feb. 23, 1994.

52 **As the *Post* said in a prominent analysis,** John Geddes, "No revolution but first shot at deficit," *ibid.*

56 **Indeed, Mimoto's study,** An early version of Mimoto's study is an untitled 64-page document. It was obtained from Statistics Canada by researcher Ken Rubin in July 1991 under access-to-information legislation.

59 **So, in typically scholarly fashion,** Frances Russell, "Political interference suggested by StatsCan move," *Winnipeg Free Press,* Oct. 9, 1991. Russell was the first to draw attention to Mimoto's work. Her columns in the *Free Press* in the spring of 1991 may have helped fuel concern within the Finance department that his findings would hurt the government's attempt to gain public support for social spending cuts.

59 **After months in the bureaucratic hopper,** H. Mimoto and P. Cross, "The Growth of the Federal Debt, 1975-1990," *Canadian Economic Observer* (published under the authority of the Minister of Supply and Services, Canada), June 1991.

60 **Indeed, the research department of the Bank of Canada,** ""Federal government revenues, expenditures and deficits since 1970," *Bank of Canada Review,* October 1985.

64 **The costs of all this,** Diane Bellemare, Lise Poulin-Simon, *What is the Real Cost of Unemployment in Canada* (Ottawa: Canadian Centre for Policy Alternatives, 1994).

65 **Even the widely-trumpetted,** Vincent Truglia; interview.

66 **We can see this most clearly,** OECD, *Economic Outlook 53* (Paris: Organization for Economic Co-operation and Development, June, 1993).

67 **"Strip out that,** "Stripping down the cycle," *The Economist,* July 3, 1993.

68 **From the mid-50s,** Numbers represent the ratio of public sector investment (excluding public enterprises) to national GDP in Canada.

68 **Pierre Fortin, an economist at,** Fortin; correspondence with the author.

69 **We can see this clearly,** OECD, *op. cit.*

70 **This was the conventional wisdom,** Thomas Wilson, Peter Dungan, Steve Murphy, "The Sources of the Recession in Canada: 1989-1992," *Canadian Business Economics,* Vol. 2, No. 2, Winter 1994.

70 **As the economy experienced,** *Economic and Fiscal Reference Tables* (Ottawa: Department of Finance, September 1994). table 64.1, p.115.

70 **George Vasic,** George Vasic, "Down the Slippery Slopes of National Debt," *Canadian Business*, Feb. 1991.

CHAPTER THREE
John Crow and the Politics of Obsession

72 **"We cannot afford to give up,** John Crow, dinner address to meeting of the Board of Directors, Bank of Canada, Halifax, June 30, 1987.

73 **"It was pretty consistent with,** Michael Wilson; interview.

74 **"I realize that parts,** John Crow, "The Work of Canadian Monetary Policy," (Eric J. Hanson Memorial Lecture), delivered at the University of Alberta, Edmonton, Jan. 18, 1988.

75 **The Globe ran a story,** Canadian Press, "Bank of Canada governor wants interest rates low," *Globe and Mail*, Jan. 19, 1988.

81 **In the preamble,** cited in George S. Watts, *The Bank of Canada: Origins and Early History* (Ottawa: Carleton University Press, 1993). p. 16.

82 **Yet advocates of price stability,** Some commentators have questioned whether "price stability" really meant zero inflation, or simply very low inflation. Here is what Crow said on the subject: "I've caused people's eyebrows to jump about two meters when I say this. They say, what do you mean by price stability, what rate of inflation? I say zero. And that seems rather shocking to people. How could you possibly mean zero inflation? Well price stability means zero inflation..." Verbatim transcript of Crow's remarks to the Executive Committee meeting of the Canadian Labour Market and Productivity Centre, May 4, 1989.

82 **In outlining the evils of inflation,** David E.W. Laidler and William B. P. Robson, *The Great Canadian Disinflation: the Economics and Politics of Monetary Policy in Canada 1988-93* (Toronto: C.D. Howe Institute, Dec. 1993). p. 16.

83 *Business Week* was blunt, "Who's Hurt by Rate Hikes? Hint: It's not the Rich," *Business Week*, Nov. 21, 1994.

84 In 1991, Canadians with incomes, *Taxation Statistics* (Ottawa: Revenue Canada, 1993).

85 Peter Spiro, interview. (Spiro's views are his own and do not necessarily represent those of the Ontario government.) For further elaboration on the relationship between low inflation and high real interest rates, see Peter S. Spiro, *Real Interest Rates and Investment and Borrowing Strategies* (New York, Quorum Books, 1989).

85 Since Crow began, real interest rates, compiled from Statistics Canada data, cited in Pierre Fortin, "Let's Turn the Policy Mix Upside Down," *Policy Options*, July-August 1993.

85 The Canadian real interest rate, comparative real interest rates cited in John Liscio, "The Battered Buck," in *Barron's*, July 18, 1994.

86 He argues that, Peter Spiro "The Differential between Canadian and U.S. Long-term Bond Yields," *Canadian Business Economics*, Vol. 2, No. 2, Winter 1994.

88 As the *Wall Street Journal* noted, Lucinda Harper, Thomas T. Vogel Jr., Fred R. Bleakley, "Heated Reaction: Edgy Markets Looking for Signs of Inflation, Find Some—and Drop," *Wall Street Journal*, March 2, 1994.

88 *Business Week* was even blunter, James C. Cooper, Kathleen Madigan, "Bondholders Have Little to Fear from a Stronger Economy," *Business Week*, Nov. 8, 1993.

88 Conversely, when growth expectations, "Investors take heart in U.S. slowdown," *Financial Post*, July 30, 1994. Lisa Grogan-Green, "Finally something to cheer," in *Financial Post*, July 30, 1994.

90 As Paul Volcker, quoted in William Greider, *Secrets of the Temple* (New York: A Touchstone Book, Simon and Schuster, New York).

92 Michael Wilson acknowledged that intense, Wilson; interview.

94 For most developed countries, data cited in Lars Osberg, "Digging a Hole or Laying the Foundations? The Objective of

Macroeconomic Policy in Canada," Luncheon address to first annual Economic Policy Conference, Laurentian University, Sudbury, March 27, 1993.

95 **"The issue in Canada,** *ibid.*

96 **Of 62 countries surveyed,** data cited in *ibid.*

96 **In 1990, real interest rates in Canada,** OECD *Economic Outlook,* Dec. 1994.

97 **Crow had started life,** for an excellent portrait of Crow's early years, see Edward Greenspon, Harvey Enchin, "Profile: Bank of Canada Governor has gone from playing Julius Caesar in a school play to holding sway over Canadians' economic future," *Globe and Mail,* Sept. 1, 1990.

103 **But in 1990, as Crow pushed,** Spiro, *op. cit.* "The Differential between Canadian and U.S. Long-Term Bond Yields."

103 **The combination of high interest rates,** Ernie Stokes; interview.

105 **Wilson acknowledges that the high Canadian dollar,** Wilson; interview.

106 **The interest costs on the national debt,** *Economic and Fiscal Reference Tables* (Ottawa: Department of Finance, September, 1994). Reference Table 64, p. 114.

107 **Contrary to much media rhetoric,** Fortin, "Canada's Rising external Debt," in Richard G. Harris (ed.) *Deficits and Debt in the Canadian Economy.* Policy Forum #29 (Kingston: John Deutsch Institute, Queen's University, 1993).

107 **Economist Pierre Fortin,** Fortin, "Slow Growth, Unemployment and Debt: What happened? What Can We Do?", paper presented at the second annual Bell conference on Economic and Public Policy, Queen's University, Kingston, Ont. Oct. 15-16, 1993.

108 **Paul Volcker commented,** Paul A. Volcker, Toyoo Gyohten, *Changing Fortunes: The World's Money and the Threat to American Leadership* (New York: Times Books, 1992). p. 178.

108 **According to John Grant,** John Grant; interview.

109 **"The Bank put its little piggy in the water,** Michael Wilson; interview.

111 **The final targets**, The Budget 1991 (Ottawa: Department of Finance, Feb. 26, 1991). p. 112.

112 **For instance, the proposition**, Wilson, Dungan, Murphy, *op. cit., The Sources of the Recession in Canada.*

114 **The findings of the U of T economists**, Ernie Stokes, "Has Monetary Policy Been Too Tight?" *Canadian Business Economics*, Vol 1, No. 1, Fall 1992.

116 **The problem, insists *Globe* columnist**, Peter Cook, "Save Canada! Boycott bonds!" *Globe and Mail*, Nov. 28, 1994.

116 **Indeed, almost twenty years ago**, *Economic and Fiscal Reference Tables* (Ottawa: Department of Finance, Sept. 1994). Table 64.1, p. 115.

116 **As the *Financial Post* put it**, Greg Ip, "Surging rates hurt attack on deficit," *Financial Post*, Dec. 13, 1994.

116 **So, although social spending**, *op cit., Economic and Fiscal Reference Tables*, Reference Table 64.1, p. 115.

117 **In 1990-91, Ottawa actually collected**, *ibid.* Reference Table 64. p. 114.

117 **As Paul Martin noted**, Paul Martin, A *New Framework for Economic Policy* (Ottawa: Government of Canada, Oct. 1994). p. 26

118 **We'd have to raise**, Submission to the House of Commons Standing Committee on Finance by the Canadian Auto Workers. Pre-Budget Consultations, Nov. 16, 1994.

118 **The dramatic crash in the Japanese**, for details on the Japanese real estate market crash see interview with Wall Street analyst William Sterling by John Liscio in *Barron's*, July 18, 1994.

119 **"It is remarkable**, Peter Spiro, *op. cit.* "The Differential between Canadian and U.S. Long-term Bond Yields."

119 **Economist Pierre Siklos**, Pierre Siklos, "The Deficit-Interest Rate Link: Empirical Evidence for Canada," *Applied Economics*, No. 20, 1988. pp. 1563-1577.

120 **Similarly, when interest rates shot up**, quoted in Greg Ip, "Inflation, rates put squeeze on economy," *Financial Post*, Jan. 21-23, 1995.

121 "Nothing else needs to change, Cook, *op. cit.*, "Save Canada! Boycott Bonds!"

CHAPTER FOUR
Jack Selody and the Power of Faith

122 **Economist Lars Osberg explains**, Osberg, *op. cit.* "Digging a Hole or Laying the Foundations."

127 **Much to their delight**, J. Peter Jarrett and Jack G. Selody, "The Productivity-Inflation Nexus in Canada, 1963-1979," *The Review of Economics and Statistics*, Vol. LXIV, No. 3, August 1982.

129 **Once again, the story**, Peter Howitt, "Zero Inflation as a long-run Target for Monetary Policy," in Richard G. Lipsey (ed.) *Zero Inflation: The Goal of Price Stability* (Toronto: C.D. Howe Institute, 1990).

131 **A report by the Economic Council**, Economic Council of Canada, *A Joint Venture: The Economics of Constitutional Options*, Twenty-Eighth Annual Review (Ottawa: Minister of Supply and Services, 1991).

132 **As economists Brian MacLean**, Brian MacLean and Mark Setterfield, "Nexus or Not? Productivity and Inflation in Canada," *Canadian Business Economics*, Vol. 1, No. 2, Winter 1993.

132 **Asked about his reliance**, Peter Howitt; correspondence with the author.

133 **John Helliwell, an economist**, John F. Helliwell, Stagflation and Productivity Decline in Canada, 1974-82," *Canadian Journal of Economics*, 17, 2, 1984.

134 **Let's look at the work**, Laidler, Robson, *op. cit.*, *The Great Canadian Disinflation*.

137 **In a thoughtful essay**, Robert M. Solow, "The Intelligent Citizen's Guide to Inflation," *The Public Interest*, No. 38, Winter 1975.

138 **If we look at inflation rates**, Fortin, "The Unbearable Lightness of Zero-inflation Optimism," *Canadian Business Economics*, Vol. 1, No. 3.

138 **In the U.S., for instance,** W. Lee Hoskins, "Defending Zero Inflation: All for Naught," *Federal Reserve Bank of Minneapolis Quarterly Review*, Spring 1991.

138 **(Interestingly, also,** Proceedings of the conference were published in the *Journal of Money, Credit and Banking*, August 1991 supplement.

140 **John Smithin, an economist,** John N. Smithin, *Macroeconomics after Thatcher and Reagan,* (Aldershot, England: Edward Elgar Publishing Ltd., 1990). p. 53.

143 **But, once again, Selody was not deterred,** Jack Selody, *The Goal of Price Stability: a review of the issues.* Technical Report No. 54 (Ottawa: Bank of Canada, 1990).

145 **Another fact that the Finance department,** The internal Finance department studies were described to me in an off-the-record interview. They have apparently been destroyed.

147 **A recent study reported in the Lancet,** cited in Reuter, "Out of a job? Check immune system," *Globe and Mail*, July 22, 1994.

148 **The profoundly important role,** M. Jahoda, "The Psychological Meanings of Unemployment," *New Society*, September 1979, p. 492.

152 **In its 1980 annual report,** cited in Joyce Kolko, *Restructuring the World Economy* (New York: Pantheon Books, 1988). p.234.

152 **The following year,** cited in *ibid.* See also Bank for International Settlements, *Annual Report* (Basel, 1981). p. 34.

154 **Although economists like to portray,** Edward Herman, "The Natural Rate of Unemployment," *Z Magazine*, November 1994.

154 **Far from being scientific,** M.A. Setterfield, D.V. Gordon, L. Osberg, "Searching for a Will o' the Wisp: An empirical study of the NAIRU in Canada," *European Economic Review 36,* 1992.

154 **Economists at the Bank of Canada,** Shawn McCarthy, "Inflation fears rise as jobless rate falls," *Toronto Star*, Nov. 5, 1994.

155 **Selody thus presents us with,** Selody, *op. cit., The Goal of Price Stability.*

155 **This phenomenon was noted,** cited in Lars Osberg, *The Ratchet Effect of Economic Theory on Unemployment: Constraints, Choices and Blind Spots,* Working Paper No. 87-01, Department of Economics, Dalhousie University, Halifax, 1987.

156 **Pierre Fortin's research suggests,** Fortin, *op. cit.* "The Unbearable Lightness of Zero-inflation Optimism."

158 **"Monetary policy directed towards,** Bank of Canada, *Annual Report* 1990, p. 9.

159 **Yet as inflation fell,** see Andrew Sharpe, "Comparison of Canadian Productivity Performance between the Early 1980s and 1990s," *Canadian Business Economics,* Vol. 2, No. 2, Winter 1994.

161 **In January 1994, when it looked,** Laidler, Robson, *op. cit.,* *The Great Canadian Disinflation.*

164 **"Yes, tight-money and balanced budgets,** Solow, *op. cit.,* "The Intelligent Citizen's Guide to Inflation."

CHAPTER FIVE
Death of a Usurer (and Other Cautionary Tales)

165 **Amid the elegant glitter,** The account of Canada's debt problems and the early role of the Bank of Canada has been drawn primarily from the following sources:

Robert B. Bryce, *Maturing in Hard Times: Canada's Department of Finance through the Great Depression* (Montreal, Kingston: McGill-Queen's University Press, 1986).

Douglas H. Fullerton, *Graham Towers and his Times* (Toronto: McClelland and Stewart: 1986).

J.L. Granatstein, *The Ottawa Men: The Civil Service Mandarins, 1935-1957* (Toronto: Oxford University Press: 1982).

Linda Mary Grayson, *The Formation of the Bank of Canada 1913-1938* University of Toronto. Ph.d. Thesis, 1974.

Douglas Owram, *The Government Generation: Canadian Intellectuals and the State 1900-1945* (Toronto: University of Toronto Press).

David W. Slater, *War Finance and Reconstruction: The Role of Canada's Department of Finance 1939-46.* Unpublished manuscript.

David W. Slater, "Birthing the Bank," *Canadian Banker*, Jan.-
Feb. 1992.
George S. Watts, *The Bank of Canada: Origins and Early
History* (Ottawa: Carleton University Press, 1993).

180 **The death of a usurer,** see Jacques Le Goff, "The Usurer and
Purgatory," in *The Dawn of Modern Banking* (New Haven: Yale
University Press, 1979).

182 **The development of the purgatory option,** The account of
the role of goldsmiths and the development of the Bank of
England is drawn primarily from:
A. Andreades, *History of the Bank of England 1640-1903*
(London: P.S. King & Son Ltd., 1924).
John Francis, *History of the Bank of England, Its Times and
Traditions* Vol.1 (London: Willoughby & Co., 1884).

188 **Adam Smith himself emphasized,** cited in William F. Hixson,
*Triumph of the Bankers: Money and Banking in the Eighteenth and
Nineteenth Centuries* (London: Praeger, 1993, p. 3.

189 **But the acute gold shortage,** for a good discussion of the colo-
nial money experience, see Richard A. Lester, "Currency
Issues to Overcome Depressions in Delaware, New Jersey, New
York and Maryland, 1715-37," *Journal of Political Economy*,
Vol. XLVII, February-December, 1939.

193 **Even Adam Smith,** cited in Hixson, *op. cit.*, p.49.

194 **When the colonies declared independence,** see Ralph V.
Harlow, "Aspects of Revolutionary Finance 1775-1783," *The
American Historical Review*, Vol. XXXV, Oct. 1929 to July
1930.

194 **With the outbreak of the Civil War,** for a detailed account of
the greenback issue, see Robert P. Sharkey, *Money, Class and
Party: An Economic Study of Civil War and Reconstruction*
(Baltimore: The Johns Hopkins Press, 1959). See also Irwin
Unger, *The Greenback Era: A Social and Political History of
American Finance, 1865-1879* (Princeton: Princeton
University Press, 1964).

203 **President Abraham Lincoln,** quoted in Hixson, *op. cit.* p. 134.

204 **As one outspoken critic,** quoted in *ibid*, p.135.

206 **Even President Andrew Johnson,** quoted in Sharkey, *op. cit.*,
p. 123.

207 **"The demoralization of society,** quoted in *ibid,* p. 252.

207 **In a speech to the U.S. Senate,** quoted in *ibid,* p. 126.

207 **Among those hardest hit,** for an account of the Populist movement, see Lawrence Goodwyn, *The Populist Moment: A Short History of the Agrarian Revolt in America* (New York: Oxford University Press, 1978).

213 **While we naively leave our fate,** for an insightful account of the biased nature of apparently neutral experts, see Thomas Walkom, "Curious how crises always preceded budgets," *Toronto Star,* Jan. 21, 1995.

CHAPTER SIX

Revenge of the Bondholders

214 **In a speech to the Dominion Grange,** W.C. Good, *Farmer Citizen: My Fifty Years in the Canadian Farmers' Movement* (Toronto: Ryerson Press, 1958). pp. 97, 98.

215 **Although the farmers' protest movement,** for an account of the Canadian farm protest movement and the rise of Social Credit, see Alvin Finkel, *The Social Credit Phenomenon in Alberta* (Toronto: University of Toronto Press). Also see Grayson, *op. cit., The Formation of the Bank of Canada.*

218 **On the other hand, a central bank,** This is the continuation of the story, begun in Chapter Five, of the establishment and early years of the Bank of Canada. See the same sources cited above at beginning of notes for Chapter Five.

225 **Astonishingly, despite the wonderful successes,** Neufeld's critique cited in Fullerton, *op. cit., Graham Towers and his Times.* p. 249.

227 **"After the demonstration the war is providing,** cited in *ibid.* p. 185.

229 **In the U.S., frustration was building,** for an excellent account of Volcker's years as chairman of the Federal Reserve System, see Greider, *op. cit., Secrets of the Temple.*

232 **"After all, no one likes to risk recession,** Volcker, *op cit., Changing Fortunes,* p. 166.

233 **As Volcker put it,** *ibid,* p. 167.

299

237 **Bouey's announcement of the targets,** cited in Thomas J. Courchene, *Money, Inflation and the Bank of Canada. Vol II. An Analysis of Monetary Gradualism 1975-80* (Toronto: C.D. Howe Institute). p. 12.

242 **"People do care about the value,** Verbatim transcript of Executive Committee Meeting, Canadian Labour Market and Productivity Centre, May 2, 1989.

244 **As he told an audience,** John W. Crow, "Monetary policy and responsibilities and accountability of central banks," The Gerhard de Kock Memorial Lecture, delivered at the University of Pretoria, South Africa. Feb. 10, 1993. Copy provided by the Bank of Canada.

245 **Pierre Fortin described it,** Fortin, *op. cit.,* "The Unbearable Lightness of Zero-Inflation Optimism."

246 **"The Bank is performing well,** David E. W. Laidler, "How Shall We Govern the Governor?" *A Critique of the Government of the Bank of Canada* (Toronto: C.D. Howe Institute, May 1991).

248 **A key stimulus to the establishment,** First Report of the Sub-Committee on the Bank of Canada, *The Mandate and Governance of the Bank of Canada* (Ottawa: Queen's Printer, Feb. 1992).

249 **In keeping with the discreet nature,** Canadian Press, "Crow sent off in style," *Globe and Mail,* March 3, 1994. Guest list for parties obtained from Bank of Canada under access-to-information legislation, with names deleted but corporate affiliations included.

251 **"The recession has had such,** Alanna Mitchell, "Young face turmoil, study says," *Globe and Mail,* March 3, 1994.

CHAPTER SEVEN

The Executioners' Song

254 **In the first week of October, the government,** Lloyd Axworthy, *Improving Social Security in Canada: A Discussion Paper* (Ottawa: Government of Canada, October 1994).

254 **Summoning the media to a press conference,** Thomas E. Kierans and William B.P. Robson, *The Courage to Act: Fixing*

Canada's Budget and Social Policy Deficits (Toronto: C.D. Howe Institute, October, 1994).

255 **Andrew Coyne, a Globe and Mail columnist,** Coyne, "Now is the time for Mr. Martin to forget about the deficit," *Globe and Mail*, Oct. 24, 1994.

256 **In fact, the Axworthy proposals,** for a good journalistic summary of how RRSPs are more beneficial to those in upper income groups, see Margaret Philp, "RRSPs tempting revenue source: Tax shelter costs billions," *Globe and Mail*, Feb. 5, 1994.

256 **Indeed, Robson had written,** Laidler and Robson, *op. cit., The Great Canadian Disinflation*, p. 22.

258 **But, lest anyone get the idea,** Greg Ip, "Thiessen warns of deficit risks...": *Financial Post*, Oct. 13, 1994.

258 **Leo de Bever,** cited in *ibid.*

259 **As the storm over the deficit,** Fortin, A *Diversified Strategy for Deficit Control: Combining Faster Growth with Fiscal Discipline,* paper presented at the Conference on the Gap Between Actual and Potential Output, Institute for Policy Analysis, University of Toronto, August 8-9, 1994.
An abbreviated version of the paper appeared as "A Strategy for Deficit Control Through Faster Growth," *Canadian Business Economics*, Vol. 3, No. 1, Fall 1994.

262 **For the powerful gentleman,** for a good discussion of the fight for public education in Upper Canada, see "The Pre-Ryerson Years," in Neil McDonald and Alf Chaiton (ed.), *Egerton Ryerson and His Times* (Toronto: Macmillan of Canada, 1978).

265 **The C.D. Howe publication that promoted,** Thomas Courchene, *Social Canada in the Millenium: Reform Imperatives and Restructuring Principles* (Toronto, C.D. Howe Institute, 1994). See especially Chap. Five.

269 **"[I]t has become dismally apparent,** Deirdre McMurdy, "The tie that binds," *Maclean's*, Oct. 31, 1994.

270 **This was vividly illustrated,** Greg Ip, "Majority benefits from spending, Fraser warns," *Financial Post*, Oct. 25, 1994.

271 **The late U.S. economist,** Henry C. Simons, *Economic Policy for a Free Society* (Chicago: University of Chicago Press, 1948). p. 51.

272 **A study prepared in the Economics department**, Sadettin Erksoy, *Winners and Losers from the Great Disinflation 1981-1987*. Working Paper No. 92-13, Department of Economics, Dalhousie University, Dec. 1992.

273 **The largest increases in unemployment**, Andrew Sharpe, "The Rise of Unemployment in Ontario," paper presented to first annual Economic Policy Conference, Laurentian University, Sudbury, Ont. March 26-27, 1993.

273 **Across Canada**, data cited in Courchene, *op. cit.*, *Social Canada in the Millenium*. Figure 14, p. 140.

274 **Thus, David Bercuson**, Bercuson, "Our national Identity not shaped by social programs," *Financial Post*, Oct. 15, 1994.

274 **Diane Francis even tried**, Francis, "We are no kinder or gentler than the U.S.," Financial Post, Oct. 29, 1994. For a look at Canada's social welfare system in comparison with U.S. and European systems, see my *The Wealthy Banker's Wife: The Assault on Equality in Canada* (Toronto: Penguin Books, 1993).

274 **But Deirdre McMurdy**, McMurdy, *op. cit.*, "The tie that binds."

274 **And Frank Stronach**, Art Chamberlain, "Magna payday for Stronach: $13 million," *Toronto Star*, Nov. 1, 1994.

275 **As Michel Belanger**, quoted in Shawn McCarthy, "Martin Stresses Equity in Taxes," *Toronto Star*, Jan. 23, 1994.

276 **Donna Dasko, vice-president**, Dasko; interview.

278 **"Our late delusions have much exceeded**, David Hume, *The History of England from the Invasion of Julius Caesar to the Revolution in 1688*, in Appendix 3, following Chapter 44 (Abridged by R.W. Kilcup, University of Chicago Press, 1975), Note, p.158.

279 **"Such was the origin of that debt**, Lord Macaulay, *History of England* (London: Longmans Green, 1872), Vol. 6, Chap. 19, p. 329 ff.

282 **Pierre Fortin suggests that much of the high and persistent unemployment**, Fortin, *op. cit.*, "The Unbearable Lightness of Zero-Inflation Optimism."

284 **In the sun-dappled offices**, Greg Ip, "Crow to be consultant for U.S. insurer," *Financial Post*, Oct. 14, 1994.

Index

McMurdy, Deirdre, 269-270, 274
Mazankowski, Don, 48
Meredith, Carol, 30
Miller, William, 229-230
Mimoto, Hideo, 53-62, 117
Morgan, J.P., 210
Mulroney, Brian, 2, 110
Murphy, Steve, 112

Neufeld, Edward, 226
Nixon, Richard, 229
Norman, Montagu, 179

Osberg, Lars, 95, 122, 154

Parker, John, 126
Paterson, William, 184-190
Perry, David, 59, 62
Pichea, Luciano, 37
Plumptre, A.F.W., 175
Poloz, Stephen, 154
Poulin-Simon, Lise, 64

Rae, Bob, 2, 217
Reagan, Ronald, 234-236
Rehak, Peter, 15, 25, 27, 31
Robinson, Heather, 124
Robson, William, 134-139, 156-163, 252-258
Romanow, Roy, 217
Rosenbluth, Gideon, 151
Rush, Benjamin, 197
Russell, Frances, 12

Salutin, Rick, 9, 12
Savage, Tom, 242

SHOOTING the HIPPO